Pressure Cooking Day by Day

Kathleen Broughton is a leading authority on pressure cooking and a distinguished home economist. She worked with the Prestige Group for twenty-eight years, joining them as a demonstrator at the time when their original work on pressure cookers was being undertaken.

She has travelled widely, demonstrating pressure cookers in places as far apart as Paris and Moscow. She has taken the opportunity to illustrate the universal appeal of this method of cooking by demonstrating not only familiar recipes but also the national regional dishes of the many countries she has visited. She is a Fellow of the Association of Home Economists.

Her leisure time is filled with making clothes and growing flowers, vegetables and herbs in the garden of her London home. She also collects historic household equipment.

D0229662

Kathleen Broughton

Pressure Cooking
Day by Day

Pan Books London and Sydney

ACKNOWLEDGEMENTS I wish to thank sincerely my colleagues,
friends and family for their help in the preparation of this book.

NOTE ON METRICATION When metricating any recipe the only
really important point to bear in mind is that the ingredients
must remain in the same proportion. Throughout this book,
the following conversions are generally used: 25 g to 1 oz,
225 g to 8 oz, 450 g to 1 lb, 6 dl to 1 pint, and 2·5 cm to 1 inch.
Please note that when following a recipe it is important to be
consistent in using either imperial measures or metric measures,
to ensure that the quantities are right. Metrication has been
done to the nearest workable equivalent: although 8 oz is
usually taken to be 225 g, in certain cases the quantity has been
adjusted to keep the proportions constant.

First Published 1970 by Kaye & Ward Ltd
This revised edition published 1977 by Pan Books Ltd,
Cavaye Place, London SW10 9PG
2nd printing 1977
© Kaye & Ward Ltd 1970, 1977
ISBN 0 330 25067 1
Printed and bound in Great Britain by
Richard Clay (The Chaucer Press) Ltd, Bungay, Suffolk.

Contents

Foreword

Perhaps as you pick up this book you are still one of those who have not yet made up their mind about pressure cookers and whether they really are as useful as they are claimed to be. Of course, you will have heard of this quick and easy way to make light of cooking while serving even more delicious, varied and nourishing meals, but there are still so many things you want to know about it. How do pressure cookers work; are they safe; can they really keep and improve the flavour, appearance and goodness of food; would it be worth while to change one's way of cooking and above all, would it be money well spent?

You may know someone with a pressure cooker which has never been used or which was tried unsuccessfully and now languishes up on a shelf or tucked away in a cupboard. Or you could be one of those who has had a pressure cooker in use for so long that you cannot imagine life without it, particularly when you think back on those long hours you used to have to spend in the kitchen and which happily are now a thing of the past.

Whatever your situation, it is hoped you will find pleasure in this book; that with its help you will be able to take advantage of all that a pressure cooker can mean in these busy, rushing days; that it will answer all your questions and provide new ideas to give you added interest and satisfaction in the preparation and serving of meals, not only every day but also when entertaining. It will have served its purpose if, with its help, your pressure cooker becomes both a servant and a friend.

Introduction

The advantages

Food and nutrition in relation to methods of cooking have, in recent years, been the subject of much discussion. Pressure cooking, a method by which foods are cooked in super-heated steam, has a definite role to play now that the necessity of conserving food values is recognized along with the advantages of speeding up cooking times for the busy cook. It is therefore natural that a pressure cooker should find a place in the modern kitchen as an essential basic article of kitchen equipment.

Correctly used, a pressure cooker has everything to recommend it to those of us who are interested both in economy and in obtaining the best results when preparing and serving meals. With it, most foods require no more than a third of the normal cooking time. As a result, fuel bills are noticeably smaller, the problem of condensation is reduced (less steam in the kitchen and for a shorter time) and cooking smells through the house are less pervasive – but above all there is greater retention of food values, especially of the mineral salts that are usually wasted away into the cooking liquid.

The question of the effect of pressure cooking on these food values is one which should be especially considered. When pressure cookers were first introduced careful experiments were carried out and the reports were later issued by the then Ministry of Food and printed by the *British Medical Journal*. These confirmed that an increased conservation of Vitamin C in fresh vegetables, particularly cabbage, cauliflower and spinach, and of B1 in meat and pulses, could be achieved over normal cooking methods, if the correct times were adhered to and the small amount of liquid needed for the cooking was included in the finished dish. In addition, all such tests confirmed a higher retention of flavour and colour so that the food when presented was both more appetizing and more attractive in appearance.

A pressure cooker is of course not meant to be used always on its own: it will work well in harmony with the frying pan, the grill and the oven, and can save countless kitchen hours in the preparation of those foods which do not in themselves constitute a meal but which often require the longest cooking.

In every way, then, and for everyone – the growing, the healthy and those with stomach and duodenal complaints – the economy in time and fuel and the higher retention of food values mean that a pressure cooker is an asset in the home. It achieves that which is the ultimate aim of all cooking – to maintain the natural goodness of the food while increasing its attractiveness, flavour and digestibility.

The principles

Cooking is merely the application of heat to food, and the higher the temperature, the quicker the food will cook. With nearly all liquids the highest temperature that can be reached at sea-level is 100°C (212°F). No matter how fast or how slowly the liquids boil, their temperature will not rise above this and nor will that of the steam into which the liquids turn.

A pressure cooker, however, is designed to harness and control the steam, which in an ordinary saucepan escapes and is wasted. The sealing-in of the steam which leads to a rise in pressure also causes a rise in temperature, and it is this, coupled with the fact that the steam under pressure is actively being forced through the food to soften and tenderize it, which explains the rapid cooking which results.

The relation between the rise in pressure and temperature is a simple one, and below 600 m (2,000 ft) above sea-level can be taken as follows:

Pressure			Temperature	
Atmospheric			100°C	(212°F)
L	0·35 kg	(5 lb)	109°C	(228°F)
M	0·7 kg	(10 lb)	115°C	(240°F)
H	1·0 kg	(15 lb)	121°C	(250°F)

Exposed to these high temperatures, the fibrous tissues of meat and fish are quickly tenderized, starch grains are softened, the colour and flavour of green vegetables are retained and the safe sterilization of milk, bottles, fruit, vegetables and meat is assured. While it is true that exposure to any heat leads to a partial loss of certain vitamins, the length of time that foods containing them take to come to the boil and are then boiled are important factors and here a pressure cooker has the advantage, as these times can be cut down, in many instances, by as much as seventy-five per cent.

When three pressures are available, H (1 kg or 15 lb) should be used for day-to-day cooking, M (0·7 kg or 10 lb) for softening fruits for jams, jellies and marmalade and for bottling vegetables; L (0·35 kg or 5 lb) for steaming mixtures with raising agents, for fruit bottling and for the blanching of most vegetables before deep-freezing.

When only one pressure is available, this may be 1 kg (15 lb), 0·7 kg (10 lb) or, with a low-pressure cooker, an approximate value of 0·56 kg (8 lb).

As pressure cooking is accomplished in a sealed pan and in 'minute' cooking times, only a very little liquid has to be added to provide the steam and so there need be no wastage of the stock or cooking liquor for vegetables, fish and meat, which will always contain a certain amount of the flavour and goodness of the food.

Ideally, cooking of vegetables particularly should be done in the absence of air and light and with as little liquid as possible; a pressure cooker fulfils these conditions exactly.

About pressure cookers

Many models of pressure cooker for domestic use are now available. These may be made from high-quality aluminium alloy of a drawn or spun manufacture with a mirror-finish polish, or from various qualities of stainless steel. The two most popular types of pressure cooker are the casserole version with two short side handles, particularly suited to small stoves and where storage space is limited, and the more versatile saucepan type with a conventional long handle to both cover and base. Capacities are from

3·5 litres (7 pt) upwards, but when making one's choice it is perhaps wisest to buy the largest one can afford, as a small amount can always be cooked with the same economy of time and fuel in a large pan, but it is disappointing to find that a small one cannot be stretched as the family increases or when entertaining guests.

Pressure cookers can be used on any kind of heat – gas, all types of electric hotplate, with oil, pressure stoves and solid fuel ranges (though with the latter, of course, no saving of fuel will result).

The component parts of a pressure cooker are the **cover** and the **body** and may be of varying design according to the make. The most familiar types are those with an insert rigid cover, opening and closing by a centre knob with an internal spring or screw action; and those with an outside closure in which the cover fits on to the body with matching notches, the closure of the cover handle over the body completing the locking device.

The cover of each cooker will be fitted with a pressure control, or valve, those in most general use being:

A lever type, fitted with a spring valve.

A control valve or weight giving a fixed pressure only.

A variable control with a sliding centre stem calibrated to register two or three pressures.

A variable control consisting of three pieces: an inner **L** (0·35-kg or 5-lb) weight, a sleeve screwing on to give **M** (0·7-kg or 10-lb) pressure and an outer sleeve to complete the maximum **H** (1-kg or 15-lb) pressure.

In addition, each pressure cooker conforming to British Standard Institute standards must be fitted with a safety device that will come into action automatically should excess pressure be built up. The types most commonly fitted are:

1 A rubber plug with a movable centre pintle which combines two safety factors. (The pintle will pop up should excessive pressure be built up so that this will be released and can then be reset for further cooking; the crosspiece of the pintle is made of a fusible alloy which will melt at an excessive temperature to warn that the cooker is boiling dry.)

2 A solid rubber excess-pressure plug which can be reset, with a separate rubber plug with fusible core to come into action with excess temperature.

3 A rubber plug with fusible core only.

The cover will also be fitted with a gasket or sealing ring made from a rubber compound, to ensure that no leakage of steam will occur at the join between the cover and base.

The design of a pressure cooker must always incorporate a locking device to ensure that the method of joining the cover to the base will prevent its removal during cooking or while any pressure at all remains inside the cooker.

Varying accessories are made available by the manufacturers, either at the time of purchase or as additional separate items, but each pressure cooker must come complete with a trivet or perforated tray on which certain foods should be put to keep them out of the cooking liquid. In this way several vegetables or foods can be cooked at the same time without mixing them together or causing any transference of flavour from one to another. A set of three containers or separators, which may be perforated or solid, and a container fitting the cooker which can be divided to hold two different foods, are among the extras which can be supplied.

Their use

Using a pressure cooker is basically the same in all models, varying only in the practical method by which pressure is attained in a particular type. The various steps must always be followed through and are simply to bring the liquid put into the cooker to the boil so that the pan fills with steam which will drive all the air from the pan. This steam is then sealed in by closure of the valve, when the pressure within the cooker will rise to that required and can be maintained over a low heat throughout the cooking time. Before opening the cooker, the steam pressure has to be allowed to fall back to normal, either immediately with cold water or by gently lifting and tipping the weight (not by pulling it off completely) to allow the steam to escape or else allowing the cooker to stand at room temperature for a few minutes.

Each pressure cooker comes with the manufacturer's recommended instructions for its correct use and these should be studied and followed; only when you get to know your cooker and become completely confident in its use is this precision item going to be the real asset that it can and should be.

Important things to remember when using a pressure cooker

The liquid being used for the cooking must be one which will give steam when it boils – fat alone is suitable only with low-pressure cookers when recommended by the manufacturers.

When browning or frying with fat before pressure cooking, the base should be used as an open pan.

The amount of liquid required for the entire cooking must be put in at the start.

The quantity will depend on the length of the cooking time and not on the amount of food being cooked, as sufficient must be put in to turn into steam and keep the pan filled with steam while it is under pressure.

Sufficient space must always be left in the cooker for the steam to circulate and do its work. This means that the complete cooker, taking into account the base and cover, must not be more than two-thirds full of solids.

As most liquids such as stocks, soups, milk, fruit juice or those in which cereals and pastas are being cooked tend to boil up and over, sufficient space must be left to prevent this happening; for these, the cooker base should never be more than half full.

The cover must always be in the fully closed position before attempting to bring the cooker to pressure.

Recipes should be checked to see whether the cooker is to be brought to pressure on a high, medium or low heat. A good reason will always be given for this.

The first stage in pressure cooking is the expulsion of all the air in the pan as the liquid comes to the boil and turns to steam. If the control valve has to be left open to allow for this, close it when you SEE the steam.

The second stage is the building up to pressure (which occurs when the steam is no longer able to escape through the control) until the required pressure is reached. This will only be when a LOUD hissing sound is heard or when the indicator on the calibrated stem type of control shows, accompanied by an escape of steam which will be the signal that the actual pressure-cooking time can begin.

Once the cooking is being timed, the heat should be lowered to the point where the loud hissing stops yet a gentle and definite muttering sound continues and there is a gentle escape of steam. If the cooker is left hissing loudly it will not cook any faster, fuel will be wasted and sooner or later the cooker will run short of steam and liquid and boil dry. If, on the other hand, the cooker goes silent, then the pressure will be dropping and at the end of the cooking time the food will not be cooked.

When the cooking time is up, pressure should only be reduced according to the recipe instructions. These will be to do this immediately by standing the cooker in a bowl of cold water or under the cold-water tap; by gently lifting and tipping the pressure control, without taking it right off, until no further steam escapes; or by leaving the cooker to stand at room temperature away from the stove, for a few minutes.

Before removing the cover at any time, the valve should be opened by raising the lever or removing the set of weights.

The liquid in the base of the cooker, unless it has been used only for steaming puddings, cakes, for bottling and so on, should never be wasted but used as stock or for adding to soups, stews, gravies and sauces.

The recommended cooking times should always be scrupulously kept to. Provided the pressure cooker is in good working order and that it is being used correctly, the methods and times given for these tested recipes will be those that will ensure the best results in every way.

Foods will always cook more quickly if loose in the cooker, either in the liquid or on the trivet, according to the recipe. Perforated or solid containers need only be used when recommended in the instructions.

Only foods requiring the same pressure and cooking time should be put into the cooker together, otherwise those requiring a shorter time will be overcooked, losing their colour, flavour and too much of their goodness. It is often possible to adjust cooking times, for example, by cutting larger vegetables into halves or quarters or by packing small or quicker-cooking vegetables into the separators where, cut off from the full force of the steam, they can afford to be given a little longer.

Otherwise it is always possible to open the cooker towards the end of the cooking time by reducing the pressure, opening the valve and adding in those foods requiring a shorter time. A simple example of this would be braised steak, taking 10 minutes, and accompanying vegetables, requiring 5. After the first 5 minutes of the cooking, the cooker would be opened and the vegetables added for the last 5 minutes so that, when the cooking time was up, the meat would have had its full 10 minutes and the vegetables their correct 5.

Their care

Like any new piece of kitchen equipment, the pressure cooker should be washed in hot, soapy water, be well rinsed and then dried before first using. Soda in any form should never be used to boil up the cooker or in the washing-up water, as it reacts with aluminium, will discolour it and can lead to pitting of the material.

Any staining or darkening which may occur from cooking certain foods is not harmful in any way to the food which will subsequently be cooked and eaten or to the cooker itself. In hard-water areas, staining can be avoided by the addition of acid in the form of vinegar or lemon, and this is why it is always recommended when foods are being steamed in containers, as it prevents the base and the trivet from turning black.

For daily cleaning after use, the pressure cooker, trivet and containers should be treated like any other aluminium utensil – washed, rinsed and dried – and should as necessary be cleaned with a cleansing powder on a cloth, with any type of pot scourer, or with soap pads.

The cover may need to be rinsed and the gasket to be lifted out and washed if any food can be seen to have boiled up, but otherwise a wipe over inside and out, after lifting off, while still warm, should keep both in good condition. The vent, however, must be looked through each time after use to make sure it is clear, and a check made that the safety plug is in the correct, closed position.

To retain the high mirror polish given to the outside of the cover and body the pressure cooker should not be left standing in water. It should never really need to be scoured, which would spoil its appearance.

For storage, the lid of a pressure cooker should not be left in the closed position. Open, or with the lid reversed and tipped according to the model, the air can circulate through the cooker and this will avoid any retention of cooking smells.

For more specific instructions for the care and cleaning of your pressure cooker, you should check in the book of instructions.

The gasket and safety plug will need replacing from time to time as a rubber compound is bound to deteriorate with continuous exposure to steam and heat. This will be when steam or water is seen escaping around the cover or around the plug itself, or if steam is seen escaping anywhere but through the valve or vent. A replacement should be bought and fitted at once, otherwise the cooker cannot continue to work efficiently and an uncontrolled escape of steam will almost certainly lead, sooner or later, to the cooker boiling dry.

It is only 'dry' heating, when all the liquid has had to turn into steam to keep up the pressure, which will cause the distortion or bulging of the base. Once this has happened, the cooker must be returned to the manufacturer for servicing, otherwise it will only continue to boil dry and will not make correct contact with a flat plate, thus worsening the distortion, spoiling the cooking and making it impossible in the end to use the cooker efficiently at all.

The cooker will also boil dry if it is left boiling away on too high a heat with the valve or vent open, or again, on too high a heat after pressure has been reached. Even when a little liquid is found in the bottom of the cooker on opening it, if this is brown or if the base is bulged it must mean that the cooker was dry and the liquid will be only the steam condensed as pressure was reduced. Should you at any time smell the cooker burning, turn off the heat and lift the cooker away, but do not put it into cold water. Let it cool of its own accord. You should then check if the base has bulged and, if it has, the cooker should be returned for servicing. To test whether the gasket or safety plug has shrunk or hardened due to exposure to the 'dry' heat, just put a little water with acid into the cooker and bring it up to pressure; should any leakage of steam then be seen, replacement parts should be bought from your local stockist and fitted at once.

The safety plug comes into action if the vent or valve gets blocked because the cooker is too full, or because food is boiling up into it, or if the cooker is left too long boiling dry. The noise this causes may be a little unnerving, particularly if liquid is also expelled with the steam, but just take the cooker away from the heat and if the liquid continues to boil out put it in the sink or outside the back door. You should then check your method of using the cooker for that particular recipe to find out where you went wrong, for a safety plug will not blow of its own accord – unless, of course, it was in need of replacement and you either did not notice this or put off getting a new one.

Manufacturers of pressure cookers offer a complete recondi-tioning and repairing service, and an estimate of the cost of this can always be obtained before the work is put in hand. The various replacement parts – gaskets, safety plugs, control valves, handles and instruction booklets – are available or can be ordered through your local stockist or direct from the manufacturer. Always re-member that the manufacturer will be as interested and keen as you are that you should use your cooker and be pleased with it, and should be prepared to help you in any way he can.

Concerning the recipes

The recipes given in this book are for use with an H (1-kg or 15-lb) pressure, except where a lower pressure is recommended to obtain the best results. If the model you are using does not have a variable control or you are not sure what the pressure is, then you can still follow these recipes by taking the cooking time for the principal ingredient as shown in the handbook given by the manufacturers of your cooker. For example:

Beef stew **H** (1-kg or 15-lb) pressure: 15–20 minutes
            L (0·35-kg or 5-lb) pressure: 45–60 minutes
Chicken à la crème **H** (1-kg or 15-lb) pressure: 4 minutes
              L (0·35-kg or 5-lb) pressure: 15 minutes

When you wish to adjust recipes from other books or just your own favourite ones, again consult the time-table or a recipe given here using the same basic ingredient, then remember that the quantity of liquid must be adjusted according to the cooking time.

Because water boils at a lower temperature as altitude increases and therefore the atmospheric pressure decreases, allowance must be made for the height at which a pressure cooker is being used if this is over 600 m (2,000 ft) above sea-level.

For day-to-day cooking the adjustments are as follows:

L pressure: use **M** pressure and do not increase cooking time.
M pressure: use **H** pressure and do not increase cooking time.
H pressure: increase cooking time by one minute for every 300 m (1,000 ft).

Quantities for thickening gravies and stews, making sauces, stuffing ingredients and so on, where absolute accuracy is not essential, have been given in spoonfuls rather than grammes as this will save having to weigh small amounts. For this purpose, a spoonful is taken as being as much above as is in the bowl and a half spoonful is level with the bowl.

flour and powder ingredients	25 g (1 oz)≃1 tablespoon
shredded suet	25 g (1 oz)≃1½ tablespoons
sugar, fruit and heavy ingredients	25 g (1 oz)≃1 level tablespoon
syrup, jam	25 g (1 oz)≃1 level tablespoon
dry rice	25 g (1 oz)≃1 tablespoon
breadcrumbs, grated cheese, coconut	12 g (½ oz)≃1 tablespoon
butter or margarine	25 g (1 oz)≃1 tablespoon
	levelled along the bowl with a knife
teacup liquid	≃1·5 dl (¼ pt)
teacup dry rice	≃150 g (6 oz)
teacup dry powder ingredients	≃100 g (4 oz)

For most recipes, butter and margarine are interchangeable; for small quantities, and for sauces particularly, the difference in cost would not be noticeable and the improvement in flavour would make the use of butter well worth while.

For brown sauces and for the preliminary frying of ingredients for stews, braises and pot roasts, dripping can be used if available.

For steamed puddings and cakes where it is important that quantities are exact, and for larger amounts as in jams, marmalades and so on, the measurements are given by weight.

Here is a list of items for you to choose from to help you to get the best results from your pressure cooker and the following recipes:

A soufflé dish, 15 cm (6 in) or 17 cm (7 in), depending on your cooker size but leaving enough room to allow it to be put in and lifted out easily, holding it on one side: for milk, egg and miscellaneous sweets, for stewing fruit.

A casserole dish, size as above, but make allowances for the side grips with which a casserole is provided; for use as above.

4, 6 or 8 teacups which can be kept specially for pressure cooking or can be those which you have in daily use: for sweet and savoury custards, for infant and invalid cooking.

A stainless steel or aluminium bowl, 6–9 dl (1–1½ pt) capacity, for steamed puddings of all kinds and for cooking rice.

Boilable plastic or china basins for Christmas puddings. If your cooker is a tall one and you choose wisely you will be able to cook 2 × 675 g (1½ lb) puddings one on top of the other and at the same time.

Individual boilable plastic bowls: you may prefer these to teacups, particularly when you are camping, caravanning or boating, as they are light and unbreakable.

A second trivet, which is always available from your local stockist or the manufacturer, and which you may find useful to rest on top of other foods, for example when putting in a container of vegetables, rice etc, or, instead of just greaseproof paper, to lay fish on for easy handling.

A long-handled straining spoon for serving vegetables and for hooking into the trivet to lift it out.

A long-handled fork for turning meat, tossing pastas.

A potato masher for potatoes, swedes, turnips, apples, for dried vegetable soups which do not need sieving, for pressing the water from spinach before lifting out of the cooker, for mashing, in the cooker, the mirepoix vegetables to make a thick gravy.

A long wooden spoon for stirring milk puddings, soups, jam, marmalades.

A small ladle for filling jam etc into the jars.

A 12·5–15-cm (5–6-in) strainer for soups, purées, pulps.

A pair of lifting tongs for bottling jars.

A seamless loaf pan or round cake tin for cakes, bread, puddings, galantines.

NOTE To avoid an excessive number of cross-references, recipes which can be found listed in the index have been marked throughout the text with an asterisk.

1 Stocks and soups

You may think that this the first section will not interest you as you have never been a great soup-maker – too much time and trouble, you have perhaps thought, particularly with so many ready-made soups from which to choose. But now you have a pressure cooker you can see how easy it is to obtain delicious, nourishing soups in minutes instead of hours. A well-made pressure-cooked soup, full of flavour and goodness and served with fried croûtons, toasted French bread or fingers of toast, can often be sufficient for an evening meal. From now on no odds and ends, no left-overs need be wasted – just a few minutes' pressure cooking and you can have a rich stock to serve as the basis for meat, chicken, fish or vegetable soups. Even if you decide soup-making is not for you, be sure to use every last little bit from the joint, the fish, the chicken, the vegetables, so that you always have a bowl of stock on hand to add to sauces, gravies and stews – nothing wasted, all the goodness preserved to give extra nourishment to all your other cooking.

General instructions

Any bones should be broken up as small as possible so that all the goodness will be extracted from them.

Cooked vegetables, potatoes, bread, thickened sauces or gravies should not be added to stock or it will not keep.

Stocks and some soups may require to have the scum removed as they come to the boil. Lift this off carefully with a metal skimmer or straining spoon. All fat should be carefully taken off stocks and soups before these are used and served. This may be done when cold and the fat solid enough to be lifted off with a spoon; when hot, the best method is to use pieces of soft, absorbent paper such as a kitchen towel, tearing off small pieces and using each once only to 'blot' up the fat by drawing it across the surface of the liquid.

The water with which any green vegetable has been cooked cannot be used for stock as it may ferment; it should, in fact, never be recooked.

Every time other vegetables are pressure cooked, you will have made a concentrated vegetable stock and this can be used in making any soup, meat or fish dish. Only turnips are not always suitable as they can have too strong a flavour, and they should be used only very sparingly when making a basic stock – and not at all in hot weather. If you do not find the particular recipe you are looking for here, just remember that the pressure-cooking time of the soup will depend on that required by the principal ingredient, which will be found in the time-table given in the appropriate chapter.

Be careful, until you are a little more experienced, with the amount of seasoning you add. Because everything is more conserved and concentrated in a pressure cooker, the seasoning required is very much less, the ingredients retaining far more of their own mineral salts.

The trivet is not used when making soups or stocks as all the ingredients must cook in the liquid so that their flavours mingle and the goodness is extracted.

Your cooker must never have the base more than half full when all the ingredients and liquid have been added. This is to leave room for the liquid to boil up – as it will do during the cooking – without boiling over, to leave plenty of room for the steam that will form, and to ensure that the vent in the cover does not get blocked up. As there is little loss of liquid by evaporation during pressure cooking, the result is always a very concentrated soup. Therefore, if more soup is wanted for serving but would more than half fill the cooker base, extra liquid can always be added after the pressure cooking.

For stock or soup which is to be stored for another day, it is useful to be able to make it very concentrated so that it will take up less space in the refrigerator. For serving, hot water, vegetable or other stock, or milk can be added to obtain the required amount. If you have not all the ingredients mentioned in a recipe just when you decide to make a particular soup, do not let this deter you. You are sure to have a suitable substitute in the cupboard and this is when your soup-making experience will stand you in good stead. For instance, a spoonful or two of sweet-corn, cooked peas, sliced cooked beans heated and put into the serving dish before a soup is poured in, the addition of an unusual herb such as basil or fennel, a pinch of saffron or nutmeg, a garnish of chopped sorrel or watercress, may be just the touch you were looking for.

The following recipes are proportioned to serve up to six helpings for soup as a first course or four helpings as a meal in itself. Use High (1-kg or 15-lb) pressure.

White stock (also called **Foundation stock**)
Pressure-cooking time: 45 minutes

This recipe will give approximately 1·2 litres (2 pt) of a very concentrated jellied stock which can be diluted with an equal quantity of water, vegetable water etc before use, and which will give extra richness and goodness when added to packet or tinned soups, gravies, meat and cereal dishes.

900 g (2 lb) meat bones – fresh or from the cooked joint	1 teaspoon salt pinch of pepper *or* 3 peppercorns

1·5 litres (2½ pt) cold water
2 large onions
2 sticks celery
2 medium carrots

sprig each of parsley and thyme
bay leaf
blade of mace
pinch of mixed herbs

Wash the bones well and break or chop as small as possible. Put them into the cooker with the water and bring to the boil over a high heat. While waiting, wash and scrape or peel the vegetables and cut them into rough pieces. When the stock is boiling, carefully lift all the scum from the top. Add the rest of the ingredients, turn the heat to **medium**, bring the cooker to pressure and cook for 45 minutes. Allow the pressure to reduce at room temperature. Strain the stock, leave until cold, then remove the fat before use.

If a marrow bone is used, add sufficient water to half fill the base, omit the vegetables, add the herbs and seasoning, and pressure cook for 2 hours. Continue as above.

If a **brown stock** is required, the onions must be fried first in hot fat either in the base of the open cooker or in a frying pan.

Chicken soups

Chicken soup stock
Pressure-cooking time: 20 or 30 minutes

The carcass and any left-overs of chicken should never be wasted. This stock is quick and easy to pressure cook, and will serve as a basis for a delicious home-made soup or for adding to packet or tinned soups.

carcass, bones, skin and left-over
  scraps of a boiled, roasted or
  uncooked chicken
1 onion stuck with 2 cloves
1 carrot, sliced
1 leek, sliced
½ teaspoon salt
pinch of pepper

as available:
  sprig each of parsley and thyme
  small bay leaf
  small blade of mace
  ¼ teaspoon celery salt
  6–12 dl (1–2 pt) cold water

Break the carcass and bones of chicken as small as possible, roughly cut up any meat and put with all the other ingredients into the cooker. (The amount of water added should depend on how much chicken there is and how concentrated one wants the stock to be.) Bring to the boil in the open pan and skim if necessary. Bring to pressure and allow 20 minutes if the chicken has been cooked before and 30 minutes if uncooked. Allow the pressure to reduce at room temperature, strain and when cold remove the fat from the top.

To use, dilute with an equal quantity of water.

Chicken consommé reine
Pressure-cooking time: 30–40 minutes

1 chicken or boiling fowl,
  1·35–1·8 kg (3–4 lb)
1·2 litres (2 pt) water
1 onion stuck with 3 cloves
2 sticks celery
1 carrot, sliced

as available:
  sprig each of parsley and thyme
  bay leaf
1 teaspoon salt
½ teaspoon pepper

Clean the chicken well, inside and out. Wash the giblets thoroughly in salted water. Put the chicken, giblets and all other ingredients into the cooker and, when boiling, remove all the scum. Bring to pressure and cook for the required time, allowing 10 minutes per 450 g (1 lb). Allow the pressure to reduce at room temperature. Lift out the chicken, carefully strain the stock and remove the fat from the top by passing small pieces of soft, absorbent paper across the surface. Remove the legs from the chicken, take off the skin and cut the meat into fine slices. Return this and the stock to the open cooker. Boil, taste and correct the seasoning and serve piping hot.

The rest of the chicken can be eaten cold with fresh vegetables or salad; in a pie; in a white sauce to fill pastry cases or to serve as a supper dish with a border of mashed potatoes; sprinkled with cheese and grilled; or in a border of cooked, savoury rice.

Chicken noodle soup
Pressure-cooking time: 3–4 minutes

6 dl (1 pt) chicken stock
6 dl (1 pt) water
100 g (4 oz) fine noodles

to garnish:
  1 hard-boiled egg
chopped parsley or watercress

Dilute the chicken stock with the water in the cooker and bring to the boil in the open pan. Add the noodles broken into 5-cm (2-in) lengths, bring to pressure and cook for 3–4 minutes according to the thickness of the noodles. While allowing the pressure to reduce at room temperature, prepare the garnish by chopping the hard-boiled egg and mixing with the chopped parsley or watercress. Just before serving, taste to correct seasoning and sprinkle with the garnish.

Cream of chicken soup

2 tablespoons margarine or butter
2 tablespoons flour
3 dl ($\frac{1}{2}$ pt) milk

9 dl ($1\frac{1}{2}$ pt) chicken stock
salt and pepper
chopped parsley or chives

Melt the margarine or butter in a large saucepan, add the flour and cook gently for 2–3 minutes, stirring all the time and without allowing it to colour. Lift from the heat, gradually add the milk, then stir and cook until thick. Add the chicken stock, taste and correct the seasoning and just before serving sprinkle thickly with chopped parsley or chives.

For a complete supper dish, serve with fried croûtons.

Mulligatawny soup

Pressure-cooking time: 7 minutes

1·2 litres (2 pt) good stock made
  from carcass of cooked chicken
2 tablespoons long rice
bouquet garni*
2 tablespoons margarine
2 tablespoons flour
1 cooking apple

1 medium onion
1 tablespoon curry powder (less
  or more according to taste)
juice of $\frac{1}{2}$ lemon
2 tablespoons cream
seasoning

Before making the stock, take any remaining meat from the chicken carcass and put on one side. Lift the trivet from the cooker, put in the stock, washed rice and bouquet garni, bring to pressure, cook for 7 minutes and allow pressure to reduce at room temperature. During the cooking, melt the margarine in another saucepan and gently fry the finely chopped onion, sliced apple, flour and curry powder for 10 minutes without discolouring. Lift the bouquet garni from the stock, strain the rice and keep warm.

Gradually add the stock to the saucepan, stirring all the time. Add the diced chicken meat and the lemon juice, bring to the boil and skim if necessary. Taste and add seasoning, throw in the rice and reheat. Add cream and serve piping hot.

Fish soups

Fish soup stock
Pressure-cooking time: 15 minutes

This stock should be made and used on the same day.

cod's head, trimmings of white
    fish heads, tails, bones, skin left
    after filleting and so on
sufficient water to cover fish
1 onion, sliced
1 carrot, sliced

1 leek, chopped
12 peppercorns
2 thin slices lemon peel
bouquet garni*
1 small teaspoon salt

Wash the fish well, put into the cooker with all the other ingredients and bring to the boil in the open pan. Carefully remove all the scum, then bring to pressure and cook for 15 minutes. Allow the pressure to reduce at room temperature, strain at once.

Use as the basis for fish soups, sauces, curries and other dishes.

Fish tomato soup
Pressure-cooking time: 5 minutes

2 cutlets cod or fresh haddock
9 dl (1½ pt) fish stock*
salt and pepper
1 small glass white wine
3 tablespoons tomato purée

2 tablespoons flour blended with
    1·5 dl (¼ pt) milk
2 tablespoons coarsely chopped
    parsley
to serve:
    toasted french bread*

Put the fish, stock and seasoning into the cooker, bring to pressure, cook for 5 minutes and allow the pressure to reduce at room temperature. Carefully lift out the fish, remove skin and bone and divide the fish into portions. Strain the soup, stir in the wine, tomato purée and blended flour, return to the heat, bring to the boil and cook for a minute or two stirring all the time. This soup should be very smooth and not too thick; thin if necessary with a little more fish stock or milk. Taste and correct seasoning. It is best served in individual cups. Put a portion of fish into each, pour over the soup, garnish thickly with the parsley. Serve with slices of toasted French bread.

Lobster bisque

2 tablespoons butter
2 tablespoons flour
1·5 dl (¼ pt) milk
9 dl (1½ pt) fish stock*
1 small tin lobster

3 tablespoons crushed cream crackers
1 small glass white wine
1 tablespoon lemon juice
salt and pepper
2 tablespoons single cream

Melt the butter in a large saucepan, add the flour and cook for a minute or two over a low heat without allowing to colour. Lift from the heat, gradually add the milk, then stir and cook until thick. Add the fish stock and the juice from the strained lobster; then, when again boiling, stir in the crushed biscuits and leave to stand on one side for 2–3 minutes until the biscuits are softened. Stir in the wine, lemon juice and the finely chopped lobster, reserving a little for garnish. Bring to the boil rapidly and taste and correct for seasoning. Lift from the heat, stir in the cream and serve at once, garnished with the rest of the lobster.

If a fresh-boiled lobster is available, pressure cook the fish stock for 10 minutes with the shells, then continue as in recipe.

Meat soups

Beef and mushroom soup
Pressure-cooking time: 7 minutes

2 tablespoons margarine
1 onion, sliced
225 g (8 oz) lean minced beef
100 g (4 oz) mushrooms
1·2 litres (2 pt) brown stock

salt and pepper
chopped parsley
to serve:
   fingers of dried toast

Melt the margarine and fry the onion and meat until golden-brown, stirring to prevent any sticking or burning. Add the very finely diced mushrooms and fry gently for a further minute or two. Lift the cooker from the heat, stir in the stock (use a meat cube dissolved in water if stock is not available) and add seasoning. Bring to pressure, cook for 7 minutes, then reduce pressure immediately. Taste and correct seasoning, and serve sprinkled with chopped parsley. Hand the fingers of dried toast separately. Three tablespoons of tomato purée, dissolved in the stock, may be added for extra flavour.

For a complete supper dish, rice may be added. When the stock is boiling in the open cooker, throw in 3 tablespoons of washed rice and continue as in recipe.

Oxtail soup
Pressure-cooking time: 40 minutes

This soup should be made the day before as it is necessary to remove all the fat which is extracted from the oxtail during the cooking. If a large oxtail is bought there will be enough meat left over to make a delicious oxtail stew for another day.

1 oxtail	bouquet garni*
1 sliced onion	pepper and salt
1 tablespoon dripping	1 tablespoon margarine
1·2 litres (2 pt) water	1 tablespoon flour
1 carrot, sliced	1 tablespoon redcurrant jelly
1 turnip, sliced	1 teaspoon Worcestershire sauce
2 sticks celery	

Wash the oxtail, cut into joints and fry with the sliced onion in the heated dripping in the open cooker until well browned all over. Add the water, sliced vegetables, bouquet garni and seasoning. Bring to pressure, cook for 40 minutes, allow the pressure to reduce at room temperature, then strain the soup into a bowl. Lift out the oxtail joints, take away any fat, then remove the meat from the bones while still hot and leave pressed between 2 plates (if it was a large oxtail, remove the meat from 3 or 4 joints only, using the rest for an oxtail stew). The next day, lift all the fat from the cold soup and cut the pressed meat into small dice. Melt the margarine in a large saucepan, add the flour and cook, stirring and allowing it to turn a good brown colour but without burning.

Lift from the heat, gradually mix in the soup, then stir until boiling. Add the diced meat, the redcurrant jelly and the Worcestershire Sauce; taste and correct seasoning and serve.

For a special occasion, leave out the Worcestershire Sauce and add 2 tablespoons of a dry Madeira or port wine.

Scotch (mutton) broth
Pressure-cooking time: 7 minutes

This soup is a meal in itself, excellent for children who need feeding up after illness and for filling up the energetic members of the family. It is best made the previous day so that all the fat can be easily removed.

1 tablespoon pearl barley	1 stick celery
225 g (8 oz) middle or best end of neck of mutton	small piece turnip
	bouquet garni*
1·2 litres (2 pt) water	salt and pepper
1 leek	chopped parsley
1 onion	
1 carrot	

Wash the barley well, put into a small pan of cold water, bring to the boil and strain. Remove all the fat from the meat. Put the water, the diced vegetables, the bouquet garni, the meat and seasoning into the cooker and bring to the boil in the open pan. Throw in the prepared barley, bring to pressure, cook for 7 minutes and allow the pressure to reduce at room temperature. Lift out the meat and cover when cold. Turn the soup into a basin and remove the bouquet garni. Next day (or when cold) lift the fat off the soup, put back into the cooker and bring to the boil in the open pan. Take all the meat off the bones, cut into small dice, add to the soup, taste and correct seasoning. Serve sprinkled with parsley.

Game soup
Pressure-cooking time: 30 minutes

As game is expensive and rather a luxury it is a pity to waste any of it and this delicious soup will make sure that the last ounce of goodness and flavour is extracted.

Carcass and left-over meat of game-birds	bouquet garni*
6–9 dl (1–1½ pt) water	2 tablespoons rice
1 small onion stuck with 2 cloves	3 cooked and skinned chipolata sausages
1 leek, sliced	salt and pepper
2 sticks celery	1 glass red wine

Break up the carcass, put into the cooker with the water, vegetables, bouquet garni and seasoning, bring to pressure, cook for 25 minutes and allow the pressure to reduce at room temperature. Strain the soup, return to the open cooker, bring to the boil, throw in the washed rice, pressure cook for a further 5 minutes, allow the pressure to reduce at room temperature. Add the finely sliced sausages, reboil, taste and correct seasoning and just before serving add the red wine.

Any gravy left over from the previous cooking of the birds may be used to give a thickened soup; leave out the rice and, after 30 minutes' cooking, gradually add the strained soup to the gravy, then continue as in recipe.

Fresh vegetable soups

Clear vegetable soup
Pressure-cooking time: 5 minutes

3 rashers streaky bacon	2 sticks celery, chopped
2 small onions	2 tomatoes, skinned and finely chopped
2 carrots	bouquet garni*
2 turnips	salt and pepper
1 tablespoon flour	
1·2 litres (2 pt) brown stock (or a stock cube, dissolved)	

Cut the bacon into very small pieces and cook gently in the open cooker until all the fat has run out. Add the onion, carrot and turnip, finely sliced, and fry until golden-brown. Put in the flour and continue browning slowly, stirring frequently to prevent sticking. Lift the cooker from the heat, gradually add the stock, then the rest of the ingredients. Return to the heat, stir until boiling, and skim if necessary. Bring to pressure over a **medium** heat, cook for 5 minutes, then allow pressure to reduce at room temperature. Remove the bouquet garni, taste and correct seasoning, and serve.

If a thick soup is required, strain, sieve the vegetables, combine again with the liquid and reheat before serving.

French onion soup
Pressure-cooking time: 4 minutes

Use full quantity for a complete supper dish, half quantity as one course of a meal.

2 tablespoons butter	salt
4 large onions, thinly sliced	1 thin slice toast per person
pepper	*to serve:*
1·2 litres (2 pt) good brown stock	grated parmesan cheese

Lift the trivet from the cooker, heat the butter and fry the well-peppered onion slices slowly until golden-brown. Add the hot stock (if cold, allow the cooker to cool) and salt; bring to pressure, cook for 4 minutes and reduce the pressure with cold water. During the cooking, make the toast and keep the grill hot. Pour the soup into individual heat-proof soup bowls, dividing the onion rings evenly among them, put a piece of toast on top of each, sprinkle thickly with the cheese and brown quickly under a hot grill. Serve at once.

Variations
For added richness, a little fresh or sour cream can be stirred in and the soup reheated but not allowed to boil.

An added piquancy can be given by putting a dash of Worcestershire sauce into each bowl before adding the toast and cheese.

Tomato soup with rice
Pressure-cooking time: 7 minutes

1 tablespoon margarine	pinch of sugar
1 medium onion, finely chopped	bay leaf
450 g (1 lb) tomatoes, skinned and sliced (or a large tin)	2 tablespoons rice, washed
	salt and pepper
1·2 litres (2 pt) white stock* (if tinned tomatoes are used, make juice up to quantity)	

Melt the margarine in the open cooker, add the onion and cook until transparent but do not allow to brown. Add the tomatoes, stock, sugar and bay leaf, and bring to the boil. Throw in the rice, bring to pressure on a **medium** heat, cook for 5 minutes, then reduce pressure with cold water. Lift out the bay leaf, taste to correct seasoning and serve.

To add extra interest to this soup, a dash of Worcestershire sauce or 2 tablespoons of sherry may be added just before serving.

Cream soups

Cream soups are those made from fresh vegetables cooked in stock and tenderized so that they may be easily passed through a sieve or mashed into a purée; they are then thickened with a white sauce or by the addition of cream.

Proportions: about 450 g (1 lb) fresh vegetables to 9 dl (1½ pt) stock/milk.

Cream of celery soup
Pressure-cooking time: 10 minutes

1 large head celery	1 large tablespoon margarine
1 small onion, finely chopped	1 tablespoon flour
6 dl (1 pt) chicken stock	3 dl (½ pt) milk
(or a stock cube, dissolved)	*to garnish:*
salt and pepper	young celery leaves, chopped

Wash celery well, slice it finely (reserve the young green leaves for garnish), put into the cooker with the onion, stock and seasoning. Bring to pressure, cook for 10 minutes, then allow pressure to reduce at room temperature. During the cooking, melt the margarine in another saucepan, add the flour and cook for 2–3 minutes while stirring, without allowing it to colour. Remove from the heat, gradually add the milk, return to a low heat and stir until thickened. Strain the soup, sieve or mash the vegetables and add this purée to the sauce. Then, beating well, stir in sufficient of the celery stock to give the required consistency to the finished soup. Reheat, taste and correct seasoning. Serve garnished with some of the very finely chopped leaves.

A small teaspoon of cream poured into the centre of each serving at the last moment will make this soup even more delicious.

Cream of fresh pea
Pressure-cooking time: 4 minutes

325 g (12 oz) fresh shelled peas
  (or thawed frozen peas)
1·2 litres (2 pt) foundation stock
sprigs of mint

salt and pepper
to serve:
  2 tablespoons cream
  cayenne pepper

Put the peas (add a few washed pods if fresh peas are used), stock, mint and seasoning into the cooker, bring to pressure, cook for 4 minutes, then allow pressure to reduce at room temperature. Strain the soup, lift out the pods and mint, sieve or mash the peas into a purée and return to the open cooker. Add sufficient of the stock to give the correct consistency and reboil. Taste to correct seasoning and just before serving, add the cream and sprinkle lightly with cayenne pepper.

A ham bone cooked with the peas or a little of the stock from a boiled ham added to the purée will give an extra flavour to this soup.

Cream of leek and potato
Pressure-cooking time: 10 minutes

1 large tablespoon margarine
2 leeks, sliced (white part only)
450 g (1 lb) potatoes, peeled
  and quartered
9 dl (1½ pt) white stock*
salt and pepper

2 egg yolks thinned with
  2 tablespoons milk or cream
knob of butter
to garnish:
  finely chopped green of leeks

Melt the margarine in the open cooker and without allowing them to colour, lightly fry the leeks and the potatoes (which should be thoroughly rinsed, after quartering, in cold water). Add the stock and seasoning, bring to pressure, cook for 10 minutes, then allow the pressure to reduce at room temperature. Mash the vegetables into a smooth purée in the cooker, reheat and taste to correct seasoning (use plenty of pepper). When the soup is really boiling, lift from the heat and stir in the egg yolks and cream and the butter. Serve at once, sprinkled with a little of the very finely chopped green from the leeks.

Serve immediately the eggs have been added; if this soup is allowed to boil again, the eggs will curdle it.

Cream of mushroom
Pressure-cooking time: 4 minutes

325 g (12 oz) fresh mushrooms, peeled and finely sliced
9 dl (1½ pt) water
a few bacon rinds, if available
salt and pepper
½ teaspoon celery salt

1 tablespoon margarine
1 tablespoon flour
3 dl (½ pt) milk
to serve:
2 tablespoons cream
knob of butter

Put the mushrooms, water, bacon rinds and seasoning into the cooker, bring to pressure, cook for 4 minutes and then allow the pressure to reduce at room temperature. During the cooking, melt the margarine in another saucepan, add the flour and, while stirring, cook for 2–3 minutes without allowing it to colour. Away from the heat, gradually add the milk; return to a low heat and stir until thickened. Strain the soup. Lift out the bacon rinds, chop the mushrooms finely and add them to the sauce; then, beating well, stir in sufficient of the stock to give the required consistency. Reheat, taste and correct seasoning, and just before serving, add the cream and a knob of butter.

Cream of tomato
Pressure-cooking time: 5 minutes

1 tablespoon butter
450 g (1 lb) tomatoes, skinned and sliced
1 onion, sliced
1 carrot, sliced
6 dl (1 pt) white stock*
1 heaped teaspoon sugar
salt and pepper
bay leaf

2 cloves
1 tablespoon margarine
1 tablespoon flour
3 dl (½ pt) milk
to garnish:
chopped parsley
2 tablespoons cream
to serve:
fried croûtons*

Melt the butter in the open cooker and gently fry the tomatoes, onion and carrot without allowing them to colour. Add the stock, sugar, seasoning, cloves and bay leaf, bring to pressure, cook for 5 minutes, then allow the pressure to reduce at room temperature. During the cooking, melt the margarine in another saucepan, add the flour and, while stirring, cook for 2–3 minutes without allowing it to colour. Away from the heat, gradually add the milk, return to a low heat and stir until thickened. Strain the soup, lift out the bay leaf and cloves, sieve the vegetables and add this purée to the sauce, then, beating well, add sufficient of the stock to give the required consistency. Reheat, taste and correct seasoning.

In the serving dish, mix well together the chopped parsley and cream, pour the hot soup on and serve at once. Hand the croûtons separately.

If you are lucky enough to have your own home-grown vegetables, you will be able to make many more of these soups, using the vegetables when they are at their best and most plentiful. For example:

Cream of broad bean
Make as for **Fresh Pea**; cook 5 minutes; serve with croûtons.

Cream of cucumber
Make as for **Celery**, using 2 large cucumbers. Wash, cut in half (remove seeds if the cucumbers are getting old), slice finely. Cook 5 minutes. Before serving, add 2 tablespoons very finely diced gherkin but reheat very carefully so that the vinegar will not curdle the soup. Garnish with chopped chives.

Cream of onion
Make as for **Leek and Potato**, using 3 large Spanish onions; cook 7 minutes; garnish with chopped chives.

Dried vegetable soups

Overnight soaking is not necessary. Wash the dried vegetables, put into a basin, boil half the quantity of the liquid given in the recipe, pour over, cover with a plate and leave for 1 hour.

Proportions: about 100 g (4 oz) to 9 dl (1½ pt) water or stock.

Haricot bean purée
Pressure-cooking time: 20 minutes

1 large onion or 3 leeks	9 dl (1½ pt) stock or water
2 sticks celery	bouquet garni*
1 small turnip	1·5 dl (¼ pt) milk
225 g (8 oz) potatoes, peeled	salt and pepper
100 g (4 oz) small haricot beans	
2 tablespoons margarine or	
dripping	

Cut up the prepared vegetables roughly and put into the cooker with the strained, soaked beans (saving the liquid) and margarine. Allow to cook gently for 5 minutes, stirring occasionally. Make the liquid up to 9 dl (1½ pt), and add the bouquet garni and seasoning. Bring to pressure on a **medium** heat, cook for 20 minutes, then allow the pressure to reduce at room temperature. Remove the bouquet garni, sieve or mash the vegetables into a purée, return to the cooker, and add the milk. Taste and correct seasoning, reheat and serve. If using large haricots, increase the cooking time to 30 minutes.

Lentil soup
Pressure-cooking time: 20 minutes

1 large onion	bouquet garni*
1 carrot	1 tablespoon margarine
2 leeks	1 tablespoon flour
2 sticks celery	1·5 dl (¼ pt) milk
100 g (4 oz) lentils	if available, 3 cooked, skinned
9 dl (1½ pt) water	frankfurter sausages
1 ham bone (or small piece of the	*to serve:*
cheapest bacon joint)	fried croûtons*

Cut up the prepared vegetables roughly. Put them in the cooker with the soaked lentils, the soaking liquid made up to the correct quantity, the ham bone, water and bouquet garni. Bring to pressure over a **medium** heat, cook for 20 minutes, then allow the pressure to reduce at room temperature. During the cooking, melt the margarine in another saucepan, add the flour and cook without allowing to colour. Away from the heat, gradually add the milk, return to a low heat and stir until thickened. Lift out the ham bone, sieve or mash the vegetables into a purée, beat into the sauce and add sufficient of the stock to give the required consistency. Put in the sliced sausages, taste and correct the seasoning, reheat and serve, handing the croûtons separately.

Split pea soup
Pressure-cooking time: 12 minutes

4 slices streaky bacon	bay leaf
2 leeks, sliced	salt and pepper
2 sticks celery, chopped	*to serve:*
100 g (4 oz) split peas	fried croûtons*
9 dl (1½ pt) water	

Cut the bacon into small pieces, put into the open cooker and fry gently so that the fat runs out. Add the leeks and celery and cook for a few minutes without allowing to brown. Add the washed peas, the water, bay leaf and seasoning. Bring to pressure over a **medium** heat, cook for 12 minutes, then allow the pressure to reduce at room temperature. Lift out the bay leaf, mash the vegetables into a purée, reheat, taste and correct seasoning. Serve piping hot, handing the croûtons separately.

Cold soups

The real secret of making these refreshing soups, just right to start a summer meal or hostess occasion or taken outdoors for picnics, barbecues and so on, lies in their consistency, which must never be stiff or solid. They must be set, but should 'tremble' when shaken and must be more strongly flavoured and seasoned than a hot soup. Their basis must always be a meat, chicken or fish stock made well in advance and chilled so that its 'jell' can be checked.

Consommé madrilène

1·5 dl (¼ pt) fresh or tinned tomato juice	6–9 dl (1–1½ pt) rich chicken stock*
1 teaspoon sugar	dash of Worcestershire sauce
1 clove garlic, crushed	*to garnish:*
small sprig of mint	red pimento
salt and pepper	

Put the tomato juice, sugar, garlic, mint and seasoning into a saucepan and boil gently for 5 minutes. Strain and add sufficient stock to ensure a 'trembling' set. Add the Worcestershire Sauce, taste and correct seasoning. Reheat and, when cool, put to chill in the refrigerator. Serve, spooned into individual soup cups, garnished with very fine strips of pimento.

Iced shrimp or prawn bisque
Pressure-cooking time: 10 minutes

6 dl (1 pt) good fish stock*
6 dl (1 pt) cooked shrimps or
  prawns
1 slice lemon peel
3 tablespoons crushed cream
  crackers
pinch of nutmeg

juice of ½ lemon
1 egg yolk
1·5 dl (¼ pt) cream
to garnish:
  watercress

Put the fish stock, shells of shrimps and lemon peel into the cooker, bring to pressure, cook for 10 minutes, then allow the pressure to reduce at room temperature. Strain the stock on to the crushed biscuits and allow them to soak. Leave a few shrimps aside for garnish, and either pound the rest with the nutmeg and a good squeeze of lemon juice in a mortar, liquidize them, or pass them through a parsley/mint cutter. Gradually stir into the stock with the biscuits to give a really creamy mixture. Put into a saucepan, cook for 5 minutes over a low heat, stirring all the time, and then sieve. Beat the egg yolk and cream together in a small basin, add 2 tablespoons of the hot soup, stir this mixture into the rest of the sieved soup, return to the pan and gently reheat, stirring all the time. Do not allow to reboil or it will curdle. When cool, chill thoroughly in the refrigerator and serve, very cold, garnished with some finely chopped shrimps and watercress.

Crème vichyssoise
Pressure-cooking time: 7 minutes

2 tablespoons butter
4 leeks, sliced
1 medium onion, diced
5 potatoes, diced
2 medium carrots, diced
6 dl (1 pt) chicken stock* (or
  a stock cube, dissolved)

salt and pepper
1·5 dl (¼ pt) double cream
3 dl (½ pt) milk
to garnish:
  finely chopped chives

Lift the trivet from the cooker, melt the butter and gently fry the leeks and onions until evenly golden. Add the potatoes, carrots, stock and seasoning, bring to pressure, cook for 7 minutes and allow the pressure to reduce at room temperature. Add half the cream to the milk, stirring well; pour into the soup and quickly bring to the boil in the open pan, lifting it from the heat at the exact moment when boiling point is reached. Allow to cool slightly; sieve, taste and correct seasoning, and put to chill.

Just before serving, stir in the rest of the cream, pour into chilled individual soup cups and sprinkle with the chives.

2 Vegetables

This section deals with those foods on which the reputation of a pressure cooker – and its user – most often rests. With vegetables of all kinds there are certain points to know and watch for; then a little trial and error, a little experience of their cooking in and out of season, young and old, fresh or a little tired, and you will soon be serving them with all their goodness, colour and flavour.

In every way, pressure cooking is *the* way to treat fresh vegetables: to cook in the absence of air conserves the vitamins; to cook in steam means little loss of minerals, sugar and soluble proteins; to cook with the small amount of liquid necessary to provide steam means that no goodness need be wasted, as the vegetable water will be used for sauces and gravies or as stock for soups, stews etc.

When pressure cooking, do not forget that the age, freshness and the size of the pieces into which you cut the fresh vegetables will all affect their cooking times, just as when using an ordinary saucepan. This being so, all the times suggested in the following tables and recipes are intended as a guide, not as hard and fast rules.

Here are a few general rules for the preparation and pressure cooking of fresh vegetables which will ensure your success in obtaining the best possible results.

General instructions

Fresh vegetables, except onions, should be carefully washed in plenty of cold water and all should have any doubtful parts removed.

Vegetables are best prepared as near cooking time as possible, particularly if they are to be cut up or shredded. If they must be prepared well in advance they will keep best if put directly into plastic bags and then into the refrigerator. Otherwise they should be left in cold water; do not put them into the cooker itself ready for cooking as this will cause them to discolour and dry out.

The minimum quantity of liquid, 1·5 dl + 1·5 dl ($\frac{1}{4}$ pt + $\frac{1}{4}$ pt), should be used except in the cases of certain fresh and all dried vegetables – see the special recipes given in the following pages.

All fresh vegetables, unless otherwise stated, should be cooked in steam, not in liquid; so the trivet must be used for the larger, easily served vegetables such as potatoes and carrots, while the separators or containers are reserved for the smaller ones such as peas and shredded cabbage. Pressure-cooked in this way, a selection of different vegetables with different cooking times and different flavours can be cooked together and still be served separately, as they will not move around or mix together during the cooking, nor will their flavours mix as they would if all were being cooked in water instead of steam.

Where fresh vegetables to be cooked together are of different sizes or thicknesses they should be cut down so that all can be given the same pressure-cooking time. As green vegetables require the shortest cooking, root vegetables should be cut into halves, quarters or cubes if they are to be cooked with them. A method for cooking vegetables together is given on p 48.

You may find that much less seasoning is needed in a pressure cooker than in an ordinary saucepan because vegetables retain their own mineral salts, so add it sparingly at first. Salt should always be sprinkled directly on the vegetables as they are being put into the cooker or as they are packed, layer by layer, in the separators or divisions. To ensure even distribution and complete dissolving of the grains in the steam, it is better to use table salt rather than the cooking variety. Spices and herbs are also included before cooking, but pepper is best added just before serving.

Unless the instructions or recipe states otherwise, pressure should be reduced at once, with cold water, when the cooking time is up.

A time-table for frozen vegetables with suggested cooking instructions is given separately.

Fresh vegetables (general)

Type	Preparation and cooking
Artichokes (Jerusalem)	Wash, scrape or peel, cook on trivet. Cut in quarters if large; cut in halves if medium and stand in water with a squeeze of lemon juice to keep white
Aubergines (eggplant)	Wash, do not peel, cut in 1·2-cm ($\frac{1}{2}$-in) slices
Beetroots	Wash carefully without breaking the skin, cut off tops leaving 2·5 cm (1 in) of stem. Cook alone in water without trivet. Allow pressure to reduce at room temperature
Carrots	Wash, scrape or peel. Slit tops, when young, whole; slice lengthwise for medium and large
Carrots and peas	Wash carrots, peel, cut into really small dice. Cook with shelled peas, sprig of mint, knob of butter and pinch of sugar in solid container

Dried vegetables must be treated quite differently from the fresh ones and instructions, a time-table and recipes for these are also given separately.

Sauces, melted butter and mayonnaise for serving with vegetables are prepared separately and the recipes will be found in Section 13. Do try and find the pressure-cooking time that suits you, your family and the vegetables best – and then stick to it. Over-cooking will do no good at all and can only lead to disappointment all round.

Use **H** pressure.

Pressure-cooking time	Method of serving
4–5 minutes	Plain, with melted butter; with a rich white sauce to which is added lemon juice when boiling; after cooking toss in butter in another pan, serve, pour butter over and sprinkle with golden crumbs
1–2 minutes	Lift on to absorbent paper. Egg, crumb, and fry in hot melted butter
Small, 6 dl (1 pt) water, 10 minutes Medium, 9 dl (1½ pt) water, 20 minutes Large, old 12 dl (2 pt) water, 30 minutes	Skin after cooking. Serve hot, sliced or diced, with white sauce. Serve cold, sliced or diced, with dressing of vinegar with a pinch of sugar added
Young, whole, 4 minutes Medium, halved, lengthwise, 4 minutes Large, quartered, lengthwise, 4 minutes	With melted butter and garnished with chopped parsley
4 minutes	Strained, with melted butter

continued

Fresh vegetables (general)

Type	Preparation and cooking
Celeriac	Wash, peel thickly, cut in 2·5-cm (1-in) strips or dice, and stand in water with a squeeze of lemon juice to keep white
Courgettes	Wash, top and tail, cook whole
Cucumber	Cucumbers that are too old to eat raw are excellent as a cooked vegetable. Wash, peel if skin is not tender, remove pips; halve lengthwise, cut in slices, quarters or large dice
Kohl-rabi	Wash, remove leaves, peel and cut into $\frac{1}{2}$-cm ($\frac{1}{4}$-in) slices or as for potato chips
Leeks	Cut off the tops and roots, slice into the stem from the top to open up and wash thoroughly
Marrow (vegetable)	Skin, unless very young and tender, cut in thick slices, remove centre core and ends
Mushrooms	
Onions	Peel off the brown skin, cut off the roots
	Wash well, leave skins on
	For pre-cooking before roasting: leave on outer skin

Pressure-cooking time	Method of serving
3 minutes	With white sauce (to which a little lemon juice was added when boiled) poured over celeriac in serving dish. Garnished with hard-boiled egg, the white chopped and the yolk sieved
4 minutes	Slice, put in ovenproof dish, pour over melted butter, sprinkle with chives, leave covered in moderate oven until served
1–2 minutes	With a white or onion sauce, plenty of pepper and garnished with chopped parsley
4 minutes	With cheese or hollandaise sauce; fried in deep or shallow fat, like potato chips
4 minutes	With a white or cheese sauce, using some of the cooking liquid, garnished with parsley
4 minutes	With white or cheese sauce, garnished with chopped parsley. For **Stuffed Marrow**, see recipe on p 49
Sliced, in solid container, 4 minutes	Drain, stir into white sauce, thinned with a little of the cooking liquid See recipe on p 50
Whole, 6–8 minutes	Lift out carefully, skin, coat with cheese sauce, sprinkle with parsley
Whole, 4–5 minutes	Remove outer skin. Continue roasting round the joint in hot oven, basting occasionally

continued

Fresh vegetables (general)

Type	Preparation and cooking
Parsnips	Wash, peel, cut in thin lengths or cubes. Put in 1·5 dl ($\frac{1}{4}$ pt) salted water under trivet; other vegetables may then be cooked on trivet or in containers
	Wash, peel, cut as for potato chips For precooking before roasting: wash, peel, cut in half or leave whole if not too large
Peppers (pimento): red or green	
Potatoes: new	Scrub, scrape or cook in skins and peel afterwards
old	Wash, peel. Small, slit through to centre; medium, halved; large, quartered; precooking for frying or roasting
Swedes	Wash, peel thickly cut into 1-cm ($\frac{1}{2}$-in) chunks or slices. Put into 1·5 dl ($\frac{1}{4}$ pt) water in cooker (under trivet if other vegetables are to be cooked at the same time)
Sweet corn (on cob)	Remove husks, brush away 'silk' with nail brush. Cook on trivet
Tomatoes: for juice	Wash but do not dry. Cut up finely, put in cooker without water or trivet and bring first to boil in the open pan. Allow pressure to reduce at room temperature
Turnips	Wash, peel unless very young and tender

Pressure-cooking time	Method of serving
3–4 minutes	Serve other vegetables, take out trivet, strain off liquid. Put in 2 tablespoons butter, 2 tablespoons sugar and heat in open pan, stirring, until the parsnips are lightly browned
2 minutes	Lift out, drain, dip in batter and deep fry
8–10 minutes	Lift out, continue roasting round the joint in the oven, basting frequently
	See recipe on p 50
Small, whole, 4–5 minutes Medium, whole, 5–6 minutes Large, quartered or halved, 6–8 minutes	Toss with melted butter, sprinkle with chopped mint; when cold leave whole or slice and fry in shallow fat
4 minutes 4–6 minutes 4–6 minutes Whole, 4–6 minutes	As boiled or steamed; lift out other vegetables, lift trivet from under potatoes and use to strain off liquid, toss potatoes over low heat until dry, serve sprinkled with chopped parsley
4 minutes	Strain off liquid, add butter and plenty of pepper and mash thoroughly. Serve sprinkled with chopped parsley
Small, 3 minutes Large, 5 minutes	Serve thickly coated with melted butter
1 minute	For cooking: strain only, or put through a fine sieve; add 1 teaspoon salt to 12 dl (2 pt) sauce. For drinking: add sugar, Worcestershire Sauce to taste, see p 51
Whole, young, 4 minutes Sliced or diced, 4 minutes	With melted butter mashed as for swedes; diced with carrots and peas (cooked together in perforated container), served hot as macédoine or cold as Russian salad in mayonnaise

Potatoes, carrots and shredded cabbage
Pressure cooking root and green vegetables together
in the same time.
Pressure-cooking time: 4 minutes

Put into the pressure cooker 3 dl ($\frac{1}{2}$ pt) water and the trivet. On
this, in two separate piles, put the potatoes and carrots (whole,
halved or quartered according to their size and so that they will
cook in 4 minutes). Season each layer of vegetables well with table
salt as it is being put in. Put the cooker on the heat without the
cover and allow the water to come to the boil. In the meantime,
pack the shredded cabbage tightly into the perforated containers,
salting each layer as it is put in. When the cooker is filled with
steam, put the containers in on top of the other vegetables if there
is room or if not, at the side, where space has been left on the
trivet. Cover, bring to pressure and cook for exactly 4 minutes.
Reduce the pressure immediately with cold water and serve the
vegetables, which will require no straining or draining, according
to the methods suggested in the time-tables or recipes in this
section.

Courgettes à la grecque
Pressure-cooking time: 10 minutes

6–8 courgettes
for the stuffing:
  2 tablespoons minced beef,
    veal or ham
  1 dessertspoon minced onion
  1 teaspoon chopped parsley
  1$\frac{1}{2}$ tablespoons rice
  pepper and salt
  a little oil and vinegar to mix
3 dl ($\frac{1}{2}$ pt) water for the cooker

for the sauce:
  2 eggs
  a little lemon juice
to garnish:
  chopped parsley and grated
  cheese

Wash the courgettes but do not peel. Cut a small slice off either end
of each, loosen the pith with a small knife or a potato peeler and
push it out one end. Scrape a little of the pulp away, chop it and
mix with the other filling ingredients, adding a little mixed oil and
vinegar to give a moist consistency. Stuff the courgettes, leaving

room at either end for expansion. Put the water and the trivet into the cooker, then the courgettes, and cover with a piece of buttered greaseproof paper. Bring to pressure, cook for 10 minutes and allow the pressure to reduce at room temperature. During this cooking, beat the eggs with a squeeze of lemon juice and 2 teaspoons cold water in a small bowl until frothy. Serve the courgettes and keep hot. Take a spoonful of the hot stock and add it to the basin, gradually adding 5 or 6 more; put into a small saucepan and heat gently, stirring all the time until thick, but do not allow to boil or it will curdle. Taste and correct seasoning, pour over the courgettes and sprinkle with the mixed cheese and parsley.

Stuffed marrow
Pressure-cooking time: 12 minutes

1 medium marrow	about 150 g (6 oz) cooked minced
1 tablespoon butter	meat
1 medium onion	salt and pepper
2 tomatoes	mirepoix* for braising
1 tablespoon rice	brown stock* or vegetable water

Peel the marrow, cut a slice from the stalk end, then scoop out the centre pulp with the seeds, using a knife with a long blade or a long-handled spoon. In a frying pan, melt the butter and gently fry the finely chopped onion, the sliced, peeled tomatoes and the washed rice for about 5 minutes. Lift the pan from the heat, add the minced meat and seasonings and mix thoroughly. Fill the mixture into the marrow case, tapping it occasionally to make sure the mixture is evenly packed. Lift the trivet from the cooker, prepare the mirepoix, adding the required amount of liquid, put the marrow on top, replacing the cut-off slice to close the end, and cover with a sheet of greased greaseproof paper. Bring to pressure, cook for 12 minutes and reduce the pressure with cold water. Lift out the marrow, cut into thick slices, lay overlapping in a deep serving dish and keep hot. Mash or sieve the mirepoix vegetables, taste and correct seasoning and if necessary add a little gravy colouring; reboil with the liquid in the open cooker, then pour round the sliced marrow.

Stuffed mushrooms
Pressure-cooking time: 3 minutes

2 large mushrooms per person
2 shallots
2 teaspoons chopped parsley
1 tablespoon butter
2 tablespoons fresh breadcrumbs
salt and pepper
a little gravy or brown sauce*
3 dl (½ pt) water for the cooker

Have the mushrooms of the same size, peel and cut off the stalks. Chop these with the shallots and parsley and fry gently in the butter, in a small saucepan. Add the breadcrumbs, seasoning and sufficient sauce to make a moist stuffing. Pile this evenly on the mushrooms. Put the water and the trivet in the cooker, then the mushrooms (if they will not all go on the trivet, put in a sheet of greaseproof paper and then a second layer). Bring to pressure, cook 3 minutes and reduce the pressure with cold water. Serve on buttered toast or on triangles of fried bread.

Stuffed green peppers
Pressure-cooking time: 5 minutes

2 green peppers
for the stuffing:
   100 g (4 oz) minced fresh or cooked beef
   1 large cup cooked rice
   2 tablespoons minced onion
   1 egg
   a little tomato soup or purée
   salt and pepper
golden crumbs
butter
3 dl (½ pt) water for the cooker

Cut the peppers in half and remove the seeds. Mix together the other ingredients, adding plenty of seasoning and sufficient tomato soup or purée to bind the mixture, and then pile into the pepper shells. Put into the cooker the water, the trivet and then the stuffed peppers, covering them with a piece of buttered grease-proof paper. Bring to pressure, cook for 5 minutes, then allow the pressure to reduce at room temperature. Lift the peppers into an ovenproof dish, sprinkle each with golden crumbs, dot with butter and pop under a hot grill for a moment or two.

Scalloped potatoes
Pressure-cooking time: 5 minutes

1 tablespoon butter or margarine	1 tablespoon flour
3 dl (½ pt) milk and water	grated cheese
450 g (1 lb) potatoes, sliced	paprika
salt and pepper	butter
3 spring onions or 1 medium	
onion, chopped	

Lift the trivet from the cooker, melt the butter in the open pan, pour in the milk and water and bring to boil. Put in a layer of potatoes, sprinkle with salt, pepper, some onion and a little of the flour, and repeat until all ingredients have been added. Bring to pressure, cook for 5 minutes and reduce the pressure immediately with cold water. Lift out into an ovenproof dish, sprinkle thickly with grated cheese and lightly with paprika, dot with butter and brown under a hot grill.

Stuffed tomatoes
Pressure-cooking time: 5 minutes

4 large tomatoes
3 dl (½ pt) water with a little lemon
  juice or vinegar for the cooker
espagnole*, madeira* or cheese*
  sauce, or hot gravy, if served
  as supper dish on its own

for the stuffing:
  1 tablespoon butter
  2 tablespoons minced fresh or
    cooked meat
  2 shallots or 1 small onion,
    finely chopped
  finely chopped parsley
  2 tablespoons white breadcrumbs
  1 egg
  a little grated lemon rind
  salt, pepper and pinch of nutmeg
  dash of Worcestershire sauce

Wash the tomatoes, cut a small circle from the stalk end and, with a tablespoon, carefully remove the centres without piercing the skin. In a separate pan, melt the butter and carefully brown the minced meat and onions. Away from the heat stir in the parsley, breadcrumbs, the tomato pulp, the beaten egg and the seasonings. Stuff the tomatoes with the filling and put each into a buttered cup. Put the water and trivet into the cooker, then the cups covered with a piece of buttered greaseproof paper. Bring to pressure, cook for 5 minutes and reduce the pressure with cold water. Lift out the cups, scoop underneath each tomato with a tablespoon so that they can be served the right way up and put back the cut-off slice as a cap. Garnish with sprigs of parsley and serve with a suitable hot sauce or with heated gravy, if any is left over from a joint.

If more than 4 or 5 are to be done at one time, put one lot of cups in the water in the bottom of the cooker, then the piece of grease-proof paper, then the trivet, with another lot of cups and another piece of paper, making a second layer.

Cream of sweet corn
Pressure-cooking time: 3 minutes

3–4 corn cobs
3 dl (½ pt) water for the cooker
2 tablespoons butter

1 tablespoon double cream
salt and pepper

Remove husks and silk, put water and trivet in the cooker, then the corn, bring to pressure, cook for 3 minutes and reduce pressure immediately. Cut the kernels from the cob, scraping every bit off. Melt the butter, add the cream and then the corn, taste and correct

Type	Preparation and cooking
Artichokes (globe)	Wash, cut stems level, so that the heads can stand upright on trivet
Asparagus	Whole stalks: wash, cut off tough ends (use for soup stock), scrape scales off stalks, tie in bundles of 6–8 Tips: wash, cut off green tips, put in perforated or covered solid container with a knob of butter and seasoning

seasoning. This may be served as a vegetable, with a poached egg on top or in fillings for stuffed vegetables etc in place of rice.

Fresh green vegetables

When items in the following table are to be pressure cooked, whether on their own or with other vegetables or foods, the water which has been put into the cooker must always be allowed to boil so that the pan is filled with steam before the vegetables are added. This principle is the same as with an ordinary saucepan; green vegetables started from 'cold' lose their colour and a lot of their goodness; green vegetables started from 'hot' keep their bright green look and more of their vitamins and flavour. Similarly, these vegetables should not be in water when pressure cooked; piled on the trivet or into containers they will lose much less of their minerals and salts.

With fresh green vegetables timing must be exact; this is 'minute' cooking and 'I'll give them just another minute' will only lead to overcooking and consequent loss of colour, texture and flavour.

Pressure-cooking time	Method of serving
Small, 6 minutes Large, 10 minutes	With browned butter with lemon juice added; with hollandaise sauce
According to thickness, 2–4 minutes	With melted butter over tips; with hollandaise or mousseline sauce
Perforated container, 1–2 minutes Solid container, 3–4 minutes	As garnish just with melted butter; with hollandaise sauce; cold, combined with a mayonnaise

continued

Type	Preparation and cooking
Beans	Broad: shell, cook on trivet if alone, or in perforated container if with other vegetables French or runner: wash, remove ends, string and slice. If very young, may be cooked whole. Put in a sprig of mint Princess: wash, remove ends, break into 2 or 3 pieces
Broccoli	Wash in salted water. Cut off thick stalks, then snick ends. Cook on trivet or separated from other vegetables underneath by a piece of greaseproof paper
Brussels sprouts	Wash in salted water. Remove discoloured old outer leaves. Cut cross in stem
Cabbage	Wash in salted water. Remove discoloured, wilted outside leaves. Red should be cooked on its own; green or white can be separated from other vegetables underneath by a piece of greaseproof paper White or green: cut in quarters, cut away some of hard white core; or shred roughly Red: shredded
Cauliflower	Wash in salted water; remove all but young, inner green leaves. Cut away thick stalk. Flowerets: break into small pieces, quartered or halved; cut away white core. Always separate from other vegetables underneath with a piece of greaseproof paper
Celery	Scrub in salted water, cut off green leaves, string; cut the outer stems in half, lengthwise; cut in 2–5-cm (1–2-in) pieces

Pressure-cooking time	Method of serving
On trivet, 2 minutes In container, 4–5 minutes	With melted butter or parsley sauce
On trivet, 2–4 minutes In container, 4–5 minutes	With melted butter
As above	As above
3–4 minutes	With melted butter, either whole or chopped
On trivet, 2–3 minutes In perforated container, 3–4 minutes	Whole, plain, or dotted with knobs of butter
	Add white or black pepper and toss in butter
On trivet, 2–3 minutes In perforated container, tightly packed, 3–4 minutes	Dot with knobs of butter
On trivet, 4–5 minutes	See recipe on p 60
On trivet, 3–4 minutes On trivet, 2–3 minutes (flowerets)	With browned breadcrumbs; with a white, parsley or cheese sauce; with grated cheese and chopped parsley
In perforated container, 3–4 minutes	With white or parsley sauce; braised as hors d'oeuvre with french dressing or hollandaise sauce

continued

Type	Preparation and cooking
Chicory (endive)	Wash under gently running cold water, remove any yellowing leaves. Do not cut in any way as this may make it taste bitter when cooked. Lift out trivet, melt 50 g (2 oz) butter without colouring, put in 2 tablespoons water, 1 teaspoon lemon juice, salt and pepper. Cover with buttered greaseproof paper
Peas	Shell, cook with a few washed pods and a sprig of mint. If peas are getting old or it has been a very dry season, cook in solid container as above but with a pinch of sugar also and allow pressure to reduce at room temperature to prevent the peas from bursting
Spinach	Wash several times in fast running water; remove stalks and the spines of the larger leaves. Cook alone. Do not use trivet. After final rinse, do not drain; pack a layer into cooker, put on high heat and as the water boils pack in further layers, seasoning in between; press down as hard as possible until cooker is two-thirds full
Various **dandelion leaves**	Use only young leaves from plants which have not yet flowered
Kale (curly)	Wash in plenty of running water
Turnip tops	Wash in plenty of running water

Pressure-cooking time	Method of serving
Alone in cooker, 4–6 minutes	Lift on to serving dish, boil liquid in open cooker until well reduced, then pour over chicory. See recipes for serving as supper, vegetarian dish
In perforated container, 2–4 minutes In solid container, 5 minutes	Tossed in melted butter, sprinkled with finely chopped mint; with diced carrots, turnips, etc, for macédoine As above, with vegetables tossed when cold in mayonnaise, as Russian salad
Up to pressure only	Serve well drained, in leaf, with melted butter; chopped with melted butter; sieved with a little nutmeg, melted butter and cream or milk added before reheating
As for **Spinach**	Chop well, toss in melted butter
As for **Shredded Cabbage** As for **Shredded Cabbage**	As above As above

Asparagus

For the following recipes prepare and cook the bundles of asparagus as given in the time-table:

AU GRATIN

1·5 dl (¼ pt) cheese sauce*
1 tablespoon grated cheese
knobs of butter

During the pressure-cooking make the sauce, using half quantity of milk only. After reducing pressure, drain the asparagus well, put into a heatproof serving dish and untie the bundles. Add sufficient of the stock to give the sauce a coating consistency, pour over the asparagus, sprinkle with the grated cheese, add small knobs of butter and put under a hot grill until the cheese is melted and the surface an even brown.

POLONAISE

4 tablespoons melted butter
1 hard-boiled egg
chopped parsley and chives
golden crumbs

After reducing pressure, drain the asparagus well, put into a hot serving dish, untie the bundles, coat with the foaming-hot melted butter and sprinkle thickly with the mixed chopped hard-boiled egg, parsley, chives and golden crumbs.

SUISSE

2 tablespoons grated gruyère cheese
a little single cream
chopped parsley

After reducing pressure, drain the asparagus well, put into a hot serving dish. Melt the gruyère cheese over a low heat, add sufficient cream to give a coating consistency and pour over the tips. Garnish with finely chopped parsley.

AS SALAD

4–6 spears per portion
lemon juice
shredded lettuce

french dressing
thin strips of red pepper

After reducing pressure, drain the asparagus well, untie the bundles and allow to get quite cold. (You may prefer actually to chill it in the refrigerator.) Allow to marinate in a shallow dish with lemon juice for 2–3 hours, carefully turning over once, during this time. Strain well, then serve each portion on finely shredded lettuce, pour over a french dressing and garnish with a thin strip of red pepper across the stalks.

Broad beans provençale
Pressure-cooking time: 3–4 minutes

2 tablespoons butter	1·5 dl ($\frac{1}{4}$ pt) white stock* or water
3 tomatoes	salt and pepper
2 tablespoons finely sliced green pepper	450 g (1 lb) shelled broad beans

Lift the trivet out of the cooker, melt the butter in the open pan, add the skinned, roughly chopped tomatoes and the finely sliced green pepper and allow to cook gently for a minute or two. Put in the liquid, season well, add the young, shelled beans, cover, bring to pressure and cook for 3–4 minutes, according to size. Reduce pressure with cold water, lift the beans into the serving dish and keep warm. Reduce the liquid remaining in the open pan carefully so that it does not burn and until it is thick. Taste and correct seasoning, then pour over the beans.

French beans lyonnaise

french beans, coarsely sliced
2 onions
2 tablespoons butter

Prepare and cook the coarsely sliced beans as given in the time-table (p 54). During the cooking, fry the finely chopped onions gently in butter in a frying pan until an even golden-brown colour. After reducing pressure, add the beans to the onions, tossing all well together and serve, pouring over any butter that remains.

Broccoli
This is delicious if, after cooking and just before serving, the spears are thickly sprinkled with grated cheese and then hot, foaming butter is poured over.

Green or white scalloped cabbage
Pressure-cooking time: 3 minutes

1·5 dl (¼ pt) water
1 onion
1 cabbage
1 tablespoon chopped red or green
pepper

salt and pepper
3 dl (½ pt) white sauce*
1 teaspoon Worcestershire sauce

Lift the trivet from the cooker, put in the water, the finely chopped onion, the shredded cabbage, the chopped red or green pepper and seasoning. Cook for 3 minutes, reducing pressure with cold water. During the cooking, make a thick white sauce in another pan, using half the quantity of milk and adding the Worcestershire Sauce. Stir in the strained vegetables, using the cooking liquid to thin the sauce; taste and correct the seasoning, using plenty of pepper, and reheat quickly before serving piping hot.

Red cabbage flamande
Pressure-cooking time: 5 minutes

2 slices streaky bacon
1 medium onion
2 tablespoons vinegar
2 tablespoons water or ham stock
1 red cabbage
2 sharp eating apples
2 cloves

for thickening:
1 tablespoon butter
1 tablespoon flour
1 tablespoon sugar
pepper, salt and nutmeg

Lift the trivet from the cooker, put in the slices of bacon, cut into small pieces, and cook over a gentle heat until the fat runs out. Gently fry the chopped onion until soft but not brown, then add the vinegar and water or ham stock, the finely shredded cabbage, the peeled, cored and sliced sharp eating apples and the cloves. Bring to pressure, cook for 5 minutes, then allow the pressure to reduce at room temperature. For the thickening, melt the butter in another pan, add the flour and cook gently without colouring. Strain the liquid into the thickening, allow to boil, stirring all the time, then all the vegetables, together with at least 1 tablespoon of sugar (more may be added to taste) and a good sprinkling of pepper and nutmeg. Taste and correct seasoning and reheat before serving.

Braised celery
Pressure-cooking time: 4 minutes

1·5 dl (¼ pt) good brown stock*
 (or a stock cube, dissolved)
1 large or 2 small heads celery
salt and pepper

2 tablespoons tomato purée
pinch of sugar
to garnish:
 chopped parsley

Lift the trivet from the cooker, put in the stock, the prepared celery sticks cut in half and the seasoning. Bring to pressure in the usual way and cook for 4 minutes. After reducing pressure, lift the celery into a heatproof dish and put into the oven to keep warm. Boil the stock in the open pan quickly until reduced by half, then stir in the tomato purée and the sugar, taste and correct seasoning and pour, piping hot, over the celery. Garnish with the chopped parsley.

Cauliflower cheese
Pressure-cooking time: 4 minutes

1 large cauliflower
3 dl (½ pt) water for the cooker
3 dl (½ pt) cheese sauce*
2 large tomatoes
salt and pepper

knobs of butter
a little grated cheese
to garnish:
 sprigs of parsley
 12 bacon rolls*

Wash and trim the cauliflower and divide in two; cut small triangles from the thick stems. Put the water, trivet and the cauliflower, cut sides down, in the cooker; bring to pressure, cook for 4 minutes and reduce the pressure with cold water. Make the cheese sauce and keep hot; grill the bacon rolls; in four individual buttered ovenproof dishes lay slices of the skinned tomatoes, season well, dot with butter and put under grill. Divide the cauliflower into four portions, put each in its dish and coat with the cheese sauce. Sprinkle with grated cheese and leave under the grill to brown. Garnish with the bacon rolls and sprigs of parsley.

Chicory au gratin
Pressure-cooking time: 3 minutes

4 heads chicory	2 tablespoons tomato purée
1·5 dl (¼ pt) water	grated cheese
2 eggs	knobs of butter
salt and pepper	

Prepare the chicory; put into the cooker the water, the eggs and then the chicory, sprinkled with table salt. Bring to pressure, cook for 3 minutes, then allow pressure to reduce at room temperature. Drop the eggs into cold water to cool and then remove the shells. Lift the chicory into an ovenproof dish, put a half of hard-boiled egg on each head, pour over the tomato purée thinned with a little of the cooking liquid to a coating consistency, sprinkle thickly with grated cheese, add small dabs of butter and reheat, until golden-brown, under a hot grill.

Peas normandie
Pressure-cooking time: 3 minutes

450 g (1 lb) peas	1·5 dl (¼ pt) white stock* or water
1 heart of young lettuce	small teaspoon sugar
6 spring onions	salt and pepper
1 tablespoon butter	chopped parsley and chives

Shell the peas, finely shred the lettuce and peel the spring onions. Lift the trivet from the cooker, melt the butter over a low heat, put in the vegetables and toss lightly. Add the white stock or water, the sugar and seasoning, bring to pressure and cook for 3–4 minutes. After reducing pressure with cold water, lift the vegetables into the serving dish and keep warm. Boil the remaining liquid in the open pan quickly until reduced by half, and use a tablespoon or so of it just to moisten the vegetables; sprinkle with chopped parsley and chives and serve.

Frozen vegetables

As these will have already had a certain amount of cooking before the deep-freezing process, it is not recommended to use a pressure cooker if this type of vegetable only is to be cooked. Little time would be saved. But if a frozen vegetable is to be served with other fresh or green vegetables, then a very satisfactory result can be obtained if pressure cooked as follows:

Vegetables should not be allowed to defrost before cooking. Those in a solid block (such as spinach) must, however, be broken up, as otherwise the outer surfaces will cook while the centre will remain frozen. Use a sharp knife or a small kitchen saw to cut into cubes. Small vegetables, such as peas and beans, or those in pieces or spears, such as brussels sprouts or broccoli, can easily be broken up by knocking several times against a hard surface.

Small green vegetables or those difficult to serve if cooked loose should be put into perforated containers, sprinkled with table salt and as with their fresh counterparts, should be added to the cooker only when the water is boiling and the pan filled with steam.

Root vegetables, still frozen, should be cooked exactly as their fresh counterparts.

If frozen vegetables have been allowed to defrost – that is, have stood for at least an hour in the kitchen temperature – they will require only half the time given in the time-table below.

Always reduce pressure immediately with cold water.

When serving, follow the suggestions given in the previous tables for fresh vegetables.

Type	Preparation and cooking	Pressure-cooking time (minutes)
Asparagus	Separate stalks or tips	4 (in solid container)
Beans (broad)	Tap to break up	4 (in perforated container)
Beans (french)	Tap to break up	4 (in perforated container)
Beans (french, whole)	Tap to break up	4 (in perforated container)
Broccoli	Tap to break up	4 (in perforated container)
Brussels sprouts	Tap to break up	4 (in perforated container)
Carrots	Tap to break up	4 (on trivet)
Mixed vegetables	Tap to break up	4 (in perforated container)
Peas	Tap to break up	4 (in perforated container)
Spinach	Cut block into cubes	4 (in perforated container)
Sweet-corn (on cob)	Allow to defrost	To pressure only (on trivet)

Dried vegetables

Pressure cooking will save hours in the preparation of dried vegetables and is particularly useful as it is not necessary to soak them overnight. They should, however, be washed, picked over and presoaked before pressure cooking. Put them when prepared into a basin, add sufficient boiling water to just cover them, put a plate on top and leave for 1 hour.

As dried vegetables need to take up a lot of water during the cooking, the trivet is not required and 1·2 litres (2 pt) water or stock should be allowed for each 450 g (1 lb). This can be the soaking water made up to the correct amount.

The liquid in the cooker should always be boiling before the soaked vegetables are put in.

Soda should not be added as this will discolour the inside of the cooker.

After adding the vegetables, together with any seasoning, herbs etc, bring to the boil on a high heat in the open pan and skim well. Lower heat until the liquid is gently boiling but not rising up in the pan, then bring to pressure without altering the heat. This will take a little longer than normal, but it is necessary to ensure that the vegetables do not boil into the cover and perhaps block the centre vent causing the safety plug to come into action. Pressure should be reduced at room temperature.

Type	Pressure-cooking time
Haricot beans (small)	20 minutes
Haricot or butter beans (large)	30 minutes
Lentils	15 minutes
Peas (split)	15 minutes
Peas (whole)	20 minutes

Baked beans
Pressure-cooking time: 20 minutes

225 g (8 oz) small haricot beans
3–4 slices streaky bacon
1 small onion, chopped

2 tablespoons brown sugar
1 teaspoon dry mustard
1 small tin tomato juice

2 tablespoons tomato purée or
  sauce
6 dl (1 pt) water

salt and pepper
1–2 tablespoons flour

Wash and pre-soak the beans as instructed. Lift the trivet from the cooker, put in the chopped bacon and allow to heat gently in the open pan until the fat runs out. Fry the onion until golden-brown, then add the sugar, mustard, tomato juice, the purée or sauce dissolved in the water, the beans and the seasoning. Bring to pressure as instructed, cook for 20 minutes and allow the pressure to reduce at room temperature. Strain off the liquid, put the beans into an ovenproof dish and put, uncovered, into the top of a hot oven, Gas No 6, 200°C (400°F) for 15 minutes. Add a little of the liquid to 1–2 tablespoons flour and, when well blended, pour into the rest of the liquid, return to the heat and stir until boiling; cook for a minute or two. Taste to correct the seasoning, pour over the beans, cover and keep hot until served.

Pease pudding
Pressure-cooking time: 12 minutes

225 g (8 oz) split green peas
6 dl (1 pt) ham or bacon stock
1 large or 2 small eggs

large knob of butter
salt and pepper

Wash and presoak the peas as instructed. Lift the trivet from the cooker, put in the stock (a ham or bacon bone could be added with 6 dl [1 pt] of water if no stock is available, and removed when the cooking time is up) and the soaked peas. Bring to the boil in the open cooker, stirring and skimming as necessary. Lower the heat until the peas are just simmering, put on the lid, bring to pressure without altering the heat and cook for 8 minutes. Allow the pressure to reduce at room temperature.

Mash the peas well with a fork or potato masher, then stir in the well-beaten egg. Add butter, taste and correct seasoning if necessary. Put in a greased bowl or solid container and cover with greaseproof paper. For the second cooking, the Pease Pudding can be cooked on its own for 4 minutes, or as given on p 64, with a selection of other vegetables to be served at the same time.

Salad bretonne
Pressure-cooking time: 20 minutes

225 g (8 oz) small haricot beans	slices of cooked ham, liver
1 tablespoon olive oil	sausage, salami, cold fried beef
2 tablespoons vinegar	or pork sausages
1 teaspoon lemon juice	2 tablespoons chopped parsley
2 medium onions	lettuce leaves

Prepare, pre-soak and cook haricot beans as instructed. Allow the pressure to reduce at room temperature and then strain. Mix together the oil, vinegar and lemon juice and while still warm stir into the beans, mixing all well together. Allow to get quite cold, then stir in the raw, finely diced onions and the cold meat cut into neat squares. Line the salad bowl with the washed and dried lettuce leaves, pile in the haricot bean mixture and sprinkle with chopped parsley.

This makes a delicious light summer supper, served with heated French bread and accompanied by a dry white wine such as a Graves.

Dehydrated vegetables

Pressure-cooking time: 4 minutes

These can be pressure cooked most successfully, though it is not recommended if they are to be cooked on their own, as there would be little saving of time.

As a green vegetable being cooked with others for the same meal, use a solid container, adding half the amount of water given on the packet (this is because they will be cooked more quickly and there will be no loss of liquid by evaporation). Season well, add a sprig of mint with peas and pressure cook in the usual way for 4 minutes. Peas only should have the pressure reduced at room temperature to prevent them bursting. For other vegetables, reduce pressure immediately with cold water. Strain and serve tossed in butter or as in recipes given.

3 Fish

Fish is tasty and nourishing, and since it has become quite expensive, the pressure cooker is the ideal method of preparing it. Only the minimum of liquid is required to provide the steam, so all the goodness can be retained and the cooking liquid need never be wasted. Moreover, since the fish holds together better in steam than in liquid, it is easier to serve attractively.

Again, although the saving of time may not be so great as with those foods which require much longer cooking by ordinary methods, you will notice at once the much improved flavour and will be glad not to have quite so much of the cooking smell through the house.

For pressure cooking, small fish may be cooked whole; larger fish be filleted or cut into steaks. Allow approximately 450 g (1 lb) filleted fish for three people. Care should be taken when buying fish to make sure that it is fresh, with the flesh firm and not flabby and the eyes bright. If the fishmonger removes the heads or tails or fillets the fish for you, be sure to get all the bits and pieces to use either before or during the cooking to make a good fish stock.

Type	Preparation and cooking
Brill **Cod** **Haddock** **Hake** **Halibut** **Plaice** **Rock salmon** **Sole** **Turbot**	Put the prepared fish on the buttered trivet or on a piece of buttered greaseproof paper if being cooked with other vegetables or other foods. Use 3 dl ($\frac{1}{2}$ pt) water or stock or 1·5 dl ($\frac{1}{4}$ pt) water and 1·5 dl ($\frac{1}{4}$ pt) wine 1. Sprinkle with lemon juice and seasoning. Cover with paper 2. Lay thick slices of peeled tomatoes on the fish, sprinkle with finely chopped onions and seasoning. Cover with buttered paper
Salmon and **Salmon-trout**	To serve hot or cold: sprinkle with plenty of lemon juice, salt and pepper. Cook on buttered trivet covered completely with a well-buttered piece of greaseproof paper
Herrings **Mackerel** **Mullet** **Whiting**	1. Cooked whole, with or without heads. Scaled when necessary. Brown the fish all over first in hot butter in the cooker then lift out. Put in 3 dl ($\frac{1}{2}$ pt) hot water, stock or 1·5 dl ($\frac{1}{4}$ pt) water, 1·5 dl ($\frac{1}{4}$ pt) wine, then the trivet and the well-seasoned fish, covered with buttered paper 2. Scale, cut off heads, cut down soft side, open and lay flat, skin side uppermost and pressing all the way down backbone to loosen it. Turn over and lift out backbone. Wash well. Sprinkle with lemon juice and seasoning. Spread with a mixture of herbs, made mustard, chutney or a thick layer of thinly sliced mushrooms. Cook flat or folded, on the buttered trivet covered with buttered paper 3. Using fish whole or boned, fill three-quarters full with suitable stuffing and secure with small skewers, by sewing with coarse thread or parcelling securely in buttered paper. Cook on trivet, covered with buttered paper

Pressure-cooking time	Method of serving
2·5–3·5-cm (1–1½-in) steaks, 4–6 minutes Tail, middle cut or whole, weighing 450–675 g (1–1½ lb), 5–6 minutes per 450 g (1 lb)	Reduce pressure immediately. Lift out carefully and skin and bone when possible 1. Serve with a coating sauce such as anchovy, cheese, hard-boiled egg or parsley, using fish stock and milk. Garnish with lemon and parsley 2. Serve with a separate sauce such as caper, hard-boiled egg, hollandaise, mousseline or tartare. Can be dotted with butter and quickly browned under a hot grill
2·5–3·5-cm (1–1½-in) steaks, 6–8 minutes Tail or middle cut weighing up to 1·35 kg (3 lb), 6 minutes per 450 g (1 lb)	Hot: with anchovy or hollandaise sauce Cold: unwrap and cover again to keep moist. Serve with mayonnaise, tartare or vinaigrette sauce or coated with chaudfroid and accompanied by a crisp green or mixed salad
Whole, according to size, 5–8 minutes	Lift into ovenproof dish, sprinkle with golden crumbs, dot with butter and leave to further brown under a hot grill while cooking vegetables and making suitable sauce such as mustard, hollandaise, caper, using the fish stock. Garnish with chopped parsley
Whole, according to size, 5–8 minutes Boned, according to thickness, 4–5 minutes	Serve with suitable coating sauce, garnish with lemon and parsley or coat thickly with chopped almonds and parsley stirred into melted butter and brown quickly under hot grill
Stuffed, according to size, 10–12 minutes	Lift out, brush with melted butter, sprinkle with golden crumbs and brown under hot grill. Garnish with parsley and lemon quarters

Fresh fish should be washed in a little salted water during preparation and is best cooked on the day it is purchased. If it is to be kept, it should be unwrapped, rinsed in salted water and put in a cool place or the refrigerator between two plates or dishes, in an unsealed plastic bag or loosely parcelled in foil.

In the pressure cooker, fish can be steamed or poached, using the trivet; casseroled directly in the liquid or pan-fried first before pressure cooking.

If fish stock is not available, it can be made with most recipes at the same time as the fish is cooked; it must then be strained before being added to the accompanying sauce.

Certain recipes, to give the correct result, must be made with a specially prepared liquor known as court-bouillon. The recipe, quick and easy to prepare, is given below.

Frozen fish may be substituted for fresh in many of the following recipes. Do not defrost, give the same pressure-cooking time, but use only half the given quantity of liquid to allow for the juices that will come from the fish as it thaws out.

To ensure a perfect fish dish, the accompaniments must be well chosen: vegetables and garnishes of contrasting colour to give attractiveness and a well-made sauce with a sharp or piquant flavour.

Choose a Chablis or a dry Sauterne when looking for a wine to complement fish.

Use **H** pressure when cooking fish.

Court-bouillon

1 glass white wine	bay leaf
1·5 dl (¼ pt) water	salt and pepper (black pepper
1 small onion	if available)
1 clove garlic	a strip of lemon peel

Bring all the ingredients slowly to the boil in a small saucepan, simmer gently in the open pan for 10 minutes, cover and allow to cool.

Court-bouillon is used when cold and strained, or when hot, according to the recipe.

Cod creole
Pressure-cooking time: 5 minutes

1·5 dl (¼ pt) water or fish stock*
1 teaspoon lemon juice or vinegar
salt and pepper
good pinch of mixed herbs
450 g (1 lb) fresh or frozen cod,
 in the piece or in steaks

50 g (2 oz) butter
4 medium tomatoes, skinned
4 medium onions, thinly sliced
to garnish:
 thin slices of green pepper (if
  available), or chopped parsley

Heat the oven to No 4, 180°C (350°F), and set the shelf on the second runner from the top. Lift the trivet from the cooker, put in the liquid, lemon juice, a little salt, the mixed herbs and the fish covered with a piece of buttered paper. Bring to pressure, cook for 5 minutes, allow the pressure to reduce at room temperature, lift out the fish and allow to drain. During the cooking, heat the butter in a frying pan; gently cook the thinly sliced tomatoes, lift into an ovenproof dish and keep hot in the oven. Fry the very thinly sliced onions carefully so that all are an even golden-brown and have absorbed the butter. Flake the fish, seasoning lightly with pepper, and pile on to the tomatoes. Cover completely with the onions, then add the strips of green pepper and bake in the oven for 10 minutes. During this time the accompanying vegetables can be pressure cooked. If pepper strips have not been used, sprinkle the fish with parsley just before serving.

Fish au gratin with stuffed tomatoes
Pressure-cooking time: 5 minutes

3 dl (½ pt) fish stock* for the
 cooker (or water with some
 sliced carrots, onion, leek, a few
 peppercorns, mixed herbs and a
 thin slice of lemon peel)
4 stuffed tomatoes*, substituting
 2 tablespoons grated cheese for
 the meat
4 steaks fresh or frozen fish (such
 as cod, haddock, halibut)
lemon juice

for the sauce:
 1 tablespoon margarine
 1 tablespoon flour
 1·5 dl (¼ pt) milk
 50 g (2 oz) grated cheese
for topping:
 golden crumbs
 knobs of butter
to garnish:
 chopped parsley

Lift the trivet from the cooker, put in the stock or water with stock ingredients, the cups containing the stuffed tomatoes covered with a piece of greaseproof paper, and the well-buttered trivet. On this put the steaks of fish, well seasoned and sprinkled with lemon juice, and lay a piece of buttered paper on top. Bring to pressure, cook 5 minutes, then allow the pressure to reduce at room temperature. During the cooking, melt the margarine in another saucepan, add the flour and cook without allowing to colour. Away from the heat, gradually add the milk and the grated cheese, return to a low heat and stir until thickened. Slip the fish off the trivet on to an ovenproof serving dish, leaving a space between each steak for the tomatoes. Lift out the cups and keep warm. Add sufficient of the strained liquid from the cooker to give the sauce a coating consistency, pour this over the fish and sprinkle thickly with the mixed grated cheese and golden crumbs. Brown quickly under a hot grill and add the stuffed tomatoes, sprinkling each with chopped parsley.

Stuffed haddock with vegetables
Pressure-cooking time: 10 minutes

1 fresh haddock, 450–675 g
  (1–1½ lb) in weight
salt and pepper
lemon juice
stuffing
3 dl (½ pt) water for the cooker
potatoes

carrots
3 dl (½ pt) suitable sauce, such as
  tomato*, cheese* or caper
melted butter
golden crumbs
to garnish:
  chopped parsley

Wash, trim the fish and remove backbone if liked; sprinkle the inside with seasoning and lemon juice, then stuff three-quarters full, closing the fish with small skewers or folding into a parcel of buttered greaseproof paper. Put the water into the cooker, add the fish trimmings, the trivet, the potatoes and carrots (well salted), then a piece of greased greaseproof paper and the fish. Bring to pressure, cook for 10 minutes and allow the pressure to reduce at room temperature. During the cooking, make the sauce using half the milk or liquid only. Lift the fish on to an ovenproof serving dish, brush with melted butter, sprinkle with golden crumbs and brown quickly under a hot grill. Serve the potatoes and carrots sprinkled with chopped parsley. Add sufficient of the strained stock to the sauce to give a thick, pouring consistency; reheat, taste and correct seasoning. Garnish the fish with sprigs of parsley and hand the sauce separately.

A little extra, piping-hot melted butter may be served with this dish, instead of the sauce.

Stuffed plaice and vegetables
Pressure-cooking time: 4 minutes

4 large fillets of fish
lemon juice
salt and pepper
shrimp paste
potatoes
carrots
3 dl (½ pt) water for the cooker
fresh or frozen peas

for the sauce:
  1 tablespoon butter
  1 tablespoon flour
  1·5 dl (¼ pt) milk
  1·5 dl (¼ pt) fish stock*
  a drop or two of cochineal
  small packet of frozen shrimps
to serve:
  butter
  parsley, chopped and in sprigs
  lemon butterflies*

Wash the fish, skin the fillets, sprinkle with lemon juice and seasoning on the skinned side, then spread thickly with shrimp paste and roll up. Prepare the potatoes and carrots (new ones will make this a delicious summer evening dish) to a size to cook in 4 minutes. Put into the cooker the water, the trivet and the potatoes and carrots, well salted, in two piles. Parcel the rolled fillets up lightly in a buttered piece of greaseproof paper and put to one side, resting on the vegetables. Put the cooker on the heat and when the pan is filled with steam put in the salted peas, packed in a perforated container. Bring to pressure, cook for 4 minutes and reduce the pressure with cold water. During the cooking, melt the butter in a small saucepan, add the flour and cook for a minute or two without discolouring. Away from the heat, add the milk and the chopped shrimps; return to the heat and cook, while stirring, until thick. Lift out the peas, toss with a little butter and keep hot. Lift the fish on to a round serving dish, arranging the fillets in a circle, and keep hot. Serve the potatoes and carrots garnished with the parsley. Lift the trivet out and use sufficient of the fish stock to give the sauce a coating consistency. Add enough colouring to give the sauce a pinkish tinge. Taste and correct seasoning, then pour over the fish. Pour a spoonful of peas into the centre, serving the rest with the other vegetables. Garnish each fillet with a lemon butterfly and a sprig of parsley.

Sole montreuil
Pressure-cooking time: 4 minutes

1 large or 2 small fillets of fresh
  frozen sole per person
salt and pepper
lemon juice
450 g (1 lb) potatoes
small piece each of carrot
  and turnip
small onion, halved and stuck
  with 3 or 4 cloves

1 tablespoon butter
scant 3 dl ($\frac{1}{2}$ pt) milk
frozen or fresh peas
for the béchamel sauce:
  1 tablespoon margarine
  1 tablespoon flour
  1 tablespoon cream
  grated cheese
  knobs of butter

Wash and skin the fillets, sprinkle the skinned side with seasoning and lemon juice and roll up. (To help the fillets stay rolled, it is a good idea to secure each with a cocktail stick, removing this after the fillets have been put on the serving dish.) Rinse the sliced potatoes in plenty of cold water. Prepare the carrot, turnip and onion. Lift the trivet from the cooker, melt the butter, add the milk, the vegetables, the trivet and the well-salted potatoes piled on one side. Put the cooker on the heat and when the pan is filled with steam put in the container with the salted peas, then a double thickness of buttered greaseproof paper and the rolled fillets. Bring to pressure, cook for 4 minutes and reduce the pressure with cold water.

During the cooking, melt the margarine in a small saucepan, add the flour and cook for a minute or two but without colouring.

Lift the fillets on to an oval dish, laying them in a line down the centre. Lift out the potatoes and overlap them to form a border round the fish. Toss the peas with a little butter and keep warm. Lift out the trivet, add sufficient of the stock to the thickening to give a coating consistency to the sauce, taste to correct the seasoning and lastly add the cream. Coat the fish carefully, sprinkle thickly with grated cheese, dot with butter and put under a very hot grill until golden-brown. When ready to serve, pile the peas at each end of the dish as garnish.

Turbot in wine sauce
Pressure-cooking time: 6–8 minutes

2 tablespoons butter
450–675 g (1–1½ lb) turbot, in
    the piece or in steaks
1·5 dl (¼ pt) white wine
1·5 dl (¼ pt) water
2 shallots or 1 medium onion,
    diced
good pinch of mixed herbs

salt and pepper
50 g (2 oz) button mushrooms,
    finely sliced
1 tablespoon butter
squeeze of lemon juice
to garnish:
    sprigs of parsley

Lift the trivet from the cooker. Put in the butter and, when heated, lightly brown the turbot on both sides; lift out. Put in the wine, water, shallots, herbs, seasoning, the trivet and then the fish, covered with the sliced mushrooms. Bring to pressure, cook according to size and weight, reduce the pressure immediately. Carefully lift the fish out on to a serving dish and keep warm. Lift out the trivet, boil the remaining stock vigorously until reduced by half. In another small saucepan, melt the butter, then add the strained stock and boil until thick; lastly add a dash of lemon juice. Garnish the fish and hand the sauce separately.

Poached salmon with new potatoes
Pressure-cooking time: 6 minutes

3 dl (½ pt) water for the cooker
new potatoes
salt and pepper
1 salmon steak per person
lemon juice
hollandaise sauce*

fresh green peas cooked
    separately, with chopped mint
    for garnish
knobs of butter
cucumber slices

Put into the cooker the water, the containers with small, even-sized new potatoes, well salted, covered with a piece of buttered greaseproof paper, the trivet, the salmon steaks, well-seasoned, sprinkled with lemon juice and covered with a piece of buttered greaseproof paper. Bring to pressure, cook for 6 minutes, reduce pressure immediately.

During the cooking, make the hollandaise sauce. In a separate saucepan, cook the fresh green peas, toss with knobs of butter and sprinkle with the finely chopped mint. Serve the salmon on to a dish large enough to arrange the steaks in a circle with each piece pointing to the centre. Garnish each slice with a line of cucumber slices to give a wheel effect and pile the strained peas, tossed in butter, in the centre and at the edge of the dish between the salmon steaks. Hand the hollandaise sauce separately.

Trout au bleu
Pressure-cooking time: 5 minutes

This dish must be cooked with a court-bouillon prepared in advance.

1 trout per person
court-bouillon*
melted maître d'hôtel butter

Wash and clean the trout but leave the heads on. Lift the trivet from the cooker, put in the cold, strained court-bouillon and the trout and cover with a piece of greaseproof paper. Bring to pressure, cook 5 minutes, reduce the pressure with cold water. Carefully lift out the fish on to the serving dish, laying them alternately head to tail. Serve at once, handing round the hot melted maître d'hôtel butter, in a sauce boat.

Trout cooked this way are delicious served cold, with mayonnaise. They should be left to get cold in the court-bouillon after the pressure has been reduced, and allowed to drain well before serving.

Soused herrings or mackerel
Pressure-cooking time: 6–8 minutes

4 herrings or mackerel	slice of lemon peel
1·5 dl (¼ pt) vinegar	1 clove garlic, if available
1·5 dl (¼ pt) water	salt and pepper
1 onion, sliced	*to garnish:*
6 peppercorns	raw onion rings
4 cloves	chopped capers, chives or
bay leaf	parsley

Wash the fish, trim, scale and cut off heads. Lift the trivet out of the cooker, put in the liquid and the fish lying alternately head to tail. Sprinkle with the rest of the ingredients, cover with a double thickness of greaseproof paper. Bring to pressure, cook for 6 to 8 minutes according to size. Reduce pressure with cold water if serving hot. Lift out the fish on to the serving dish and keep hot. Boil the liquid rapidly in the cooker until reduced by half, then strain, piping hot, over the fish. Garnish with the capers, parsley or chives.

To serve cold: allow the pressure to reduce at room temperature, leaving the fish in the cooker until quite cold, then lift out and drain (the cooker trivet on a large plate is just right for this purpose). Boil the liquid rapidly in the cooker until reduced by half, allow to cool again then strain over the fish which may be left whole or carefully boned and divided into 'fillets'. Serve with very finely sliced raw onion rings and chopped parsley.

Spiced mackerel
Pressure-cooking time: 6 minutes

4 small mackerel	3 dl ($\frac{1}{2}$ pt) water for the cooker
for the filling:	
4 good tablespoons finely chopped parsley	2 tablespoons chopped capers
2 tablespoons finely chopped fennel leaves (if obtainable, these will make all the difference to this dish) or 3–4 crushed caraway seeds	2 tablespoons melted butter
	1 teaspoon grated lemon peel
	pinch each of cayenne and black pepper
	salt

Split the mackerel, clean and wash well. Butter 4 pieces of greaseproof paper sufficiently large to parcel up each fish completely. Mix all the ingredients for the filling well together, binding them with the melted butter. Put a quarter of this into each fish, then wrap it in the buttered paper making a secure parcel so that none of the butter or juices will run out. Put the water and the trivet in the cooker and then the parcelled fish. Bring to pressure in the usual way, cook for 6 minutes and reduce the pressure with cold water. Lift each parcel out separately and open it out, upside down, on the hot serving dish so that all the juices pour over the fish.

This is an economical, appetizing and nutritious supper dish and does not require an accompanying sauce; serve with thick slices of hot French bread, recipe on p 272.

Scallops Parisienne
Pressure-cooking time: 5 minutes

4 large or 5 small scallops
1·5 dl (¼ pt) milk
50 g (2 oz) finely sliced mushrooms
salt and pepper
1 egg
225 g (8 oz) potatoes, peeled and sliced
3 dl (½ pt) water for the cooker

for the mashed potato:
1 tablespoon butter
a little milk
for the sauce:
1 tablespoon butter
1 tablespoon flour
1 tablespoon cream, if available
grated cheese
to garnish:
sprigs of parsley

Wash the scallops well and put them into a round dish or bowl that will fit into the cooker, with the milk, the mushrooms and the seasoning. Lift the trivet from the cooker, put in the water, then the bowl covered with a piece of greaseproof paper and, at the side, the egg. Put in the trivet on top and then the well-salted potatoes. Bring to pressure, cook for 5 minutes and allow the pressure to reduce at room temperature. Lift out the potatoes with the trivet and the bowl, and drop the egg into cold water. Strain the water from the cooker, put back the potatoes over a low heat, toss until dry then mash well with the butter, milk and plenty of seasoning. Strain the liquor from the bowl and use to make a white sauce with the butter and flour. Shell the egg.

Slice the scallops and stir into the sauce with the mushrooms and chopped hard-boiled egg, reheat thoroughly and add cream. Arrange into scallop shells or individual dishes, pipe or fork a border of mashed potato round each, sprinkle thickly with grated cheese, dot with butter and put under a hot grill until golden-brown. Garnish with a sprig of parsley.

Many other fish such as salmon and lobster (tinned or fresh), turbot, haddock and cod (fresh or frozen but used when thawed), may be served in the same way, making delicious supper dishes or, in small portions, as a 'starter' for a dinner party. (When served in scallop shells these are called coquilles.)

American fish pie
Pressure-cooking time: 4 minutes

3 dl (½ pt) water for the cooker
450 g (1 lb) potatoes, peeled and
  sliced
225 g (8 oz) white fish, fresh or
  frozen
lemon juice
salt and pepper
1 egg

a little milk
3 tablespoons golden crumbs
1 tablespoon butter
1·5 dl (¼ pt) anchovy* or hard-
  boiled egg* sauce
to garnish:
  parsley sprigs, slices of lemon,
  slices of peeled tomato

Preheat the oven to Gas No 5, 190°C (375°F), and put a shelf on the middle runner. Lift the trivet from the cooker, put in the water, the trivet, the sliced potatoes (which should have been put through plenty of cold water), then the fish on a piece of greased grease-proof paper. Season well and sprinkle with lemon juice. Bring to pressure, cook for 4 minutes and reduce the pressure with cold water. Lift out the fish, the potatoes and the trivet; pour out the stock and keep on one side. Rinse the cooker. Put the potatoes back into the cooker, season well, mash thoroughly, then reheat adding nearly all the beaten egg and a little milk, and beating until creamy and white.

Grease a shallow tin or plate well. Mix the golden crumbs with the melted butter and press into the tin to make an even lining. Then spread with the mashed potato, brush over with the rest of the egg, bake until firm and crisp – about 30 minutes. Make the sauce, using a little of the fish stock as well as the milk; flake the fish, add it and keep hot. Gently lift the case on to the serving dish, fill with the hot fish mixture and garnish with the slices of tomato and lemon and the parsley sprigs.

Fish cakes
Pressure-cooking time: 5 minutes

for 8 fishcakes:
  100 g (4 oz) white fish
  100 g (4 oz) potatoes
1 tablespoon butter
a little anchovy essence
chopped parsley or chives

for coating:
  egg
  golden crumbs
to garnish:
  fried sprigs of parsley*
  3 dl (¼ pt) parsley sauce*

Prepare and cook the fish and potatoes as in the previous recipe. When cool, mix the flaked fish, mashed potatoes, melted butter, flavouring and seasonings well together and form into cakes, patting them well to make them firm so that they will hold together. Have ready a tablespoon of seasoned flour on one piece of grease-proof paper, a flat plate with the beaten egg, and another piece of paper with the golden crumbs. Toss each cake in the flour, pass it through the egg and coat thoroughly with the golden crumbs, lightly tossing from one hand to the other to shake off any loose crumbs. Fry in hot fat, lift on to kitchen paper to drain. Garnish with fried parsley and hand the parsley sauce separately.

Kedgeree
Pressure-cooking time: 5 minutes

3 dl ($\frac{1}{2}$ pt) water with a little lemon juice or vinegar for the cooker
1 egg
1 cup long-grain rice
1$\frac{1}{2}$ cups salted water for rice

225 g (8 oz) smoked haddock
2 tablespoons margarine
pepper
to garnish:
chopped parsley

Lift the trivet from the cooker, put in the water, the egg and a solid container filled with the washed rice plus 1$\frac{1}{2}$ cups of salted water and covered with greased greaseproof paper. Place the trivet on top with the haddock dotted with butter and also covered with greaseproof paper. Bring to pressure in the usual way, cook for 5 minutes, allow the pressure to reduce at room temperature. Lift out the fish and the trivet; drop the egg into cold water; turn the rice into another saucepan and shake gently over a low heat until quite dry but do not allow it to catch. Add the margarine and, as it melts, stir it into the rice; then put in the flaked fish, correct seasoning and keep hot. Chop the white of egg and put the yolk through a sieve. Pile the kedgeree high on a hot dish and sprinkle with the egg and chopped parsley.

4 Meat, poultry and game

Meat dishes are probably the most important part of the daily cooking as they provide the bulk of the protein, body-building elements. It might be nice to live all the time on roast meat, juicy steaks, fresh young chickens, but most budgets cannot run to this; here your pressure cooker is going to be invaluable. The cheaper cuts and joints can be made into an endless selection of dishes, and these cuts are often more flavourful and nutritious than many of the more expensive ones. Busy people may often be tempted to spend more than the budget can really stand because of the time required in ordinary cooking to tenderize these economical meats and the less tender chickens, but now you are going to be able to enjoy pot roasts, braises and stews in a wide selection of appetizing dishes and with a saving of cooking time and fuel which means that your pressure cooker is going to pay for itself over and over again.

Here are a few points to note with regard to meat pressure cookery, particularly if you are going to adapt a favourite recipe from ordinary cooking methods and times.

General instructions

Smaller cuts, such as chops, fillets and meat for stewing and braising, should have as much fat as possible trimmed off before cooking.

Tougher and cheaper cuts which normally take 3 to 4 hours will require approximately one-seventh of the usual time.

Pot-roasts, boiling joints, chickens normally timed 20 to 30 minutes per 450 g (1 lb)+20 minutes over will require no more than 10–12 minutes per 450 g (1 lb).

If frozen meats are used, be sure to allow them to thaw completely and then treat them as the fresh meats in the following recipes.

It is important not to overcook meats in the pressure cooker. Each additional minute at pressure is equal to about 10 minutes in the ordinary way and does not always mean that the meat will be better cooked. The protein fibres, in fact, can reach a point in any cooking where continued exposure to heat makes for a hard, stringy result instead of the done-to-a-turn, easily digested texture which we all look for in a meat dish.

As pressure-cooking times are so short, meat cookery can be done with a minimum of liquid, which means that none of the meat juices are wasted. Whether from a pot-roast, casserole, braise or stew, the gravy will be rich and concentrated and, to ensure the correct consistency, it is best to thicken after the cooking either by the addition of thickening agents or by reducing the liquor by boiling rapidly in the open pan.

The most usual thickening agent is flour; the average proportion would be 1 tablespoon to each 6 dl (1 pt) liquid. The new super-sifted flours are very easy to blend with water, stock, a little of the cooled cooking liquid or milk; for others, the easiest way is to keep a small screw-top jar or covered plastic cup for the purpose, putting a little of the liquid in the jar first, measuring in the flour, screwing on the top and then shaking vigorously.

When cut-up meats are to be floured before cooking, a good tip is to do this in a paper bag. Put in a couple of tablespoons of flour, a shake of salt and pepper, then the meat a little at a time and toss well. Any flour left over will go towards the thickening to be added at the end of the cooking.

Pressure cooked meat recipes must always include a liquid which, when boiled, will turn into the steam necessary to build up pressure. This may be stock or dissolved stock cubes, bought or home-made soups, thin gravy or sauce, or cider, beer or any wine.

As the sample recipes given show, the meat may be cooked in just sufficient liquid for the portions to be served as for stews, with a minimum quantity of liquid under the trivet as for pot-roasts, or with the cooker half full of liquid as when boiling hams or for silverside of beef.

When stewing, braising, casseroling, the root vegetables used for flavouring can be given the same pressure-cooking time as the meat, but accompanying vegetables, such as potatoes and all varieties of green vegetable, should be added towards the end of the meat's cooking time so that all will be ready to serve together. Whether this can all be done together will depend on whether there is enough space in the cooker so that it is not over-filled and whether getting the vegetables in and out is a reasonably easy proposition. If it is not, then there is little loss of time and hardly any extra work in giving the meat its full time and cooking the accompanying vegetables separately while the meat is kept hot.

To retain as much as possible of the meat juices, flavour and goodness, many of the following recipes recommend that the seasoned or floured meat be browned first in hot fat. This is known as searing and may do no more than seal the outside surface of the meat, or may continue until the meat is well-browned (and when onions included in the recipe are fried too, will give the finished dish its appetizing, rich brown colour). This preliminary browning is always done in the open cooker, without the trivet, and any surplus fat is afterwards drained off.

The liquid required for the pressure cooking should preferably be added hot; if cold, the cooker should be allowed to cool before it is put in, otherwise too much may be lost in steam as the cold liquid is poured into the hot pan and then there will not be enough left to last the cooking time. This can mean that the cooker will boil dry, spoiling the food and perhaps distorting the cooker base.

It is never a good idea to try and cook too large a joint or chicken in your pressure cooker. Better and more accurate results are obtained if the weight is kept below 1·35 kg (3 lb) in the larger cookers with proportionally smaller joints according to the cooker size, as this allows plenty of room for the steam to circulate to the centre of the joint to ensure even cooking right through.

A variation in cooking times is given in most of the recipes and a little experience will soon enable you to judge what is necessary to obtain the degree of 'doneness' that you prefer. It will be obvious that the quality of the meat, its weight, size, thickness and the proportions of lean, fat and bone are all factors to be considered when gauging the pressure-cooking time. As a general rule for cut-up meats, a coarser meat will take longer to tenderize than a finer one; the larger the amount of fat and the smaller the proportion of bone in a joint, the more minutes per weight will be required.

The suggested quantities given in the following recipes are for four people. If more or less is to be cooked remember that when the meat is cut up into cubes, even-sized pieces or joints, or is minced, the pressure-cooking time will remain the same; with joints which are timed by weight the adjustment will be for longer or shorter pressure cooking according to the weight of the piece.

A summary time-table for meats can be found on p 278 where you can check the cooking times, at a glance, should you be trying out a recipe of your own. Use H pressure.

Beef Pot-roasted

Pot-roast
Pressure-cooking time: 12–15 minutes per 450 g (1 lb)

a suitable joint (rump, topside, brisket, rolled rib) weighing not more than 1·35 kg (3 lb)
a little fat for browning
salt and pepper

hot water, stock (or a stock cube, dissolved) or thin gravy
1–1½ tablespoons flour blended with a little liquid for thickening

Trim the meat, removing any surplus fat. Wipe with a damp cloth, tie or skewer firmly into shape, weigh and decide the cooking time.

Lift the trivet from the cooker, heat the fat in the open pan and carefully brown the meat all over. Do not prick with a fork when turning the joint and be sure not to over-brown; if the outside gets too hard the steam cannot penetrate and the centre may remain underdone. Lift out the meat and dust it all over with plenty of salt and pepper. Strain the fat from the cooker, put in the hot liquid (or if cold, allow the cooker to cool) and stir well to lift from the bottom any 'brownness' from the frying, as this will give colour to the gravy. The amount of liquid added will depend on the cooking time but must not be less than 3 dl ($\frac{1}{2}$ pt). This amount will be sufficient for 450 g (1 lb) of meat at 12–15 minutes per 450 g (1 lb); an extra 1·5 dl ($\frac{1}{4}$ pt) will then be required if the joint weighs up to 900 g (2 lb) and a further 1·5 dl ($\frac{1}{4}$ pt) if up to 1·35 kg (3 lb). It will not matter if this comes above the trivet; the preliminary browning will have 'sealed' the meat so that it does not absorb the liquid.

Put in the trivet and joint, bring to pressure, cook for the required time and reduce the pressure with cold water. Lift out the joint and keep hot. Remove the trivet, add the thickening, return the pan to the stove, stir until boiling, taste to correct the seasoning and cook for 2–3 minutes.

A little gravy browning should be added if necessary.

If it is practical and there is sufficient room around and above the joint, accompanying vegetables such as potatoes and carrots or green vegetables can be added 4–5 minutes before the cooking time of the meat is up. Lift the cooker from the heat, reduce the pressure with cold water, put in the vegetables, bring the cooker to pressure again in the usual way and continue the cooking. In this way, the meat will have had its full time, the vegetables their correct time and all will be ready to serve together. The liquid too will make a delicious gravy as it will combine both the meat and vegetable juices.

Extra flavour and colour can be added by browning a sliced onion in the fat after the meat has been lifted out and leaving it in the liquid under the trivet during the cooking, straining it out or leaving it to serve in the gravy. Pot-roasted meat makes a delicious cold joint with salad and is an excellent method of quickly preparing meat for sandwiches, rolls etc for picnics and outdoor occasions.

Stuffed beef
Pressure-cooking time: 15 minutes per 450 g (1 lb)

a piece of round or topside
  weighing not more than 1·35 kg
  (3 lb) and shaped into a long roll
salt and pepper
liquid to cover the trivet, but not
  less than 3 dl (½ pt)

for the stuffing:
3 slices streaky bacon
3 medium onions, chopped
a good pinch of mixed meat herbs
2 tablespoons freshly chopped
  parsley
1 beaten egg

Trim and wipe the meat and make deep cuts along its length about
1 cm (½ in) apart and three-quarters of the way through. In a frying pan, gently heat the chopped bacon so that the fat runs out and
let it crisp, then fry the chopped onions until golden-brown. Mix
with the rest of the ingredients, add sufficient egg to bind the mixture, fill this stuffing into the cuts, tie the meat securely as if it were
a parcel and weigh it. Continue as given for the pot-roast but lifting the joint when cooked on to an ovenproof dish, basting with a
little hot fat as for a roast joint and putting it on the second shelf
of an oven heated to Gas No 5, 190°C (375°F), while the accompanying vegetables are being cooked.

Boiled

Boiled beef with dumplings
Pressure-cooking time: 15 minutes per 450 g (1 lb)

joint of salted silverside weighing
  not more than 1·35 kg (3 lb)
water for the cooker
medium carrots and onions
bouquet garni*

for the dumplings:
225 g (8 oz) self-raising flour
½ teaspoon baking powder
½ teaspoon salt
75 g (3 oz) shredded suet
cold water to mix

Trim, wipe and weigh the meat, put into the cooker without the
trivet. Cover with water, bring to the boil, lift out and throw this
water away. (This is instead of leaving to soak overnight.) Put the
joint back and add sufficient water to half fill the cooker. Bring to
pressure, cook for all but 5 minutes of the cooking time, reduce
the pressure with cold water. During the cooking, prepare the

carrots which should be neatly trimmed and shaped to an even size, and the onions. Add these to the cooker together with the bouquet garni, bring to pressure again, cook for a further 5 minutes, reduce pressure with cold water. During this cooking make the dumplings by sieving the flour, baking powder and salt, mixing in the suet and forming into an elastic dough with cold water. With well-floured hands, make this into eight even-sized dumplings. Return the cooker to the heat and when the liquid is again boiling, drop in the dumplings. Just lay the lid on top or cover with a plate and boil gently for 10 minutes.

Serve at once, lifting the meat, vegetables and dumplings on to a large serving dish. Pour a little of the liquor over and hand more separately.

A parsley or mustard sauce can be served with this dish; make it with three-quarters of the milk and a quarter of the cooking liquid from which the fat should first be removed by drawing pieces of absorbent paper across the surface.

Boiled beef with vegetables

Pressure-cooking time: 12 minutes per 450 g (1 lb)

joint of fresh brisket weighing not more than 1·35 kg (3 lb)
medium potatoes, onions and carrots
water for the cooker
1 medium cabbage, quartered

to serve:
3 dl (½ pt) mustard* or onion* sauce (see note below)

Trim, wipe and weigh the meat, prepare vegetables leaving the onions whole and cutting the carrots and potatoes to a size to cook in 5 minutes. Lift out the trivet, put in the joint and sufficient water to half fill the cooker, adding plenty of salt. Bring to pressure, cook for all but 5 minutes of the required time, reduce the pressure with cold water. Take out 1·5 dl (¼ pt) of the liquid and return the pan to the heat, reboil, then put in the potatoes, onions, carrots and the quartered cabbage. Bring to pressure again, cook for a further 5 minutes and reduce the pressure with cold water. During this cooking make the mustard sauce using half milk and half cooking liquid. Taste and correct the seasoning and keep hot. Serve the meat, either in the joint or as overlapping slices, arrange vegetables around and pour a little of the cooking liquid over. Hand the sauce separately.

If onion sauce is preferred, put 2 large onions, trimmed and well washed but with the skins still on, in with the meat. Lift these out after the first cooking, skin, chop and add to the sauce made with half milk and half cooking liquid.

Braised

This is a method of cooking meat so that the food is not actually in the liquid but resting on a bed of vegetables, known as 'mirepoix' (p 274). It is suitable for the cheaper pieces of beef, such as buttock, skirt or chuck steak (usually cut ready into individual portions), for a joint such as topside, for liver and kidneys.

Braised steak
Pressure-cooking time: 10 minutes

4 pieces chuck or other braising
   steak
seasoned flour
for mirepoix*:
   1 large onion
   1 large carrot
   1 large turnip
   1 stick celery
   bouquet garni*
   seasoning

potatoes, carrots or separate
   vegetables if wanted
1 tablespoon dripping
1 slice streaky bacon
stock for the cooker
to garnish:
   chopped parsley
sauce to choice

Trim, wipe meat and toss in seasoned flour, shaking well to remove any surplus. Slice the onion and roughly cut the other vegetables; prepare the potatoes and carrots for serving separately, leaving whole unless very large, when cut in half. Lift out the trivet and in the open cooker heat the dripping, fry the meat quickly until well browned on both sides and lift out. Put in the bacon and onions, fry in the same way; lift the cooker from the heat, add 1·5 dl (¼ pt) hot stock (if added cold, allow the cooker to cool) and stir until there are no 'browny' bits left sticking to the base of the pan; put in the rest of the vegetables and the bouquet garni and add more stock just to show through them. Put back the meat and then if cooking separate vegetables, the trivet, and the potatoes and carrots in separate piles. Bring to pressure in the usual way, cook for 10 minutes and reduce the pressure with cold water.

Lift out the vegetables and sprinkle with parsley; lift out the trivet, serve the steak and keep hot. After removing the bacon and bouquet garni, thoroughly mash the mirepoix vegetables in the cooker, taste and correct seasoning and add a little browning if necessary; served as an accompanying sauce.

Otherwise, use the strained stock to make a brown sauce*.

Beef bourguignon
Pressure-cooking time: 10 minutes

4 portions braising beef
seasoned flour
bacon fat
3 onions, sliced
3 dl (½ pt) red wine (or half wine, half brown stock*)
1 clove garlic, crushed
bouquet garni*

100 g (4 oz) button mushrooms (or a small tin)
1 tablespoon butter
salt and pepper
about 1 tablespoon flour for thickening
to garnish:
chopped parsley

Trim, wipe the meat and toss in seasoned flour. Lift the trivet from the cooker, put in some pieces of bacon fat and heat until the fat runs out. Quickly brown the meat on both sides, lift out and brown the sliced onions until dark but not burnt. Lift the cooker from the heat, allow to cool, add the liquid and stir well to lift any 'brown' bits from the bottom. Put in the meat, return the cooker to the heat and, when boiling, put in the crushed garlic, the bouquet garni and seasoning. Bring to pressure, cook for 10 minutes and reduce the pressure with cold water. During the cooking, slice the prepared mushrooms very finely and fry lightly in a little butter. Remove the bouquet garni, serve the meat and onions into a casserole dish, cover with a layer of mushrooms and keep hot. Thicken the sauce with a little blended flour or reduce it by boiling rapidly, without burning, in the open pan. Taste and correct seasoning and pour into the casserole. Garnish with the chopped parsley.

Braised oxtail Pressure-cooking time: 40 minutes

1 oxtail	bouquet garni*
salt and pepper	2 heaped tablespoons flour
2 tablespoons dripping or other fat	blended with a little water for
2–3 large onions	thickening
6 dl (1 pt) brown stock* or water	1 small glass dry red wine or port
2–3 large carrots	(optional)
	1 dessertspoon redcurrant jelly

Wipe the joints, trim off any surplus fat and season with salt and pepper. Lift the trivet from the cooker and melt the fat. When hot, fry the sliced onions until golden-brown, lift out, then brown the oxtail joints evenly all over. Strain off any fat left, put in the hot liquid (if added cold, allow the cooker to cool), the onions, the carrots cut into slices or lengths and the bouquet garni. Bring to pressure, cook for 40 minutes and reduce the pressure with cold water. Lift the joints on to a serving dish, strain the stock and put the vegetables and the meat in a low oven to keep hot. Return the stock to the cooker, add the blended flour and cook for 2–3 minutes stirring all the time. Add the wine and the redcurrant jelly, taste and correct seasoning, pour the sauce over the meat and garnish with the carrots.

As oxtail can be rather fatty, it may be found better to prepare and pressure cook it the previous day. The meat and vegetables should be lifted from the strained stock, which should be stored in a deep bowl; remove all the fat from it before the second cooking. Return the meat and stock to the cooker, bring to pressure and allow to reduce at room temperature. Continue as above.

For an extra-nourishing meal, small haricot beans can be served with oxtail. After 20 minutes' cooking, reduce the pressure with cold water, add 100 g (4 oz) prepared beans and a further 3 dl ($\frac{1}{2}$ pt) water or stock and pressure cook for the last 20 minutes. Continue as before.

Braised tongue
Pressure-cooking time: 15 minutes per 450 g (1 lb) if fresh; 20 minutes per 450 g (1 lb) if smoked

1 ox tongue	1 onion stuck with 2 cloves
water according to cooking time	1 carrot

2 sticks celery
1 small turnip
bay leaf
sprig of parsley

a few peppercorns
salt and pepper
gravy or madeira* sauce

Soak the tongue for 2 hours in cold water. Weigh and decide on cooking time (it will be easier to handle if loosely tied in a piece of butter muslin). Lift the trivet from the cooker, put in the tongue, add sufficient water to cover, bring to the boil in the open pan and throw the water away. Put back the tongue, all the ingredients (including salt if the tongue is fresh), and the water. Bring to pressure, cook for the required time and allow the pressure to reduce at room temperature. During the cooking, prepare a thick gravy or madeira sauce which can later be thinned with some of the cooking liquid. Lift out the tongue and carefully remove the skin and all the bones. Cut into thick slices, overlapping these on an oval serving dish, and put in a low oven to keep hot. Strain the stock and add sufficient to the sauce to give a rich, coating consistency. Taste and correct seasoning, pour over the tongue and serve piping hot.

A delicious accompaniment for this dish would be a quartered green cabbage and some whole young carrots pressure cooked for 5 minutes without the trivet and in 3 dl ($\frac{1}{2}$ pt) of the cooking stock; this could be done while boning and skinning the tongue and finishing off the sauce. These, well strained, should then garnish the dish.

For a smoked tongue, soak overnight in cold water. Add two tablespoons of vinegar but no salt to the cooking water and after pressure has been reduced, boil the liquid rapidly in the open pan for 2–3 minutes. Use a little of this concentrated stock to thin down some horseradish sauce. Bring this to the boil, stir in a tablespoon of cream and hand round separately.

Stewed

It is usual to allow 150 g (6 oz) raw meat per person and 6 dl (1 pt) sauce or gravy per 450 g (1 lb).

Beef stew with vegetables
Pressure-cooking time: 15–20 minutes

675 g (1½ lb) stewing steak such as skirt, shin, flank, chuck
seasoned flour
a selection of seasonable vegetables including onions, carrots, a little turnip, swede, parsnip, sticks of celery, etc
dripping or fat for frying

6 dl (1 pt) hot stock or water
bouquet garni* or a good pinch of meat herbs
salt and pepper
2 heaped tablespoons flour blended with a little water for thickening

Wipe meat, trim off fat, cut into 2·5-cm (1-in) cubes and toss in seasoned flour, shaking well to remove any surplus; prepare the vegetables and cut into neat 2·5-cm (1-in) cubes or pieces. Lift the trivet from the cooker, heat about 2 tablespoons of fat and, when hot, fry the onions until a good brown colour but not burnt. Lift out, then fry the meat, keeping it moving to brown evenly all over. Lift the cooker from the heat, take out the meat and add the hot liquid (if cold, allow the cooker to cool), stir well until there are no 'browny' bits left on the bottom of the pan, put in the onions, meat, all the other vegetables, the bouquet garni and seasoning. Bring to pressure, cook for the required time and reduce the pressure with cold water. During the cooking time, prepare the thickening and add this to the cooker returning to the heat and stirring until boiling, then cooking for a further 2 to 3 minutes. Remove the bouquet garni, taste and correct seasoning and serve piping hot.

If the meat and onions have been well browned, this stew should be a good colour, but gravy browning can be added with the thickening if necessary, or if it is preferred to cook the stew without browning the meat and onions first.

Beef strogonoff
Pressure-cooking time: 8 minutes

450 g (1 lb) good chuck or rump steak
225 g (8 oz) fresh button mushrooms
2 tablespoons butter
1 small onion, finely chopped

1·5 dl (¼ pt) good brown stock*
a sprig of marjoram or ½ bay leaf
salt and pepper
2 tablespoons cream (soured cream* is excellent)

to garnish:
  chopped parsley
as accompaniment:
  hot potato crisps

Wipe, trim the steak and cut across the grain into lengths which should be the width of a thick shoe-lace. Wash the mushrooms and slice finely lengthwise without removing the stalks. Lift the trivet from the cooker, heat the butter, brown the meat and onion quickly and evenly. Lift the cooker from the heat, add the hot liquid (or, if added cold, allow the cooker to cool), the seasonings and the mushrooms, stirring well. Bring to pressure, cook for 8 minutes and allow the pressure to reduce at room temperature. During the cooking, preheat the oven at Gas No 3, 170°C (325°F), and put the crisps in at the bottom to warm. Serve the meat and vegetables into an ovenproof dish and keep hot. Boil the liquid rapidly in the open pan until reduced and thickening, taste and correct seasoning, add cream and immediately pour over the meat. Serve garnished with chopped parsley and hand the potato crisps separately.

When serving this dish for a special occasion, the meat may first be left to marinate, the strained liquid being used for the cooking.

Curries

Everyone has their own ideas, it seems, on how to make a good curry and certainly there are many varieties of this dish, depending on the country and even the region of its origin. This standard recipe can, of course, be altered and varied; added to, perhaps, if a particular flavour or ingredient is a favourite, or changed if all the ingredients suggested are not available. Again, the 'hotness' of the curry is a matter for the individual; taste carefully to correct this during the cooking and before serving.

Basic curry sauce
This quantity will be sufficient for 450 g (1 lb) of fresh meat, a jointed chicken etc.

2 tablespoons coconut
4·5 dl (¾ pt) good white stock*
1 medium onion
1 small crisp apple
2 tablespoons butter

1 dessertspoon each flour and
  curry powder
1 tablespoon mango chutney
1 teaspoon lemon juice
1 teaspoon red jelly or jam
salt and pepper

Fresh beef curry
Pressure-cooking time: 15–20 minutes

450 g (1 lb) steak
1 teacup savoury rice
1 teacup hot, salted water

Put the coconut in a small basin, pour over the boiling stock, cover
and leave to infuse for at least half an hour. Wipe, trim the meat
and cut into 2·5-cm (1-in) cubes. Chop the onion and apple finely.
When the coconut is ready, strain off the stock. Lift the trivet from
the cooker, heat the butter, lightly fry the meat and lift out. Put in
the onion and apple and fry gently but without browning for about
10 minutes. Add the flour and curry powder and fry again for a
few minutes. Away from the heat, add the chutney and stock,
stirring to make sure no bits have been left on the bottom of the
pan. Return to the heat and, when boiling, add the meat, bring to
pressure, cook for 10 minutes and reduce the pressure with cold
water. Stir the curry and if it is getting too thick add a little more
hot stock. Put in the trivet and a solid container with the rice and
water covered with a piece of greaseproof paper. Bring to pressure
again, cook for the last 5 minutes and allow the pressure to reduce
at room temperature. During this cooking, preheat the oven to
Gas No 4, 180°C (350°F), and put into the bottom the ovenproof
dish on which you will serve the rice. Have ready a kettle of boiling
water. Lift out the rice, tip it into a colander, pour over the boiling
water and shake to separate the grains. Pile into the serving dish,
turn off the oven and leave the rice on the centre shelf to dry off.
Lift out the trivet, stir the curry, add the strained lemon juice and
jelly, reboil, taste and correct seasoning and serve piping hot,
handing the rice separately.

If a curry is to be made with cooked meat, make the sauce and
put in the rice as above, bring to pressure in the usual way, cook
for 5 minutes and reduce the pressure at room temperature. Lift

out the rice, stir the sauce, add more stock if necessary. Put in the diced, cooked meat, bring to pressure again, remove from the heat and allow the pressure to reduce at room temperature. During this time, finish the rice as in previous recipe, then add the last of the ingredients to the curry before serving.

Other suitable foods for currying are fresh lamb – cooked as for beef – prawns, hard-boiled eggs, cooked or tinned cocktail sausages, bananas halved lengthways, reheated in the curry sauce.

Gourmet meat loaf
Pressure-cooking time: 25 minutes

225 g (8 oz) each of fresh, finely minced beef, veal and pork
4 tablespoons fresh white breadcrumbs
1 medium onion
2 tablespoons butter
2 tablespoons milk
2 tablespoons red wine
1 clove garlic, crushed (optional)
salt and pepper

pinch of mixed spice
½ teaspoon each of crushed mace, thyme and bay leaf
1 large egg
2 tablespoons dripping or fat
6 dl (1 pt) hot water for cooker
as accompaniment:
   3 dl (½ pt) rich brown gravy* or tomato sauce*

Wipe and trim all fat from the meat and mince finely. Prepare the breadcrumbs, dice the onion finely. Melt the butter in a small saucepan and simmer the onion until transparent, but do not allow to colour. Add the milk and breadcrumbs, cook for a moment or two, then add the wine. Combine with the meats, seasonings, herbs and beaten egg, then with floured hands, shape into a thick roll that will fit into the cooker. Lift the trivet from the cooker, heat the fat, carefully brown the loaf all over, lift out and tie in a triple thickness of greaseproof paper which should be pleated once to allow for expansion. Drain out the fat, put in the water, the trivet and the loaf. Bring to pressure, cook for 25 minutes and reduce the pressure with cold water. If accompanying vegetables are to be pressure cooked, preheat the oven to Gas No 3, 170°C (325°F), lift the loaf on to a greased baking sheet and keep hot. Use 3 dl (½ pt) of the cooking water for the vegetables and add this stock to the gravy or tomato sauce before pouring round the loaf on the serving dish.

This loaf is excellent cold. Roll in golden crumbs while still hot, chill, then serve, sliced, garnished with sliced tomatoes and cucumber and quartered hard-boiled eggs. A potato salad with chopped chives added will make a delicious accompaniment.

Lancashire hot pot
Pressure-cooking time: 12 minutes

450 g (1 lb) good, lean stewing steak
2 large onions
775 g (1¾ lb) potatoes
2 tablespoons dripping or fat
3 dl (½ pt) good brown stock*, or vegetable stock with a little browning
  added for colour
salt and pepper
1 tablespoon flour blended with a little water for thickening
knobs of butter
to garnish: chopped parsley

Wipe and trim the meat, season and cut into neat pieces about 1-cm (½-in) square; slice the prepared onions and potatoes thickly. Lift the trivet from the cooker, heat the fat and quickly brown the meat evenly all over. Lift out and strain away the fat. Put in the hot liquid (if added cold, allow the cooker to cool), then the meat, onions and potatoes in layers, well seasoned and with potatoes as the last layer. Bring to pressure, cook for 12 minutes and allow the pressure to reduce at room temperature. During the cooking, preheat the grill and prepare a little blended flour for thickening, then carefully transfer the hot pot to an ovenproof casserole or dish, keeping the potato layer at the top. Add the thickening to the stock in the cooker, boil well to cook and pour down the side of the dish. Dot the top with knobs of butter and leave under the grill until golden-brown. Garnish with chopped parsley.

To make a delicious change of flavour to this appetizing and nourishing dish, white stock, vegetable or plain water to which tomato juice or purée is added can be used instead; a bay leaf should be put in the middle layer and lifted out during the transfer to the serving dish.

Savoury meat balls with spaghetti
Pressure-cooking time: 16 minutes

325 g (12 oz) minced lean beef
1 medium onion
4 tablespoons rice
1 tablespoon chopped parsley
salt and pepper
1 egg

6 dl (1 pt) liquid made up from
 tomato purée or soup and water
1 tablespoon Worcestershire sauce
bay leaf
150 g (6 oz) spaghetti
1·5 dl (¼ pt) boiling water if
 necessary

Mix together the beef, finely chopped onion, half the washed rice, the parsley and seasoning, bind with the beaten egg and form into eight balls, shaping carefully with well-floured hands. Lastly, press each ball firmly into the rest of the rice to give a 'prickly' appearance. Lift the trivet from the cooker, put in the liquid, sauce and bay leaf and bring to the boil in the open pan. Drop in the meat balls, bring to pressure, cook for 10 minutes, reduce the pressure with cold water.

During the cooking time, preheat the oven to Gas No 2, 150°C (300°F), and prepare the spaghetti. Lift the meat balls on to a large, deep serving dish and keep hot. Add the water to the sauce in the cooker if necessary, stir well, bring to the boil, add the spaghetti. Bring to pressure, cook for 6 minutes, reduce pressure with cold water. With a straining spoon or tongs, lift out the spaghetti and serve around the meat balls. Reboil the sauce, taste and correct seasoning and pour into the dish. If tomato purée has been used, a teaspoon of sugar may be added to the sauce before serving. As an additional flavour, 2 tablespoons diced apple may be added with the tomato liquid.

Tripe and onions
Pressure-cooking time: 15 minutes

675–900 g (1½–2 lb) blanched tripe
 as prepared by the butcher
water
4–5 medium onions
salt and pepper

1 tablespoon flour
1·5 dl (¼ pt) milk
to garnish:
 fried croûtons*
 chopped parsley

Cut the tripe in 3·5-cm (1½-in) pieces. Lift the trivet from the cooker, put in the tripe and sufficient water to cover. Bring just to the boil in the open cooker and throw the water away. Add the onions, left whole, the seasoning and sufficient cold water just to cover. Bring to pressure, cook for 15 minutes and allow the pressure to reduce at room temperature. Strain off the liquid. Blend the flour with a little of the milk and a tablespoon of hot stock, add to the cooker with the rest of the milk, then return to the heat and, stirring all the time, bring to the boil and allow to cook for 2–3 minutes. Taste and correct seasoning and, if necessary, add more stock to give a pouring consistency. Serve garnished with fried croûtons dipped in chopped parsley.

As variation, sliced carrots and mushroom stalks with a flavouring of crushed garlic may be added; this dish is then called **Tripe à la Bourgeoise**.

Veal Pot roasted

Stuffed shoulder of veal
Pressure-cooking time: 12–14 minutes per 450 g (1 lb)

a boned shoulder of veal, weighing not more than 1·35 kg (3 lb)	salt and pepper
	3 tablespoons dripping, bacon or other fat
1 rasher of bacon, diced	white stock* (or a chicken cube, dissolved in water) for the cooking
1 tablespoon chopped parsley	
1 onion, finely chopped	
4 tablespoons fresh breadcrumbs	1 level tablespoon flour blended with a little milk for thickening
grated rind of ½ lemon	
1 egg	gravy browning

Wipe, trim the meat, then lay flat with the boned surface upwards. Mix all the ingredients for the stuffing and bind together with the beaten egg. Spread evenly over the joint but not taking it too close to the outer edges. Roll the joint, tie securely with thin string or hold in position with short skewers and weigh. Rub the outside of the meat with salt and pepper and roll in flour. Lift the trivet from the cooker, heat the fat and carefully brown the joint all over. Lift out, drain away the fat, add the required amount of hot liquid (if added cold, allow the cooker to cool), return to the heat and bring to the boil stirring all the time, making sure that all the 'brown' bits are lifted from the bottom of the cooker. Put back the trivet and the meat, bring to pressure, cook for the required time and reduce the pressure with cold water. Lift out the meat and keep hot. Lift out the trivet, reduce the liquid in the cooker a little by boiling rapidly in the open pan, lift from the heat and, when cooled slightly, add the thickening and colouring. Reboil, taste to correct seasoning and hand separately.

Veal niçoise
Pressure-cooking time: 12 minutes per 450 g (1 lb)

a piece of roasting veal such as fillet, loin, shoulder, weighing not more than 1·35 kg (3 lb)
1 clove garlic
salt and pepper
2 tablespoons olive oil or dripping
450 g (1 lb) small onions
white stock* or water as required
a sprig or two of thyme, rosemary or other suitable herbs as available
900 g (2 lb) tomatoes, skinned

Wipe and trim the meat, weigh, then rub all over with the garlic, salt and pepper. Lift the trivet from the cooker, heat the fat and brown the meat carefully all over. Lift out, drain away the fat, put in the required amount of liquid, the trivet and the meat, bring to pressure, cook for all but 4 minutes of the cooking time and reduce the pressure with cold water. Lift out the meat and the trivet and strain out all but enough liquid to just cover the bottom of the cooker. Put in the whole onions, the seasonings, then the meat on top and the whole tomatoes around the joint. Bring to pressure again, cook for 4 minutes and allow the pressure to reduce at room temperature.

Lift out the meat, put the onions on to the serving dish with the meat on top and the tomatoes around. Reboil the liquid, taste and correct the seasoning and either pour around the meat or hand separately.

This sauce should not be too thick, but it can be reduced by boiling rapidly in the open cooker or by cooking together in a small saucepan 1 tablespoon butter and 1 tablespoon flour without allowing to colour, and then adding the liquid gradually for the required consistency and cooking for 2–3 minutes.

Boiled

Knuckle of veal with rice
Pressure-cooking time: 10 minutes per 450 g (1 lb)

1 knuckle of veal, not more than
   1·35 kg (3 lb)
1 carrot
1 turnip
1 onion
4 cloves
bouquet garni*

salt and pepper
water for the cooking
100 g (4 oz) rice
6 dl (1 pt) parsley sauce*
to garnish:
   lemon quarters
   bacon rolls*

Wipe, trim and weigh the meat. Peel and cut the carrot and turnip into rough cubes; peel onion and stick with cloves. Lift the trivet from the cooker, put in the meat, vegetables, bouquet garni, seasonings and enough water nearly to cover but not to fill the base more than half full. Bring to the boil in the open pan and skim well. Bring to pressure, cook for all but 5 minutes of the required time, reduce the pressure with cold water. Lift out the vegetables, return the pan to the heat, bring to the boil, throw in the washed rice, bring to pressure and cook for the last 5 minutes. Allow the pressure to reduce at room temperature. During this cooking, make the parsley sauce, but using only half the quantity of milk. Make the bacon rolls and leave under a low grill or in the warming oven. Lift the meat on to the serving dish, strain the rice (saving the stock) and put round the joint as a border. Keep hot. Use sufficient of the stock to give the sauce a thick, pouring consistency; taste and correct seasoning and hand separately. Garnish the rice with the bacon rolls and lemon quarters.

Stuffed veal rolls
Pressure-cooking time: 12 minutes

450 g (1 lb) lean veal cut into
   thin slices
100 g (4 oz) bacon, sliced
lemon juice, salt and pepper
seasoned flour
2 tablespoons butter

1 medium onion, sliced
1·5 dl (¼ pt) water plus small glass
   white wine, or 3 dl (½ pt) stock
a thin slice of lemon peel
bouquet garni*
to garnish:
   sprigs of parsley

Wipe and trim the meat and cut into strips approximately 12 × 5 cm (5 × 2 in). Stretch each slice of bacon by drawing the back of a cook's knife along its length. Sprinkle the veal strips with lemon juice and seasoning, lay a piece of bacon on each, roll up and fix with half a cocktail stick or by tying with cotton, then toss in seasoned flour. Lift the trivet from the cooker, heat the butter, gently brown the rolls and onion and lift out. Add the hot liquid (if cold, allow the cooker to cool), return to the heat and stir, making sure that any 'brown' bits from the frying have been lifted from the bottom. Put back the rolls and onion; add the seasonings, bring to pressure, cook for 12 minutes and reduce the pressure with cold water. Lift the rolls on to the serving dish, take out the sticks or remove the cotton and keep hot. Reduce the liquid by boiling rapidly in the open pan, taste and correct seasoning and then strain over the veal rolls. Garnish with sprigs of parsley.

A variation of the sauce can be made by adding tomato purée to taste.

Stewed

Veal blanquette
Pressure-cooking time: 12 minutes

450 g (1 lb) veal pieces	2 tablespoons cream
salt and pepper	1 egg yolk
1 small onion	*to garnish:*
3 dl (½ pt) white stock* or water	chopped parsley
a slice of lemon peel	lemon quarters
3 dl (½ pt) white sauce*	bacon rolls*

Wipe and trim the meat and toss in plenty of salt and pepper. Lift the trivet from the cooker, put in the meat and sliced onion, add the liquid, lemon peel and seasonings, bring to pressure, cook for 12 minutes and reduce the pressure with cold water. During the cooking, make a white sauce using only half the quantity of milk. Lift the meat into a deep serving dish, strain the stock and add sufficient to the sauce to give a rich, coating consistency. Reheat, taste and correct seasoning. Add cream and egg and cook for a minute or two, but without allowing it to boil or it will curdle.

Pour over the veal and garnish with chopped parsley, bacon rolls and lemon quarters.

Veal fricassée
Pressure-cooking time: 12 minutes

450 g (1 lb) veal pieces
salt and pepper
2 tablespoons butter
3 dl (½ pt) white stock* or water
1 teaspoon sugar
4 baby carrots
8 spring onions

12 new potatoes
2 young turnips
3 dl (½ pt) white sauce*
2 tablespoons cream
to garnish:
  chopped parsley

Wipe and trim the meat and toss in plenty of salt and pepper. In a frying pan, heat the butter, lightly cook the meat, without browning, until sealed and lift out. Take the trivet from the cooker, put in the stock, the meat and seasonings, bring to pressure, cook for 8 minutes and reduce the pressure with cold water. During the cooking, add the sugar to the butter, put in the peeled whole carrots, onions and potatoes and the turnips cut into neat pieces. Cook gently, shaking the pan often, so that the vegetables are softened and take on a glazed, light-brown look. Add these to the cooker, bring to pressure again, cook for a further 4 minutes and reduce the pressure with cold water. During this cooking, make the sauce using only half the quantity of milk. Lift the meat and vegetables into a deep serving dish and keep hot. Use sufficient of the stock to give a rich, pouring consistency; reboil, taste and correct seasoning, add cream, pour over the meat and garnish with chopped parsley.

Sweetbreads

Sweetbreads must always be precooked; they are then ready to be stewed, braised, fried and so on in any recipe.

TO PRECOOK SWEETBREADS Wash the sweetbreads, put in a saucepan with sufficient water to cover and bring slowly to the boil. Plunge at once into cold salted water, adding a squeeze of lemon juice.

Trim carefully, removing all the tubes and membranes. Press between two plates until cool. The sweetbreads are now ready to be used as required.

Creamed sweetbreads
Pressure-cooking time: 6 minutes

1·5 dl (¼ pt) white stock*
2 prepared calf's sweetbreads
1 small onion
2 or 3 small carrots
piece of lemon rind
a few peppercorns
a blade of mace
salt and pepper

6 dl (1 pt) white sauce*
2 tablespoons chopped cooked
   ham
squeeze of lemon juice
2 tablespoons cream
to garnish:
   4 triangles of fried bread
   lemon butterflies*

Lift the trivet from the cooker, put in the stock, sliced sweetbreads, the vegetables and seasonings, bring to pressure, cook for 6 minutes and allow the pressure to reduce at room temperature. During this cooking make the sauce, using only half the quantity of milk; fry the bread and cut into triangles. Lift the sweetbreads into a deep serving dish and pile chopped ham at each end. Keep hot. Strain the stock and add sufficient to the sauce to give a thick, coating consistency. Reheat, add the lemon juice and cream, taste and correct seasoning and coat the sweetbreads only with the sauce. Garnish with the fried bread and lemon butterflies.

Braised sweetbreads
Pressure-cooking time: 8 minutes

2 prepared calf's sweetbreads
4 medium onions
seasoned flour
50 g (2 oz) mushrooms
2 tablespoons butter
3 dl (½ pt) brown stock* (or a
  stock cube, dissolved)

salt and pepper
4 slices of fried bread
1 tablespoon flour blended with a
  little water for thickening
a little sherry or wine (optional)
to garnish:
  chopped parsley

Cut each sweetbread into eight pieces and roll in seasoned flour; slice the onions and mushrooms finely. Lift the trivet from the cooker, heat the butter and fry the onions and mushrooms golden-brown. Lift out, fry the pieces of sweetbread until evenly brown and lift out. Add the stock, stir well to remove any 'brown' pieces from the bottom of the cooker, put back the vegetables and the sweetbreads. Add the seasoning, bring to pressure, cook for 8 minutes and allow the pressure to reduce at room temperature. During this cooking, prepare the thickening; fry the bread and lay the slices ready in the serving dish. Lift out and serve the sweetbreads and vegetables and keep hot. Thicken the sauce, add the wine, reheat, taste and correct seasoning and pour into the dish. Garnish thickly with chopped parsley.

Lamb and mutton Pot-roasted

Rolled, stuffed breast of lamb
Pressure-cooking time: 10–12 minutes per 450 g (1 lb)

a boned breast of lamb, weighing
   about 900 g (2 lb)
salt and pepper

for the stuffing:	salt and pepper
1 finely diced onion	1 beaten egg
4 tablespoons fresh breadcrumbs	2 tablespoons dripping or fat
4 tablespoons finely chopped	stock or thin gravy
celery	1 tablespoon flour blended with
pinch of sage	a little water for thickening
1 teaspoon chopped parsley	gravy browning

Unroll the meat, wipe and season the cut surface well with salt and pepper. Mix the stuffing ingredients together and bind firmly with sufficient beaten egg (or make up packet stuffing). Spread this over the meat, roll the joint again and close securely with small skewers or tie with string and weigh. Lift the trivet from the cooker, melt the fat and fry the meat all over until really brown. Lift out, add the required amount of liquid according to the cooking time, but not less than 3 dl ($\frac{1}{2}$ pt). Put in the trivet and the meat, bring to pressure, cook for the required time and reduce the pressure with cold water. Lift out the meat and keep hot. Add the thickening and colouring to the stock, reheat, taste and correct seasoning and hand separately.

If your butcher gave you the breast bones, these should be put into the cooker with the liquid to enrich the stock. Lift them out before adding the thickening.

Boiled

Leg of mutton with caper sauce
Pressure-cooking time: 15–18 minutes per 450 g (1 lb)

1 leg of mutton weighing not more than 1·35 kg (3 lb)
medium carrots
medium onions
sprig each of thyme and parsley
2 bay leaves
1 clove garlic, crushed (optional)
salt and pepper
water for the cooking
3 dl (½ pt) caper sauce*

Wipe, trim and weigh the meat, peel the vegetables and leave whole. Lift the trivet from the cooker, put in the joint, vegetables and seasonings and sufficient water to half fill the cooker. Bring to pressure, cook for the required time and reduce the pressure with cold water. During the cooking, make the caper sauce using only half the ·quantity of milk. Lift the meat on to the serving dish, garnish with the vegetables, lifted out carefully with a straining spoon. Strain the stock and use sufficient to give the sauce a pouring consistency. Reheat, taste and correct seasoning and hand separately.

Braised

Lamb cutlets, country style
Pressure-cooking time: 7 minutes; oven time: 15 minutes

8 small lamb cutlets
6 small onions
325 g (12 oz) medium potatoes
2 tablespoons butter or other fat
3 dl (½ pt) white stock*
1 clove garlic, crushed
bouquet garni*
salt and pepper
a little nutmeg
to garnish:
    chopped parsley

Wipe and trim cutlets; peel and slice onions, peel potatoes. Lift the trivet from the cooker, melt the butter over a low heat and quickly fry the cutlets on both sides and then the onions, until golden-brown. Add the stock, garlic and bouquet garni, the trivet and the salted potatoes in a perforated container. Bring to pressure, cook for 7 minutes, reduce the pressure with cold water. During this cooking, preheat the oven to Gas No 4, 180°C (350°F), setting a shelf towards the top. Lift out the potatoes and trivet, serve the cutlets and onions into a shallow casserole, boil the stock rapidly in the open pan until reduced by half; lift out the bouquet garni, taste and correct seasoning and pour over the meat. Slice the potatoes and lay in the casserole as a top layer, seasoning well with plenty of salt, pepper and a sprinkle of nutmeg. Put as high in the oven as possible and bake until the potatoes are browned – about 15 minutes. Garnish with chopped parsley.

While the casserole is baking, use the pressure cooker for the accompanying vegetables: young carrots, fresh peas or beans sprinkled with finely chopped mint would be a good choice.

Kidneys liégeoise (in wine sauce)
Pressure-cooking time: 7 minutes

6 (550 g or 1¼ lb) lamb's kidneys
4 thin slices streaky bacon
100 g (4 oz) button mushrooms
1 tablespoon butter
2 dl (⅓ pt) wine (inexpensive
   vin rosé recommended)

for the sauce:
1 tablespoon butter
1 tablespoon flour
salt and pepper
to garnish:
chopped parsley

Wipe kidneys, skin, and cut along the rounded edge with scissors. Lay flat and, again with the scissors, trim away the tubes and membranes, then cut in quarters and season well. Make twelve bacon rolls* and put on two short skewers. Skin the mushrooms, or if very young, wash well and dry. Cut into slices lengthways. Lift the trivet from the cooker, fry the bacon rolls until golden-brown, lift out and take off skewers. If there is not enough fat in the cooker, add the butter and, when hot, lightly brown the kidneys. Lift the cooker from the heat and, when cooled, add the wine; stir well, then put in the bacon rolls and mushrooms. Cover, bring to pressure, cook for 7 minutes and reduce the pressure with cold water. During this cooking, melt the butter in a medium-sized saucepan, add the flour and cook slowly until turning a golden-brown. Strain the liquid from the cooker and add sufficient to the sauce to give a rich, coating consistency. Return to the cooker, stir while reheating, taste and correct seasoning and serve piping hot garnished with parsley.

This recipe can be made with brown stock, a dissolved stock cube or thin gravy if preferred.

Braised stuffed hearts
Pressure-cooking time: 30 minutes

4 sheep's hearts	1 onion
salt and pepper	1 carrot
stuffing – see recipe (p 273) or ready-made	1 turnip
	3 dl (½ pt) brown stock*
seasoned flour	1 tablespoon flour blended with a
2 tablespoons dripping or fat	little water for thickening

Wash the hearts thoroughly, remove all fat and tubes and slice halfway down to make a pocket. Season inside with salt and pepper and three-quarters fill with the stuffing. Then secure loosely, either sewing up, lacing with thin string round small skewers or using cocktail sticks. Toss in seasoned flour. Lift the trivet from the cooker, heat the fat and brown the hearts all over. Lift out, then lightly fry the vegetables. Pour in the hot stock (if cold, allow the cooker to cool), add seasoning, put back the hearts, bring to pressure, cook for 30 minutes and reduce the pressure with cold water. Lift the hearts on to a hot serving dish and keep hot. Mash the vegetables well into the gravy, add blended flour and colouring if necessary, bring to the boil, taste and correct seasoning and pour over the hearts.

A dash of sherry added to the strained, thickened sauce just before serving makes this dish extra special.

Stewed

Summer lamb stew
Pressure-cooking time: 12 minutes

450 g (1 lb) middle neck or breast
  of lamb
salt and pepper
2 onions
3 tablespoons butter
3 dl (½ pt) brown stock*
½ bay leaf
1 teaspoon fresh chopped mint

450 g (1 lb) new potatoes
8 young carrots
2 or 3 baby turnips
450 g (1 lb) shelled peas
flour blended with a little water
  for thickening

Wipe and trim the meat, cut from the bone and into 2·5-cm (1-in) squares; toss well in salt and pepper. Slice the onions. Lift the trivet from the cooker, melt the butter over a low heat and gently cook the meat and onions until golden-brown. Add the hot stock (or if cold, allow the cooker to cool), the bones and seasonings, bring to pressure, cook for 7 minutes and reduce the pressure with cold water. During this cooking, peel the potatoes, carrots and turnips which must be really small and left whole; but to ensure they will be cooked, just make a slit to the centre in each. Add these and the peas to the cooker, bring to pressure again, cook for the last 5 minutes, reduce the pressure with cold water. Very gently, lift out the bones, then add sufficient blended flour to give a rich, creamy sauce; taste to correct the seasoning, cook for 2–3 minutes and serve piping hot.

Irish stew
Pressure-cooking time: 12 minutes

450 g (1 lb) best end or middle cut
  of neck chops
salt and pepper
900 g (2 lb) large potatoes
4 large onions

4 small carrots, to give colour
  (optional)
1·5 dl (¼ pt) hot water
to garnish:
  chopped parsley or chives

Wipe and trim off surplus fat from chops and sprinkle well with salt and pepper; peel the potatoes and onions and cut into really thick slices. (Peel the carrots but leave whole.) Lift the trivet from the cooker, put in the hot water and the chops, then a layer of onions and lastly the potatoes (and carrots). Bring to pressure, cook for 12 minutes, then reduce the pressure with cold water. Lift the potatoes on to a hot serving dish, forming them into an over-lapping border; serve the chops and onions into the centre and pour the liquor over. Set a carrot at each corner and garnish thickly with parsley or chives.

Navarin of lamb
Pressure-cooking time: 10 minutes

675 g (1½ lb) best end of neck or cutlets or lamb pieces
salt and pepper
3 medium onions
50 g (2 oz) button mushrooms, or a small tin
2 tablespoons dripping or fat
few strips of green pepper or a small packet of frozen peas
1 tablespoon mint sauce or jelly
1 small tin tomato soup
450 g (1 lb) small or new potatoes for serving separately
a little chopped mint
to garnish:
chopped parsley

Cut the meat into 2·5-cm (1-in) cubes and toss in salt and pepper; peel and slice the onions and mushrooms. Lift the trivet from the cooker, melt the fat over a low heat and gently cook the onions, but without allowing them to brown. Add the mushrooms, the meat, the peppers or peas, the mint sauce or jelly and the tomato soup. Bring to the boil, stirring well. Put in the trivet and the potatoes, sprinkled with mint, in a perforated container. Bring to pressure, cook for 10 minutes and reduce the pressure with cold water. Serve the potatoes; lift out the trivet, taste to correct sea-soning, reheat and serve garnished with parsley.

Savoury liver with vegetables
Pressure-cooking time: 4 minutes

325 g (12 oz) lamb's liver
seasoned flour
3 medium onions
2 rashers streaky bacon
small or quartered medium potatoes and frozen or dehydrated peas (with a sprig of mint) to serve as separate vegetables
1 tablespoon butter
1·5 dl (¼ pt) water with 2 tablespoons vinegar
1 clove
sprig of parsley
salt and pepper
to garnish:
chopped parsley

Wash the liver, dry, cut in 1-cm ($\frac{1}{2}$-in) strips and toss in seasoned flour. Slice the onions, chop the bacon, prepare the potatoes and put in a perforated container and the peas in a solid container (adding the necessary amount of water if using the dehydrated kind). Lift the trivet from the cooker, heat the fat, fry the bacon and onions until golden-brown and lift out. Strain off the fat, put in the hot liquid, the bacon, onions, and seasonings with the strips of liver on top. Add the trivet and the salted potatoes, put the cooker on the heat and when the pan is filled with steam, add the peas. Bring to pressure, cook for 4 minutes and reduce the pressure at room temperature. Serve the potatoes and the strained peas and lift the liver on to a serving dish. If the gravy is a little too thin, thicken with blended flour and milk or reduce by boiling in the open pan. Taste and correct seasoning, pour over the liver and garnish with chopped parsley.

Pork Boiled

Pickled pork with haricot beans

Pressure-cooking time: 15 minutes per 450 g (1 lb)

a piece of pickled pork weighing not more than 1·35 kg (3 lb)
100 g (4 oz) small haricot beans
2 medium onions
12 peppercorns, 4 cloves and a pinch of sage or mixed herbs tied in muslin

sufficient water to cover
salt and pepper
3 dl ($\frac{1}{2}$ pt) thick brown sauce*

Weigh the joint and soak in cold water for 1 hour. Prepare the beans as given on p 64 and then tie them loosely in a piece of muslin. Lift the trivet from the cooker, put in the pork, the sliced onions and seasonings. Add sufficient water to cover but not more than half fill the base of the cooker. Bring to pressure, cook for all but 20 minutes, reduce the pressure with cold water. Put the open pan back on the heat, bring to the boil, drop in the beans, bring to pressure again, cook for a further 20 minutes and allow the pressure to reduce at room temperature. Serve the pork surrounded by the drained beans on a deep serving dish; strain the stock, add sufficient to make the brown gravy and pour this over the beans.

It may be found easier to carve this joint before taking it to table. Lay the slices overlapping on the serving dish; surround them with beans and pour the gravy over.

Pig's trotters with vegetables
Pressure-cooking time: 30 minutes

If the pig's trotters have been salted they should be soaked over-night in cold water.

4 pig's trotters	4 small turnips
salt and pepper	sufficient potatoes for 4
1·5 dl (¼ pt) vinegar	*for thickening:*
1·5 dl (¼ pt) water	1 tablespoon butter
pinch of allspice	1 tablespoon flour
4 small onions	*to garnish:*
4 small carrots	fried parsley*

Scrub the pig's trotters well, drain and dry, season with salt and pepper. Lift the trivet from the cooker, put in the liquid, the season-ings and the trotters, bring to pressure, cook for 25 minutes, reduce the pressure with cold water. During this cooking, prepare the vegetables, leaving the young carrots, onions, turnips whole and cutting the potatoes to a size to cook in 5 minutes. Add the vege-tables to the stock, put in the trivet and then the potatoes; bring to pressure again, cook for the remaining minutes, then reduce the pressure with cold water. During this cooking, prepare and fry the parsley. Serve the potatoes, lift out the trivet, dish the trotters sur-rounded with the vegetables and garnished with parsley and keep hot. Remove the fat from the stock by drawing pieces of absorbent paper across the surface. In a separate saucepan, melt the butter, add the flour and cook without browning for a moment or two. Away from the heat, add the stock gradually, stirring well; reheat, taste and correct seasoning and cook for 2–3 minutes. Hand separately.

As a delicacy, pig's trotters can be served grilled. Pressure cook for 25 minutes only, adding the carrots, turnips and onions to the stock at the beginning of the cooking. Lift out the trotters, drain, halve, dip in melted butter and then breadcrumbs, and brown under the grill, turning them from time to time. Garnish with fried parsley and serve with a mustard sauce, using half milk and half strained stock.

Braised

Braised pork chops
Pressure-cooking time: 10–12 minutes

4 pork chops about 2 cm (¾ in) thick
1 large eating apple
2 tablespoons butter
mirepoix*
stock

salt and pepper
a little gravy browning
to garnish:
a small packet of frozen or dehydrated peas

Wipe, trim off excess fat from the chops and season well. Peel and core the apple and cut into four thick slices. Lift the trivet from the cooker, melt the butter over a low heat, brown the chops on both sides and lift out. Quickly fry the apple rings, lift out and put one on each chop. Prepare the mirepoix, adding sufficient stock to come just to the top and put back the chops. Bring to pressure, cook for the required time, then reduce the pressure with cold water. During this cooking, prepare the peas in another saucepan. Lift the chops carefully on to a serving dish and keep hot. Thoroughly mash the vegetables into the gravy, reheat, taste and correct seasoning, add a little browning to give a rich colour and pour round the chops. Fill the peas into the centre of the apple rings as garnish. Alternatively strain the stock, thicken with blended flour and add colouring. Serve as above.

Piquant pork cutlets
Pressure-cooking time: 8 minutes

4 thin cutlets of pork
salt and pepper
1 tablespoon dripping
1·5 dl (¼ pt) dry cider
1·5 dl (¼ pt) water

1 clove garlic, crushed (optional)
2 or 3 cloves
a little flour blended with water for thickening

Wipe the cutlets, trim off excess fat, season well with salt and, if available, black pepper. Lift the trivet from the cooker, heat the fat, brown the chops on both sides, lift out and drain off the fat. Allow the cooker to cool, add the cider, water, cutlets and seasonings, bring to pressure, cook for 8 minutes, reduce the pressure with cold water. Lift the cutlets on to the serving dish and keep hot. Remove the cloves, add the blended flour to the sauce and reheat. Taste to correct seasoning, cook for 2–3 minutes and pour over the cutlets.

Pork fillets in cream sauce
Pressure-cooking time: 8–10 minutes

4 pork fillets about 2 cm (¾ in) thick	1·5 dl (¼ pt) stock or water
	1·5 dl (¼ pt) sour cream*
1 small onion	salt and pepper
225 g (8 oz) button mushrooms	*to garnish:*
2 tablespoons butter	chopped parsley or chives

Wipe and trim the fillets, peel and dice the onion finely, wash and dry the mushrooms (peel only if necessary) and slice finely, stalk and all. Lift the trivet from the cooker, heat the butter and lightly fry the onion and the fillets on both sides. Pour in the liquid, bring to pressure, cook for 6 minutes, reduce the pressure with cold water. Pile the mushrooms on the chops, bring to pressure again, cook 2 minutes, reduce the pressure with cold water. Carefully lift the chops on to the serving dish and keep hot. Add cream, check seasoning, reheat the sauce without allowing it to boil, whisk well and pour over the chops. Garnish with chopped parsley or chives.

Ham

When pressure cooking ham or bacon joints, the method of preparation will depend on whether it is fresh (green) or smoked, and on the type of joint – whether it is of a lean, expensive cut such as gammon, hock or back, or an inexpensive, more fatty cut such as streaky, collar or flank. The joint should not weigh more than 1·35–1·5 kg (3–3½ lb) for the largest cookers.

Boiled ham

Pressure-cooking time: 12 minutes per 450 g (1 lb)

Fresh ham and bacon joints should be put into the open cooker without the trivet, covered with water and brought to the boil; the water should be thrown away.

Smoked joints should be soaked for at least 2 hours and then be treated as above, before pressure cooking.

Lean joints, to keep their moisture, should be cooked without the trivet and with sufficient water to cover if possible but not to fill the cooker more than half full.

Fatty joints are best cooked on the trivet with just enough water to last the cooking time, but never less than 3 dl ($\frac{1}{2}$ pt).

Prepacked, boned ham should be cooked according to the instructions, but allowing just the 12 minutes per 450 g (1 lb) for pressure cooking.

A selection of vegetables, such as onions, carrots and celery, or a choice of herbs, such as a bouquet garni, may be added to the cooking liquid. If a sweet flavour is preferred, the liquid used may be diluted peach, pineapple or orange juice.

Pressure should be allowed to reduce at room temperature. If the ham or bacon is to be served cold, then the joint should be left in the cooker until quite cold before being lifted out.

TO SERVE HOT Lift out the joint, untie the string and remove the skin by slipping the prong of a fork under it at one side and rolling the fork over and over, bringing the skin with it. Have some golden crumbs ready on a piece of greaseproof paper and coat the fat side of the joint with them, pressing the paper firmly to make sure that the crumbs really adhere. Put the joint on the serving dish into the oven, to keep hot. Add about 2 tablespoons only of the stock to make 3 dl ($\frac{1}{2}$ pt) parsley sauce* and hand separately, or simply serve a little of the plain, strained stock (from which the fat should be removed before pouring into the sauce boat by drawing pieces of absorbent paper across the surface).

TO SERVE COLD When the joint and liquid are cold, skim off any fat, lift out the joint and dress as above. Serve with a green or mixed salad and new or jacket potatoes.

Baked ham

PLAIN BAKED Pressure cook according to the directions given but allow only 10 minutes per 450 g (1 lb). During the cooking, preheat the oven to Gas No 6, 200°C (400°F), lift out the ham, remove the skin, put into a roasting tin and bake in the centre of the oven until the fat is golden-brown – about 15–20 minutes.

SWEET BAKED When the skin has been removed, lightly spread with ready-made mustard, rub brown sugar into the fatty side and stick with cloves at 2-cm (1-in) intervals. Bake as above, until glazed and crisp.

Braised

Braised ham with onions
Pressure-cooking time: 12 minutes per 450 g (1 lb)

a piece of ham or bacon weighing
   not more than 1·35 kg (3 lb)
2 tablespoons dripping or fat
3–4 dl ($\frac{1}{2}$–$\frac{3}{4}$ pt) water

12–15 pickled onions
a little melted butter for glazing

Weigh the joint, preboil as given in the instructions on p 114, then carefully cut off the skin with a sharp knife and score the fat across in 2-cm (1-in) squares. Lift the trivet from the cooker, heat the fat, thoroughly brown the skinned side of the joint, lift out and drain off the fat. Put in the required amount of hot water (if cold, allow the cooker to cool), the trivet and the joint; bring to pressure, cook for the required time, then reduce the pressure with cold water. During this cooking, preheat the grill (if the joint will fit under it) or the oven to Gas No 5, 190°C (375°F). In a small saucepan, melt a little butter without allowing it to brown, and toss the drained and dried onions so that they are completely coated. Lift out the joint, put an onion on a cocktail stick in each of the scored sections and put under the grill or in the oven until browned.

    This can be served with a brown gravy or with parsley*, mustard* or madeira* sauce, using a little of the cooking liquid to obtain the correct consistency.

Ham slices – Hawaii style
Pressure-cooking time: 10 minutes

2·5-cm (1-in) thick slice of lean,
  uncooked ham
sufficient medium potatoes for 4
1 small tin of pineapple slices
2 tablespoons butter
made mustard

salt and pepper
2 or 3 cloves
large packet of frozen peas
3 dl (½ pt) parsley sauce*

Trim all fat from the ham and cut into four portions; peel the
potatoes; strain the pineapple slices, keeping the juice. Lift the trivet from the cooker, heat the butter and brown the pieces of ham
on both sides. Lift the pan from the heat, take out the ham, spread
thinly with the mustard, stick the cloves into the fat and sprinkle
lightly with pepper. Put the pineapple juice made up to 1·5 dl (¼ pt)
with water in the cooker, then the ham with a pineapple slice on
each portion, the trivet and the salted potatoes piled to one side.
Bring to pressure, cook for 6 minutes, reduce the pressure with
cold water.

During this cooking, put the peas in a perforated container and
make the parsley sauce using only half the quantity of milk. Put
the open cooker back on the heat, allow the liquid to boil and the
pan to fill with steam, put in the peas, bring to pressure again, cook
for a further 4 minutes and reduce the pressure with cold water.
Lift out the peas, serve the potatoes, take out the trivet. Put the
ham with pineapple on the serving dish and keep hot with the
vegetables. Add sufficient of the stock to the sauce to give a coating
consistency, reheat, taste and correct seasoning and pour round
the ham. Garnish with the peas, putting a few in the centre of each
pineapple slice and the rest in a pile at each end of the dish.

Sweet-sour ham balls
Pressure-cooking time: 8 minutes

450 g (1 lb) minced lean raw ham
100 g (4 oz) fresh breadcrumbs
pinch of mixed herbs
salt and pepper
1 egg
milk to mix

2 tablespoons dripping or fat
seasoned flour
for the sauce:
  100 g (4 oz) brown sugar
  1 teaspoon dry mustard

1·5 dl (¼ pt) water and vinegar mixed

3 dl (½ pt) water with lemon juice or vinegar for the cooker

Mix together the finely minced ham, breadcrumbs and seasonings; stir in the beaten egg and sufficient milk to bind into a firm mixture, form into eight balls and roll in seasoned flour. In a frying pan, heat the dripping and carefully brown balls all over. Lift into a heatproof dish or bowl which will fit easily into the pressure cooker. Add the sugar and mustard to the remaining fat in the pan and heat gently until it dissolves. Stir in the liquid and, when boiling, pour over the balls and cover with a double sheet of grease-proof paper. Put the water, trivet and then the covered dish in the cooker, bring to pressure, cook for 8 minutes and allow the pressure to reduce at room temperature.

A container of rice could be cooked with this dish if there is sufficient room in the cooker. Put the covered meat dish directly on the bottom of the cooker in the water and use the trivet on top for the container with rice to stand on. Serve the rice as a border, with the ham balls in the centre and the sauce poured over.

Meat suet puddings and pies

Steak and kidney pudding
Steaming time: 15 minutes; pressure-cooking time: 55 minutes

A china, oven-glass, metal or boilable plastic bowl can be used. The covering should be double greaseproof paper, foil or a pudding cloth.

for the filling:
450 g (1 lb) stewing steak
2 kidneys
2 heaped tablespoons seasoned flour
1·5 dl (¼ pt) brown stock* or water

for the pastry:
200 g (8 oz) self-raising flour
100 g (4 oz) shredded suet
salt
a little water to mix
9 dl (1½ pt) boiling water with lemon juice or vinegar for the cooker

Wipe the meat, remove excess fat, cut in 2·5-cm (1-in) strips; skin the kidneys, halve, remove all tubes and membranes and cut in small pieces. Toss all in well-seasoned flour, then roll up each strip of steak with a piece of kidney inside. To make the pastry, mix together the dry ingredients and mix to an elastic, not wet, dough with cold water. Roll out two-thirds into a circle and line the basin, pressing the pastry firmly against the sides and base. Put in the meat and half the liquid, moisten the edges of the lining with cold water, cover with the one-third pastry left, rolled into a circle to form a lid, and pinch the edges together all round. Tie down with a double thickness of greased greaseproof paper and put on the trivet in the boiling water in the cooker. (If you have difficulty putting the basin in the cooker or lifting it out, leave a long end of string after tying the knot securing the covering and take it across to the other side to form a handle.) Put on the lid, wait until the steam escapes from the open vent, lower the heat and steam very gently, like an ordinary steamed pudding, for 15 minutes. Raise the heat, bring to pressure in the usual way and cook for 55 minutes. Allow the pressure to reduce at room temperature. Take off the covering, cut a hole in the centre of the crust and fill the pudding with a little more boiled stock. Serve in the basin wrapped around with a white napkin.

If the same quantity is divided into four individual puddings, using small aluminium or boilable plastic bowls, they will require 10 minutes' steaming, 35 minutes' pressure cooking with 6 dl (1 pt) water for the cooker and the pressure reduced at room temperature.

Meat suet roll
Steaming time: 10 minutes; pressure-cooking time: 35 minutes

for the filling:
450 g (1 lb) stewing steak
1 sheep's kidney (optional)
seasoned flour
1 small onion, chopped
1 tablespoon chopped parsley

for the pastry:
150 g (6 oz) sieved self-raising flour
pinch of salt
75 g (3 oz) shredded suet
cold water to mix
6 dl (1 pt) boiling water for the cooker
rich gravy (foundation brown sauce*)

Cut the meat into small squares or, if cooking kidney, into thin strips, removing most of the fat. Wash the kidney in salted water, skin, cut in half, remove all the tubes with pointed scissors and cut into small pieces. Toss the squares of meat in well-seasoned flour or put a piece of kidney on each strip, roll up and dust with seasoned flour and mix in a bowl with the chopped onion and parsley. Make the suet crust by mixing together the dry ingredients and adding sufficient cold water to give an elastic, not too moist, dough. On a floured surface, roll out the paste into a long strip a little narrower than the base of the cooker, spread evenly with the meat mixture, moisten the edges with cold water and roll up like a swiss roll, pinching the ends and the long edge well together. Wrap in a double sheet of greased greaseproof paper (pleated to allow for expansion) and tie the ends loosely with string. Have ready in the cooker the boiling water and the trivet. Put in the roll, cover the cooker and when the steam escapes through the vent, lower the heat and steam very gently for 10 minutes like an ordinary steamed pudding. This is to make the suet crust nice and light. Then, turn up the heat, bring to pressure, cook for 35 minutes and allow the pressure to reduce at room temperature. Serve whole or sliced, covered with a little good brown sauce and with the rest handed separately.

Meat pasty

Pressure-cooking time: 5 minutes; oven time: 25 minutes

for the filling:
325 g (12 oz) fresh minced beef
salt and pepper
3 medium onions
1 tablespoon dripping or fat
1 tablespoon sweet chutney
dash of Worcestershire sauce, tomato sauce or tomato purée to taste

1·5 dl ($\frac{1}{4}$ pt) brown stock*, gravy or water with gravy browning added
325 g (12 oz) shortcrust pastry (frozen would be suitable)
a little beaten egg or milk to glaze

Season the meat well with salt and pepper. Dice the onions. Lift the trivet from the cooker, heat the fat and evenly brown the onions and the meat, stirring frequently. Add the other ingredients, return to the heat and boil, stirring to remove any brown bits from the bottom of the pan. Bring to pressure in the usual way, cook for 5 minutes and reduce the pressure by standing the cooker in a deep bowl of cold water and leave until the meat is cold. During this cooking, preheat the oven to Gas No 6, 200°C (400°F), and set the shelf in the centre of the oven. Make the pastry, divide in two and line a pie plate with half. Damp the edges, put on the strained, cooked ingredients, cover with the second circle and press the edges together. Trim the edges, flake with a sharp knife and make a cross in the centre. Brush with beaten egg, decorate with diamonds cut from the trimmings and bake until well risen and golden-brown. Just before serving, reboil the gravy, taste and correct seasoning and fill into the pastry or, if there is no room, hand separately.

Pork and liver pie
Pressure-cooking time: 6 minutes; oven time: 25 minutes

325 g (12 oz) lean pork
100 g (4 oz) pig's liver
seasoned flour
1 large onion
50 g (2 oz) mushrooms
1 tablespoon brown sugar
1·5 dl (¼ pt) apple juice, cider or
   small can of shandy

1·5 dl (¼ pt) water
1 tablespoon cooking fat
salt and pepper
2 teaspoons meat herbs, or
   bouquet garni*
225-g (8-oz) packet of ready-
   made puff pastry
blended flour for thickening
a little beaten egg

Wipe the meats, cut into 2-cm (1-in) pieces, toss in seasoned flour, slice the peeled onions and mushrooms. Blend the sugar with the liquids and stir until dissolved. Lift the trivet from the cooker, heat the fat and lightly fry the meats. Add the liquid and stir very well, then put in the vegetables, herbs and seasoning. Bring to pressure, cook for 6 minutes, then stand the cooker in a deep bowl of cold water to reduce the pressure and cool the meat. During this cooking, preheat the oven to Gas No 8, 230°C (450°F), and set a shelf in the middle. Roll out the pastry to the size of the pie-dish being used. Lift the meat and vegetables with a straining spoon into the dish and, if necessary, add a little blended flour to the gravy. Taste to correct seasoning and pour over the meat. Cover with the pastry, trim, then flake the edges with the blade of a sharp knife,

cut a cross in the centre and decorate with small circles or diamonds of pastry cut from the trimmings. Brush with beaten egg to
glaze. Cook for 15 minutes, then lower the heat to Gas No 5,
190°C (375°F), and continue baking until well browned and risen.

Rabbit pie

Pressure-cooking time: 10 minutes; oven time: 30 minutes

1 rabbit
4 slices streaky bacon
1 egg
3 dl (½ pt) white stock* (or a stock
  cube, dissolved in water)
1 slice of lemon rind
salt and pepper

pinch of meat spice of mixed herbs
sliced onions (optional)
150 g (6 oz) flaky or shortcrust
  pastry (can be bought ready-
  made)
a little beaten egg for glazing

Wipe the rabbit, joint neatly into 8 pieces and season well. Make 8
bacon rolls, put on two short skewers; wrap the egg in aluminium
foil. Lift the trivet from the cooker, lightly brown the bacon rolls
in their own fat, take off the skewers and leave in the cooker. Add
the hot liquid and the other ingredients, bring to pressure, cook
for 10 minutes and reduce the pressure in cold water, leaving it
until the meat is cold. Lift out the egg, unwrap and drop in cold
water. During this cooking, preheat the oven to Gas No 5, 190°C
(375°F), for shortcrust or Gas No 6, 200°C (400°F), for flaky
pastry. Make the pastry, line the edge of the pie-dish and damp
with cold water. Put in the meat, the other ingredients, the sliced
hard-boiled egg and about one-third of the stock. Cover with the
pastry, press down round the edges, trim and flake the edges with
a sharp knife. Brush with egg, cut a cross in the centre and decorate
with pastry diamonds cut from the trimmings. Bake on the middle
shelf of the oven until brown and well risen. Just before serving,
boil the rest of the stock until reduced by half, taste and correct
seasoning and fill up the pie through the hole in the centre.

Chicken and ham vol-au-vents

4 medium vol-au-vent cases (these
  can be bought fresh-baked or
  frozen)
6 tablespoons diced chicken
3 tablespoons diced ham

3 dl (½ pt) white sauce*
1 small tin of button mushrooms
to garnish:
  crisp lettuce leaves
  sprigs of parsley

Reheat the vol-au-vent cases at the top of an oven preheated to Gas No 8, 230°C (450°F), for 8–10 minutes. Make the white sauce, add the chopped chicken and ham, the drained, sliced mushrooms and reheat until piping hot. Fill into the cases, put on their lids and a sprig of parsley and serve with the lettuce leaves as decoration.

Poultry and game

	Preparation and cooking	Pressure-cooking time	Method of serving
Chicken (poussin: very young)	Halved	7 minutes	Braised or fricasseed
	Jointed	4 minutes	In a cream sauce
(roasting: 1·35 kg or 2½–3 lb)	Roasted whole, plain or stuffed	5 minutes per 450 g (1 lb)	Browned off in hot oven
	If frozen, completely thawed	5 minutes per 450 g (1 lb)	Coq au vin
	Jointed	5 minutes	Suprême
(boiling: 1·5–1·8 kg or 3½–4 lb)	Whole	10 minutes per 450 g (1 lb)	With boiled rice
	Halved or jointed	20 minutes	Casseroled or braised
	Jointed	10 minutes	As blanquette
(frozen pieces)	Completely thawed, skinned	5 minutes	As for fresh pieces
Duckling	Whole, marinated	12–15 minutes per 450 g (1 lb)	Braised
	Jointed	12 minutes	Bigarade—with oranges
Hare	Jointed	35–40 minutes	Jugged
Rabbit	Jointed	12–15 minutes	Stewed, fricasseed, blanquette
	Precooking for a pie	10 minutes	With shortcrust pastry
Partridge and pheasant	Whole	7–10 minutes	Braised with cabbage
	Halved or jointed	5–7 minutes	Braised or casseroled

When considering chicken, other poultry and game for pressure cooking it is important to decide on the recipe you intend to follow and to choose, according to size, age and condition, the type which will give the best results. Some recipes will not be successful if an old, tough boiling fowl is used, while with others where a young one or a roaster is recommended too long a cooking time could spoil the flavour, tenderness and texture. Where the chicken or fowl is to be left whole, the cooking time is given per 450 g (1 lb) so that the weight must be known; if the bird is stuffed, weigh the stuffed bird. When jointed, a choice of times is given and a little experience will soon allow you to decide whether this needs to be the shorter or the longer – but try not to give more than is necessary as poultry has a delicate flavour and texture which can easily be lost by over-cooking. Where pieces are to be coated with a sauce, it is usually preferable to skin them. If whole frozen poultry are used for roasting or boiling they must be allowed to thaw completely before cooking – and don't forget to lift out the giblets which are usually packed inside! Frozen pieces, too, must be thawed before use.

Roast stuffed chicken
Pressure-cooking time: 5 minutes per 450 g (1 lb);
oven time: 15 minutes

1 roasting chicken weighing
  1·35–1·8 kg (3–4 lb)
seasoning
for the stuffing:
  1 tablespoon breadcrumbs
  10 g (½ oz) shredded suet
  pinch of mixed herbs
  a little grated lemon rind
  1 tablespoon chopped parsley
  the giblets
  salt and pepper
  a little milk or egg

2 tablespoons dripping
at least 3 dl (½ pt) water for the
  cooker
2 or 3 slices thin streaky bacon
flour blended with a little water
  for thickening
as accompaniments:
  bacon rolls*
  bread sauce*
to garnish:
  sprigs of watercress

Put the giblets to soak in salted water for at least half an hour, then rinse thoroughly. Wipe the chicken well, inside and out, dust with salt and pepper. Finely dice the liver (be sure to remove the gall bladder carefully), heart and kidneys, and add to the other ingredients for the stuffing, binding with a little milk or egg. Stuff the chicken, closing the opening by sewing with string or with small skewers, and weigh. Lift the trivet from the cooker, heat the fat and brown the chicken well all over. Lift out and drain off the fat into a roasting tin. Put the water and the rest of the giblets, the feet etc into the cooker, then the trivet and the chicken. Lay the bacon across the breast and cover the whole chicken tightly with a piece of greaseproof paper. Bring to pressure, cook for the required time and reduce the pressure with cold water. During this cooking, preheat the oven to Gas No 5, 190°C (375°F), and set a shelf towards the top. Make the bread sauce and keep hot. Just before the cooking time is up, put the roasting tin in the oven to heat the fat. Lift out the chicken, take the bacon off, dust the breast with seasoned flour, put into the hot fat, baste the whole chicken thoroughly and leave in the oven for 15 minutes, basting once again. Cut the bacon slices in two, roll up, put on skewers and lay across the roasting tin to brown with the chicken. Dish the chicken, garnished with the bacon rolls and a bunch of watercress. Strain the stock and make the gravy in the roasting tin, handing separately with the bread sauce.

Coq au vin
Pressure-cooking time: 25 minutes

1 plump chicken, about 1·35 kg (3 lb)
salt, pepper and lemon juice
a 100-g (4-oz) slice bacon or uncooked ham
3 tablespoons butter
1 small glass brandy
1·5 dl (¼ pt) red wine such as Mâcon or Beaujolais

bouquet garni*
100 g (4 oz) button mushrooms
1 tablespoon sugar and 1 more tablespoon red wine
100 g (4 oz) baby onions
1 clove garlic, crushed, or a squeeze of prepared garlic juice

Wipe the chicken, which should be trussed securely, and season inside and out with salt, pepper and lemon juice; wash the giblets thoroughly in salted water; cut the piece of bacon into large cubes; take the trivet from the cooker, heat 3 tablespoons of the butter, brown the bacon and lift out. Fry the chicken all over, doing this on a medium heat only and turning the chicken carefully and frequently so that it is an even golden-brown. Warm the brandy in a small saucepan, pour into the cooker and set it alight with a match. When the flames have died down, pour in the red wine, add the giblets and the bouquet garni, cover the chicken with a piece of buttered paper, bring to pressure, cook for 20 minutes and reduce the pressure with cold water. During this cooking, melt the remaining butter in a small saucepan, lightly cook the mushrooms for a minute or two and lift out. Add the sugar to the butter that remains, put in the whole onions and cook until lightly brown. Put back the mushrooms and stir in the additional red wine and the garlic. Put the trivet on top of the chicken and then the mushrooms and onions in a small bowl or solid container covered with a piece of greaseproof paper. Bring to pressure again, cook for 5 minutes and allow the pressure to reduce at room temperature. Lift out the container and keep hot. Lift out the trivet, the giblets and then the chicken; carve this into portions, lay in the serving dish and surround with the bacon, lifted out with a straining spoon. Boil the sauce rapidly in the open pan until thickened to a coating consistency, taste and correct seasoning, pour over the chicken and arrange the mushrooms and onions on top.

Braised chicken with vegetables
Pressure-cooking time: 5–8 minutes

a boiling fowl, jointed, or portions of frozen chicken
seasoned flour
mirepoix*
sufficient potatoes, carrots and a green vegetable for 4
2 tablespoons dripping or fat (bacon rinds if available)

225 g (8 oz) chipolata sausages
flour blended with a little water for thickening
gravy browning if necessary
a little sherry or madeira to add to the sauce if liked

If using frozen chicken, allow to thaw completely. Skin the chicken pieces and toss in seasoned flour. Prepare the mirepoix ingredients, the potatoes, carrots or other chosen vegetables. Lift the trivet from the cooker, put in the bacon from the mirepoix and the fat, heat, then brown the sausages quickly in the very hot fat. Lift out, brown the chicken pieces and lift them out. Finish making the mirepoix, adding just enough liquid to show through the surface.

Put back the chicken pieces, the sausages, covered with a piece of greaseproof paper, the trivet and the potatoes and carrots in separate piles. Put the cooker on the heat, bring to the boil, add the green vegetables in a perforated container (in the smaller cookers there may not be room for this), bring to pressure, cook for 5 minutes if frozen chicken, 8 minutes if fresh and reduce the pressure with cold water. Serve the vegetables separately, lift the chicken and sausages into the serving dish and keep all hot. Strain the stock, thicken and colour, return to the heat, reboil, taste and correct seasoning, cook for 2–3 minutes, add the wine and pour over the chicken.

Alternatively, the mirepoix vegetables, after the bouquet garni has been lifted out, may be well mashed or put through a liquidizer, and sufficient stock added to give the gravy the required consistency.

Chicken à la crème Pressure-cooking time: 4 minutes

2 young chickens or poussins
  (weight about 675 g (1½ lb))
salt and pepper
2 tablespoons butter
1 medium onion, finely diced

1·5 dl (¼ pt) chicken stock or water
1·5 dl (¼ pt) double cream
to garnish:
  hard-boiled egg
  chopped parsley

From each chicken cut away the breast from each side in one complete piece, taking as much meat from the wing as possible, and skin them. Season well with salt and pepper. Lift the trivet from the cooker, heat the butter and cook the onion for a minute or two but without browning; put in the hot liquid (if added cold, allow the cooker to cool) and the chicken breasts, bring to pressure in the usual way, cook for 4 minutes and reduce the pressure with cold water. Pour in the cream, return to the heat and boil rapidly until the sauce thickens, but be sure it does not burn. Turn the chicken pieces over once in the sauce, taste and correct seasoning. Lift the pieces on to the serving dish, laying them down the centre and standing up against each other. Coat with the sauce, then garnish alternately with lines of chopped egg and parsley.

The legs, wings and carcasses left can be used to make stock.

Chicken blanquette Pressure-cooking time: 7–10 minutes

4 portions or frozen pieces of
  boiling fowl
salt and pepper
1 large onion
2 or 3 sticks celery
1·5 dl (¼ pt) water
bouquet garni*
1 clove garlic, crushed, or a squeeze
  of prepared garlic juice (optional)

to garnish:
  chopped parsley
  fried bread
for the sauce:
  1 tablespoon butter
  1 tablespoon flour
  1·5 dl (¼ pt) milk

Wipe the chicken joints, trim off the fat, skin, and toss in seasoning. Quarter the onion and slice the celery. Lift the trivet from the cooker, put in the water, chicken, vegetables, seasoning and herbs, bring to pressure in the usual way, cook for 7 minutes if frozen chicken, 10 minutes if fresh and reduce the pressure with cold water. During this cooking, fry two slices of bread without crusts and cut into triangles. Make the sauce by melting the butter in a small saucepan, adding the flour and stirring for a minute or two over the heat before stirring in the milk. Lift the chicken on to a deep serving dish, and keep hot. Strain the stock and add sufficient to the sauce to give a coating consistency. Reheat, taste and correct seasoning. Dip half of each triangle of bread into the sauce and then into the chopped parsley. Pour the sauce over the chicken and garnish with the prepared fried bread.

To enrich this recipe, 2 tablespoons cream with a yolk of egg may be added to the sauce and cooked for 2–3 minutes, but without boiling again or the sauce will curdle.

Chicken suprême Pressure-cooking time: 5 minutes

4 pieces chicken wing with breast,
  fresh or frozen
1·5 dl (¼ pt) double cream
seasoned flour
100 g (4 oz) button mushrooms
2 tablespoons butter
4 slices uncooked ham about
  5 mm (¼ in) thick
3 dl (½ pt) chicken stock* (or a
  stock cube, dissolved in water)

for the sauce:
  2 tablespoons butter
  2 tablespoons flour
  1·5 dl (¼ pt) chicken stock*
  1·5 dl (¼ pt) milk
  1 egg yolk
  salt and pepper
to garnish:
  sprigs of parsley

If using frozen pieces, allow to thaw completely. Carefully lift the chicken from the bones in each piece and skin. (Save these and the skin to make chicken stock in the cooker afterwards or, if chicken is bought the day before, bone it and make the stock straight away for this dish.) Take a little of the cream, brush the chicken pieces with it and roll them in seasoned flour. Wash the mushrooms and slice them lengthwise, stalks and all. Lift the trivet from the cooker, heat the butter, brown the slices of ham on both sides and lift out. Brown the chicken all over until a golden colour only and lift out. Add the hot stock (if added cold, allow the cooker to cool), put back the ham and on each slice a piece of chicken, placing them close together so that they touch. Lay the mushrooms in a thick layer on the top, dot with butter and cover with a piece of grease-proof paper. Bring to pressure, cook for 5 minutes and reduce the pressure with cold water. During this cooking make the sauce by melting the butter in a small saucepan, adding the flour and stir-ring for a minute or two over the heat; gradually pour in the milk, but do not add the cream or egg. Lift each piece of ham with its own chicken and mushrooms on to a serving dish and keep hot. Reboil the sauce, check seasoning; mix the cream with the beaten yolk and add, away from the heat, cooking for a further 2 minutes but without allowing the sauce to boil, otherwise it will curdle. Pour round the dish and garnish each portion with a sprig of parsley.

Sherry to taste, may be added to the sauce, just before serving, for extra richness.

Southern chicken casserole
Pressure-cooking time: 15–20 minutes

1·5–1·8 kg (3½–4 lb) fowl	4 firm tomatoes
seasoned flour	3 dl (½ pt) water
4 slices streaky bacon, thick-cut	1·5 dl (¼ pt) chilli sauce
2 carrots	salt and celery salt
2 medium onions or 6 shallots	flour for thickening if required
1 green pepper	

Ask your supplier to cut the fowl into 4–6 portions; wipe the chicken pieces, skin them and roll in seasoned flour; cut the bacon into large dice. Coarsely chop the carrots and the onions or shal-

lots. Wash the pepper, cut in half, remove all seeds and slice finely.
Skin and halve the tomatoes and remove the pips. Lift the trivet
from the cooker, put in the bacon and cook until nicely brown and
the fat runs out. Add the chicken and brown the pieces evenly all
over. Lift out the chicken, put in the prepared vegetables and cook
for 3–4 minutes. Add the hot water (if cold, allow the cooker to
cool), the chilli sauce and the chicken in layers, sprinkling each
lightly with the salts. Bring to pressure, cook for 15–20 minutes
according to the size of the joints, reduce the pressure with cold
water. Lift the chicken into a casserole dish, add the thickening, if
required, to the sauce, bring to the boil again, taste and correct
seasoning and pour into the dish.

Braised duckling with cherries
Pressure-cooking time: 10–12 minutes per 450 g (1 lb)

1 duck, cleaned and trussed	2 or 3 cubes turnip
4 slices streaky bacon	1 stick celery, sliced
seasoned flour	bay leaf
2 medium onions, sliced	small glass wine (optional)
3 dl (½ pt) brown stock*	2 tablespoons fat or dripping
2 medium carrots, cut in rounds	a dish of maraschino cherries

Wipe the duck and weigh. Lift the trivet from the cooker, put in
the bacon and allow to cook until the fat runs out. Carefully brown
the breast of the duck only, on both sides, lift out and dust with
seasoned flour. As it is essential to have a brown stock for this
dish, if you have none ready cook the onions now until really dark
brown. Put in the liquid, the rest of the vegetables, bay leaf, and
then the duck. To make it extra special, pour a small glass of
white or red wine over the duck; otherwise, spoon over a little of
the juice from the cherries. Bring the cooker to pressure, cook for
the required time, reduce the pressure by standing the cooker in a
deep bowl of cold water. During the cooking, preheat the oven to
Gas No 5, 190°C (375°F), and have ready a roasting tin with a
little hot fat in it. Lift out the duck (but leave the cooker in cold
water), baste with the hot fat and put as near to the top of the oven
as possible to brown. When the cooker contents are nearly cold,
skim off as much fat as possible, then sieve; return this thick gravy
to the pan, reheat, taste and correct seasoning, then pour into a

deep casserole. Put the duck on top. It may be served whole, as it will be so well cooked that it will joint easily; but you may prefer to cut it into portions before taking it to table. Hand the cherries separately.

Duckling bigarade
Pressure-cooking time: 10 minutes

1 duckling	3 dl ($\frac{1}{2}$ pt) white stock*
knob of butter	2 onions, sliced
peel of 1 bitter orange	2 carrots, sliced
3 slices streaky bacon	small glass white wine (optional)
pinch of mixed herbs	*for the sauce:*
a little fresh chopped parsley and chives	1 tablespoon butter
	1 tablespoon flour
pinch of nutmeg	a little orange juice
salt and pepper	*to garnish:* watercress

Wipe the duckling and put a knob of butter and a large piece of orange rind inside it. Cut the bacon slices in half; mix the herbs together. Lift the trivet from the cooker, fry the bacon lightly until the fat runs out and while still hot roll in the herb mixture. Brown the breast of duck on both sides, lift out, season well with salt and pepper and lay the prepared bacon slices over the breast. Put into the cooker the stock and vegetables and then the duck (if using wine pour it over now), bring to pressure, cook for the required time, reduce the pressure in a deep bowl of cold water. During this cooking, shred the rest of the orange peel very finely, put 2 table-spoons water in a small saucepan and when boiling put in the shreds, boil quickly for 2–3 minutes and drain. Melt the butter in the saucepan, add the flour and cook gently for a minute or two. Lift out the duck and keep hot. Strain the stock and beat gradually into the saucepan, return to the heat and cook for 2–3 minutes. Check for a pouring consistency, add the cooked peel and a little strained orange juice, taste and correct seasoning and hand separately. Garnish the duck with the watercress.

Fricassée of rabbit

Pressure-cooking time: 20–25 minutes

This dish can be made a real delicacy if the rabbit joints are first marinated for a couple of hours in 3 dl (½ pt) white wine or cider. They should be turned over 2 or 3 times whilst marinating.

1 rabbit, jointed (and marinated)
2 slices streaky bacon
2 tablespoons dripping
3 onions, finely sliced
3 dl (½ pt) white stock* or the
 liquor from the marinade

a piece of lemon rind if stock is
 used
salt and pepper
to garnish:
 2 slices fried bread
 chopped parsley

Wipe the rabbit joints and season well. Lift the trivet from the cooker, heat the diced bacon until the fat runs out, and add the dripping. Then brown the joints and the onions. Add the liquid, lemon rind and seasoning, bring to pressure, cook for the required time and reduce the pressure in cold water. During this cooking, fry the bread, cut into triangles and dip half of each in the chopped parsley. Lift the joints into a casserole dish and keep hot. Boil the contents of the cooker rapidly until reduced and thick, taste and correct seasoning, pour over the joints and garnish with the fried triangles of bread.

Braised or jugged hare

Pressure-cooking time: 30–40 minutes

1 hare
2 tablespoons dripping or lumps
 of bacon fat
seasoned flour
2 chopped onions
1 or 2 field mushrooms
1·5 dl (¼ pt) brown stock*
small glass red wine

1 clove garlic, crushed
blade of mace
salt and pepper
the blood of the hare, if liked
to garnish:
 2 slices fried bread
 redcurrant jelly

Joint the hare and clean thoroughly. Lift the trivet from the cooker, melt the fat and brown the joints, lift out and toss in seasoned flour. Brown the onions, drain away the fat, add the sliced mushrooms, the stock and wine, the seasonings and the joints, bring to pressure, cook for the required time and reduce the pressure with cold water. During this cooking, fry the bread and cut in triangles. Lift the joints into a casserole dish and keep hot. Boil the contents of the pan until well thickened. If the blood is to be used, add it now, but do not allow the sauce to reboil. Taste and correct the seasoning and pour over the joints. Dip one point of each triangle in redcurrant jelly and serve as garnish.

Braised pheasant chartreuse
Pressure-cooking time: 7–10 minutes

1 large or 2 small pheasants
1 large white cabbage
2 medium carrots
2 thick bacon rashers
2 tablespoons dripping
salt and pepper
1 medium onion, sliced

3 dl ($\frac{1}{2}$ pt) brown stock* or water
4 frankfurter or cocktail sausages
a little red wine to enrich the
  gravy (optional)
flour blended with a little water
  for thickening
to serve:
  small bunch of watercress

Wipe the pheasant and see it is securely trussed. Cut the cabbage into quarters, the carrots in four lengthways and the bacon slices in four pieces. Lift the trivet from the cooker, heat the bacon until the fat runs out, then add the dripping. Carefully brown the pheasant all over, lift out and dust with salt and pepper. Lightly fry the onions, then drain off the fat, put in the liquid, the cabbage, the onion and carrots, the pheasant on top and the sausages around it. Bring to pressure, cook for the required time and reduce the pressure with cold water. Lift the pheasant out and put on one side. Put the cabbage quarters on the serving dish, the pheasant on top and the sausages, bacon and carrots around as garnish. Strain the stock, removing any fat by drawing small pieces of absorbent paper across the surface; add the thickening, reboil, cook for 2–3 minutes, taste and correct seasoning and add the red wine if available. Put the watercress in a bunch on the dish; hand the sauce separately.

Cold meats

Brawn
Pressure-cooking time: 35 minutes

½ salted pig's head (cow head or pig's cheek could be used instead)
small knuckle of veal
6 dl (1 pt) cold water
2 small onions
2 small carrots
½ teaspoon nutmeg

blade of mace
3 cloves
few peppercorns
pinch of meat herbs or of mixed herbs
salt and pepper
to garnish:
  1 hard-boiled egg
  slices of gherkin or cucumber

Lift the trivet from the cooker, put in the meats and the water, bring to the boil in the open pan and skim until there is nothing more coming to the surface. Add the rest of the ingredients, bring to pressure, cook for 35 minutes and allow the pressure to reduce at room temperature. Lift out the joints, remove all the meat and cut into 1-cm (½-in) dice. Strain the stock, boil rapidly with the bones in the open pan until reduced to about 3 dl (½ pt), taste and correct seasoning. Put back the meat and reboil, then turn into a wetted mould or basin to three-quarters fill it, cover completely with the stock and leave to set. Turn out, just before serving, by dipping quickly in and out of boiling water.

Serve garnished with overlapping alternate slices of hard-boiled egg and gherkin or cucumber.

Chicken liver pâté
This should be made a day or two before required so that it can mature.
Pressure-cooking time: 3 minutes

225 g (8 oz) chicken livers
1 tablespoon melted butter
3 dl (½ pt) water with a little lemon juice or vinegar for the cooker
2 tablespoons butter
2 tablespoons cream cheese

salt and pepper
pinch of mixed spice
pinch of herbs (thyme, basil, marjoram, rosemary, as available)
1 tablespoon brandy
1 tablespoon sherry

Wipe the livers and put into a deep saucer or dish that will fit into the cooker with 1 tablespoon melted butter, covering with a piece of greaseproof paper. Put the water, trivet and livers in the cooker, bring to pressure, cook for 3 minutes and reduce the pressure with cold water. During this cooking, mix the butter, cheese, herbs and seasoning to a smooth consistency. Lift the livers from the cooker, strain the stock into the brandy and sherry and whisk well. Sieve the livers or put through a liquidizer; combine all the ingredients together, beat well, smooth into a 450-g (1-lb) loaf tin or small soufflé dish and refrigerate until firm. Serve in individual portions with slices of hot toast and garnished with crisp heart of lettuce leaves.

Galantine of beef
Pressure-cooking time: 35 minutes

450 g (1 lb) minced lean beef
100 g (4 oz) raw ham
100 g (4 oz) sausage meat
2–3 large mushrooms
1 small onion
100 g (4 oz) fresh white
  breadcrumbs
2 tablespoons fresh chopped
  parsley

dash of Worcestershire or
  HP sauce
1 beaten egg
salt and pepper
2 hard-boiled eggs (optional)
4·5 dl (¾ pt) water for the cooker
golden crumbs for coating

Mince together the meats, chop the mushrooms and onion very finely. Mix all the ingredients together and bind with the beaten egg. Put into a seamless 450-g (1-lb) loaf tin or suitable container rinsed in cold water and tie with a double thickness of greaseproof paper; or form into a roll and tie in a triple thickness of grease-proof paper, pleating this to allow for the roll expanding. If hard-boiled eggs are used, lay these end to end in the middle of the mixture. Lift the trivet from the cooker and put in the water. If the galantine is in a container, add a little lemon juice or vinegar and then the trivet; if in a roll, put directly into the water. Bring to pressure, cook for 35 minutes and allow the pressure to reduce at room temperature.

Lift out the container, take off the paper, put on a clean piece and press under heavy weights. (If a loaf tin has been used, a carton of sugar, on its side, usually forms a good base for the weights.) If a roll has been made, re-roll very tightly in clean paper and press between two large plates.

When cold, coat in golden crumbs and serve with salad.

Pressed tongue
Pressure-cooking time: 15 minutes per 450 g (1 lb)

1 ox tongue	2 or 3 cloves
2 dessertspoons vinegar	bay leaf
12 peppercorns	cold water to cover

The easiest way to handle the tongue is to tie it loosely in a piece of butter muslin. If the tongue has been smoked, soak overnight in cold water. Lift the trivet from the cooker, put in the tongue and other ingredients, add sufficient water to half fill the cooker or just cover the tongue, whichever is the less; bring to pressure, cook for the required time and allow the pressure to reduce at room temperature. Lift the tongue on to a large dish, untie, skin carefully and remove all the small bones. While still hot, curl the tongue into a basin or a soufflé dish which is just a little too small for it, put a saucer or plate which just fits inside the container on top and press with weights from the household scales (or packets of sugar, etc). Leave overnight. To turn out the tongue, dip the dish just to the level of the top, in boiling water; count to about twenty, then turn on to the serving dish and give a shake.

Serve with new potatoes and a mixed or green salad.

5 Cereals, rice and pasta

While pressure cooking cereals and other such foods does not represent quite such a spectacular saving in time as for meats, vegetables, soups and so on, it does mean that rice, for example, can be pressure cooked at the same time as many of the dishes it is to accompany; this does away with a second saucepan and represents a considerable saving in fuel and work. Nowadays there are so many varieties and forms of these foods, with new ones coming on to the market every day, that it is not possible to mention them all. However, the timetable and recipes in the following section should give a good idea of average times from which to work out the correct one for a particular type.

There are also many new varieties specially treated for quick cooking; here, unless the time given on the packet is considerably longer than the pressure-cooking time, it is probably more sensible to cook them on their own, following the instructions on the packet.

It is, however, true to say that the completeness of the cooking under pressure does bring out an extra-good taste in cereals such as oatmeal, and ensures that macaroni, spaghetti and rice are really swollen, al dente and very absorbent of other flavours such as cheese, tomato and garlic.

A choice of rice, macaroni, spaghetti and noodles will add a very welcome as well as nourishing variety to the diet and substitute most satisfactorily for potatoes.

General instructions

The trivet is not used for any of these foods, as all require to be cooked in plenty of salted water or sauce to swell and absorb liquid during cooking. As a general rule, pastas such as macaroni, spaghetti, noodles etc will require approximately one-third of the normal cooking time when pressure cooked, e.g.:

Normal cooking time: 8–10 minutes; pressure cooking time: 3–4 minutes.
Normal cooking time: 10–15 minutes; pressure cooking time: 5–6 minutes.
Normal cooking time: 15–25 minutes; pressure cooking time: 8–10 minutes.

If the recipe being followed requires further cooking of the pasta when other ingredients are added, then the first pressure-cooking time should be cut by 2–3 minutes.

As these foods usually require to be plunged into boiling salted water, do not try to put the cover on with the weight on or the valve closed. As the pan will be filled with steam, it may be difficult or even impossible to close the cover completely and therefore safely; once the cover is correctly closed the weight can be put on or the valve be closed immediately.

As all cereals tend to froth and boil up during cooking, the pan must never be more than one-third full when ready to be brought to pressure. Use H pressure and allow to reduce at room temperature.

During the actual pressure cooking the heat can be kept a little lower than normal. If the contents of the pan begin to boil through the valve, just keep an eye on it to make sure that the steam still continues to escape. As the cooking is so short and the meal usually waiting to be dished up it is not difficult to do this. Should a floury-looking liquid begin to boil out of the valve, take the cooker away from the heat for a moment, give it a good shake backwards and forwards, then put it back on the heat and continue for the rest of the cooking time, still watching it carefully.

In the following recipes, the small cereals, pasta and the rice are measured in cups: 1 full teacup=150 g (6 oz) approximately; the larger cereals and those cooked in lengths are given by weight. For most dishes, 50 g (2 oz) should be allowed per person.

Cereal	Amount	Water	Salt	Time (mins.)
Barley (pearl)	1 cup	4 cups	1 teaspoon	20
Macaroni				
(short lengths)	225 g (8 oz)	1·2 litres (2 pt)	1 tablespoon	4–5
(elbow)	225 g (8 oz)	1·2 litres (2 pt)	1 tablespoon	5–6
Noodles				
(fine)	225 g (8 oz)	1·2 litres (2 pt)	1 tablespoon	2–3
(medium)	225 g (8 oz)	1·2 litres (2 pt)	1 tablespoon	3–4
(alphabet)	1 cup	3 cups	1 tablespoon	3–4
(small shells)	1 cup	4 cups	1 tablespoon	3
Oatmeal (coarse)	1 cup	4 cups	½ teaspoon	15–20
Rice (long-grain)	1 cup	2 cups	½ teaspoon	5
Spaghetti				
(fine)	225 g (8 oz)	1·2 litres (2 pt)	1 tablespoon	3–4
(regular)	225 g (8 oz)	1·2 litres (2 pt)	2 tablespoons	5–6
Vermicelli	225 g (8 oz)	1·2 litres (2 pt)	1 tablespoon	3–4

Barley

This is most usually added to clear soups such as vegetable or chicken to give them plenty of bulk and to make them more of a meal in themselves. It is an excellent food too, for invalids and can be made into a cream soup or barley water, recipes for which will be found in the appropriate section.

Macaroni

To serve as a course of a meal, allow 50 g (2 oz) per person. After pressure cooking, reduce the pressure with cold water and drain through a colander.

Macaroni cheese

225 g (8 oz) macaroni	knobs of butter
6 dl (1 pt) cheese sauce*	*to garnish:*
2 tablespoons butter	paprika pepper
3 tablespoons grated cheese	fried croûtons*

Cook the macaroni as directed; during this cooking make the cheese sauce and have the butter ready, melted in a large saucepan. Turn the drained macaroni into the saucepan, toss until well coated with the butter. Add the cheese sauce, stir, and put into a buttered ovenproof dish. Sprinkle thickly with the cheese, dot with knobs of butter and while it is browning lightly under the grill, fry the bread. Sprinkle with paprika and garnish with triangles of fried bread.

Macaroni rarebit

100 g (4 oz) macaroni	1 large tomato
3 dl (½ pt) cheese sauce* with	1 tablespoon butter
Worcestershire sauce and	1 tablespoon grated cheese
mustard	1 tablespoon chopped chives
2 slices streaky bacon	

Cook the macaroni as directed. During the cooking, make the cheese sauce but add ¼ teaspoon mustard to the flour and a good dash of Worcestershire sauce with the milk; fry the diced streaky bacon in its own fat until crisp; cut the tomato into slices. Toss the drained macaroni in a saucepan with the melted butter, then divide into 4 individual buttered ovenproof dishes or scallop shells. Pour over the sauce, sprinkle with cheese, arrange the tomato slices and brown under a hot grill. Garnish with the fried bacon and chopped chives.

Savoury macaroni

225 g (8 oz) macaroni
2 tablespoons butter
1 onion, finely chopped
some strips of red or green pepper
  if available
50 g (2 oz) sliced mushrooms

4 tomatoes
1·5 dl (¼ pt) brown stock* or gravy
dash of Worcestershire sauce
salt and pepper
225 g (8 oz) cooked ham, meat,
  chicken or sausages

Cook the macaroni as directed, and pile on the serving dish to keep hot. During this cooking, heat the butter in a frying pan and gently cook the onion, mushrooms and pepper if used. Add the quartered tomatoes, cook for a moment or two, stir in the liquid, seasonings and finally the cooked meat. Cover and leave over a low heat until ready to serve. Add the Worcestershire sauce, taste and correct seasoning and pour over the macaroni. Serve with or without grated cheese handed separately.

Noodles

To serve as a course of a meal, allow 50 g (2 oz) per person. After cooking, reduce the pressure with cold water and drain through a colander.

The larger, broader, kinds of noodle may replace macaroni in the recipes already given and the finer types may replace spaghetti in those following. Alphabet and shell noodles may be served in thin or clear soups such as chicken, vegetable etc, when they give an attractive as well as a nutritious addition.

Fine noodles would make an excellent accompaniment for a pot-roast, for Swedish meat balls (Köttbullar*) etc, and as they cook quickly it does not mean keeping these dishes hot for too long. If served with a boiled meat such as silverside or mutton in place of dumplings, they can be added to the cooking liquid 3–4 minutes before the end of the full cooking time.

Buttered noodles

225 g (8 oz) fine noodles
3 tablespoons butter

to garnish:
  chopped parsley or chives

Cook the noodles as directed. Have ready the melted butter, which should be allowed to turn brown over a low heat.

Serve the noodles, pour over the browned butter and garnish with the parsley or chives.

Noodle supper

225 g (8 oz) medium or broad
  noodles
2 tablespoons butter
100 g (4 oz) grated cheese
  (cheddar and parmesan mixed)

salt, pepper and nutmeg
to accompany:
  a crisp green salad

Cook the noodles as directed. Melt 1 tablespoon butter in the cooker, put back the drained noodles and toss until they are well coated. Stir in the cheese, the rest of the butter, the seasoning and a pinch of nutmeg and reheat. Serve with individual green salads.

Shrimp shells

100 g (4 oz) small shell noodles
1 packet of frozen shrimps
2 tablespoons mayonnaise with 1
  tablespoon thin cream or top of
  the milk

squeeze of lemon juice
1 tablespoon butter
a little grated cheese
golden crumbs
to garnish:
  lemon butterflies*
  sprigs of parsley

Cook the shells as directed. During the cooking, wash the thawed-out shrimps quickly in cold water. In a small saucepan heat the mayonnaise with the cream over a low heat, stir in the shrimps and add pepper and lemon juice to taste. Put the noodles back into the cooker with the butter and toss until well coated and glistening. Arrange the noodles in buttered individual ovenproof dishes or scallop shells, leaving a shallow well in the centre of each. Fill this with the shrimp mixture, sprinkle with the cheese and golden crumbs and brown under a hot grill. Garnish each with a lemon butterfly and a sprig of parsley.

Oatmeal

Now that quick-cooking oats are so popular it is really only for the coarse whole oatmeal that pressure cooking is such a time-saver. Be sure to stir the oatmeal well after adding to the boiling water, and watch the pan during the cooking to make sure that it is not frothing up to block the valve. Allow the pressure to reduce at room temperature and if the porridge is not quite thick enough, it can be boiled while stirring in the open pan until the desired consistency is reached.

Rice

One cup of rice will give approximately 4 cups when cooked, so allow 1 full teacup, approximately 150 g (6 oz), for 2 people as an accompaniment or as part of a complete dish.

If cooked on its own, the rice should be thrown into the salted boiling water in the cooker and the pressure should be reduced with cold water.

In many of the recipes, the rice is cooked with other ingredients and it is then put into a solid container in the proportion of 2 cups water to 1 cup rice, the container being covered with a piece of greaseproof paper. At the end of the cooking time, the pressure is allowed to reduce at room temperature to ensure that the rice will absorb all the water.

With either method, the rice should be finished off as given in the following recipe:

Boiled rice as an accompaniment
Cook long-grain rice as directed but add half a lemon to the water. During the cooking, preheat the oven to Gas No 3, 170°C (325°F), and boil a kettle of water. As soon as the rice has been strained, pour the boiling water over to separate the grains. Put into a hot dish and then in the oven on the middle shelf. Turn off the oven and leave to dry out for a few minutes.

Buttered rice
Cook the long-grain rice as directed and leave to dry out in the oven for a few minutes as explained for boiled rice. Melt 2 tablespoons butter in a saucepan, stir in the rice, add a beaten egg, a sprinkling of chopped parsley or chives, reheat and serve piping hot with a bowl of grated cheese handed separately.

Curried rice
For serving with cooked chicken, veal or lamb heated in a cream or tomato sauce.

After rinsing, put back in the pan, add 1 teaspoon curry powder which has been heated in 1 tablespoon melted butter and stir until mixed through.

Yellow rice
For vegetarian dishes, using mixed vegetables and hard-boiled eggs, in a tomato* or curry* sauce.

While the rice is cooking, melt a little butter or oil in a frying pan, add a finely diced onion and cook gently. When the rice has been rinsed and dried, add to the frying pan and stir slowly until the rice turns golden brown.

Arabian rice
Delicious with cooked poultry or game reheated in a rich brown gravy or espagnole* or madeira* sauce.

When the rice has been rinsed, stir in 2 tablespoons melted butter, 50 g (2 oz) sultanas or small raisins and 50 g (2 oz) finely shredded blanched almonds, and mix well together.

Chinese-style rice
While the rice is cooking, beat an egg and scramble it very lightly in butter, in a frying pan. Add a cup of diced fresh or tinned lobster or crabmeat and the drained rice, and allow to cook gently for 3–4 minutes without browning. Stir in 1 teaspoon soy sauce, season using fresh ground black pepper if possible, and serve.

Spanish-style rice
While the rice is cooking, melt 2 tablespoons butter or oil in a frying pan, add 1 finely chopped onion, 1 clove garlic (or a squeeze

of garlic juice) and 2 tablespoons diced green peppers and cook gently until soft. Add 3 or 4 large peeled, chopped tomatoes, a crushed bay leaf and seasoning, and simmer gently until the drained rice is ready. Stir in the rice, reheat and serve.

Risotto
Pressure-cooking time: 6 minutes

This dish should always be made with the Italian or round-grain rice. It is not really satisfactory if made with the long-grain rice as this type is not sufficiently absorbent to give the desired result.

2 tablespoons olive oil	4 cups boiling, well-seasoned
1 medium onion, finely sliced	chicken stock*
1 clove garlic, chopped	4 heaped tablespoons grated
1 cup rice	parmesan cheese

Lift the trivet from the cooker, heat the oil and cook the onion until just turning brown. Add the garlic and rice and stir until the rice begins to look transparent. Pour in the boiling stock, stir for a moment or two until the liquid is boiling again, bring to pressure, cook for 6 minutes and allow the pressure to reduce at room temperature. The rice should have absorbed all the stock, but if it has not, allow it to cook for a moment or two in the open pan. Stir in the grated cheese and serve at once piled high on the serving dish.

Risotto with mushrooms
During the cooking as given in the preceding recipe, gently cook 100 g (4 oz) finely sliced button mushrooms in a little oil and add these to the rice in the cooker just before serving. The grated cheese should be handed separately.

Risotto with chicken livers
During the cooking of the rice as given for **Risotto***, thinly slice 3 chicken livers and fry them very carefully so that they do not dry up, in 1 tablespoon mixed butter and olive oil, then lift out. Add the strained juice of ½ lemon or 1 tablespoon white wine to the juices in the pan, then 1·5 dl (¼ pt) thickened brown stock* or chicken gravy. Taste and correct seasoning, put back the livers, reheat without boiling and serve piled into the centre of a rice ring.

Pilaff
Pressure-cooking time: 5 minutes

2 tablespoons chopped onion
50 g (2 oz) butter
1 cup long-grain rice
2 cups hot chicken or veal stock

to garnish:
a little paprika or chopped
parsley

Lift the trivet from the cooker and lightly cook the onion in the melted butter, but without allowing it to colour. Add the rice and stir until it begins to look transparent. Add the hot stock and allow to boil again, stirring well; cover, bring to pressure, cook for 5 minutes and allow the pressure to reduce at room temperature. Return to the heat and flick with a fork until each grain is separate. Arrange in a ring or as a bed on the serving dish with any of the following accompaniments:

Diced cooked turkey in a cream sauce, the rice garnished with bacon rolls.

Diced cooked lamb or mutton in a cream sauce, with raisins stirred into the rice.

Add some diced celery with the onions in the frying pan.

Diced cooked duck in a cream sauce, the rice garnished with slices of peeled oranges or cooked, stoned prunes.

Spaghetti

As a complete dish, spaghetti is usually cooked in the long lengths in which it is sold. To do this, wait until the salted water in the cooker is boiling fast, then taking a fistful of spaghetti, plunge the ends in the water but don't let go. As the spaghetti softens, it can be bent until it all slips under the water and the cover can then be fitted on easily. After reducing the pressure with cold water, the spaghetti should be strained and should be tender but still quite firm.

Spaghetti bolognaise
Pressure-cooking time: 10 minutes and 5 minutes

3 tablespoons olive oil or butter
1 onion, diced
100 g (4 oz) lean minced raw beef
    (or half beef, half chicken
    livers)
50 g (2 oz) mushrooms (stalks
    only will do)
a little diced carrot and celery
    (optional)
1·5 dl (¼ pt) dry white wine
a piece of lemon rind, bay leaf or
    a little basil, as available

salt, pepper, nutmeg
2 lumps of sugar
2 good tablespoons tomato purée
    or paste stirred into 1·5 dl (¼ pt)
    brown stock made with beef
    cube
325 g (12 oz) spaghetti
a little olive oil or butter
to serve:
    2 tablespoons grated parmesan
    cheese

Lift the trivet from the cooker, heat the oil and gently brown the diced onion. Add the meat, chopped mushrooms and other vegetables if used. Cook for 2–3 minutes only, stirring all the time as the meat must not be allowed to harden. Pour in the wine and boil rapidly for a moment or two, then add the seasonings, sugar and the tomato liquid. Stir again, bring to pressure, cook for 10 minutes and reduce the pressure with cold water. Turn the sauce into another saucepan and while it is cooking very gently, without a lid, to reduce it to a really creamy consistency, rinse out the cooker and prepare the spaghetti as directed. While it is draining, put a little oil or butter in the cooker, allow it and the cooker to warm thoroughly, put back the spaghetti and stir it around off the heat until it is well coated. Serve in a deep, really hot dish, pour over the sauce and hand the cheese separately.

Spaghetti milanaise
Pressure-cooking time: 5–6 minutes

325 g (12 oz) spaghetti
2 tablespoons olive oil or butter
150 g (6 oz) strips of cooked
    ham and tongue
1 tablespoon tinned button
    mushrooms, sliced

2 tablespoons tomato purée or
    paste added to 1·5 dl (¼ pt) beef
    stock (made with cube)
salt and pepper
to garnish:
    2 tablespoons grated cheese
    chopped parsley

Cook the spaghetti as directed, drain and rinse with boiling water. Heat the oil in the cooker, put back the spaghetti and stir with a fork until well coated. Add the meat, mushrooms and the tomato liquid. Heat thoroughly, stirring gently, correct seasoning and serve in a deep dish, sprinkled with the cheese and parsley.

Quick spaghetti savoury
Pressure-cooking time: 5–6 minutes

100 g (4 oz) spaghetti
4 large tomatoes
salt and pepper
4 circles of fried bread

3 dl (½ pt) cheese sauce*
to garnish:
2 tablespoons grated cheese
chopped parsley

Cook the spaghetti as directed. During the cooking, grill the halved, seasoned tomatoes; fry the circles of bread, put ready on four individual dishes with the tomatoes on top and keep hot. Make the sauce and when the spaghetti is drained stir it in, reheat, season well and pile on to the tomatoes. Sprinkle with the cheese and chopped parsley.

6 Puddings

Nowadays many people just do not have sufficient time to prepare the great variety of steamed puddings and hot sweets which used to be such a great standby and which were so welcome on cold winter evenings and such a good way to satisfy growing children's appetites. Then again, because of the long time necessary for steaming sponge and suet puddings and the length of time that the oven must be on for milk puddings cooked in the usual way, the cost of the fuel has to be taken into consideration. But a pressure cooker means that now you can make these dishes again, with speed, great economy of fuel, with no need to watch to see that the saucepan is not running short of water – and with hardly any steam to add to the problem of condensation in the kitchen.

If you are serving cold meat or grilling for the first course, then your pressure cooker would be free for one of these puddings. They can also be a great help in providing extra bulk to a meal which may have to be a little light on the more expensive foods such as meat, fish and poultry.

In the following recipes you will find a selection of the different kinds of pudding which are suited to pressure cooking both at home and outdoors – where you can still end the meal with a flourish even when no oven is available.

Steamed puddings

The method of pressure cooking these corresponds to the usual way of steaming or boiling on top of the stove but there are one or two points to remember which will ensure complete success from your very first attempt.

Any type of bowl or container in metal, china, ovenglass or boilable plastic can be used as long as it is watertight; it should be well greased.

It should not be more than two-thirds filled, to allow room for the pudding to rise during the cooking.

A fitted lid is not recommended as this does not allow the release of the steam nor the quick penetration of the heat which is essential if the super-heated steam under pressure is to do its work properly. A double thickness of greased greaseproof paper is recommended and is all that is required for the covering. If it is a little difficult to put the bowl in and lift it out when hot, the string tying the paper firmly down should be taken loosely across from one side to the other and tied there, to form a handle.

Sufficient water must be put into the cooker before the pressure cooking starts to last the cooking time. The minimum required is 1·5 dl ($\frac{1}{4}$ pt) for every $\frac{1}{4}$ hour or part of $\frac{1}{4}$ hour's cooking, plus 3 dl ($\frac{1}{2}$ pt) to make quite sure. This must be boiling before the pudding is put in and should have a little lemon juice or vinegar added to prevent the darkening of the metal in hard-water areas. Do not put the water on and allow it to boil rapidly while you are making the pudding; if you are then delayed, too much water may boil away causing the pan to boil dry before the cooking time is up.

The trivet should be used to stand the pudding on.

All mixtures which contain a raising agent and which should have a light texture when cooked must be allowed to steam gently as in an ordinary steamer before beginning the pressure cooking. (If the cooker was brought to pressure in the usual way the pressure of steam building up in the pan would prevent the raising agent from working and the mixture would remain heavy.) The exact steaming time needed is given in the sample recipes; this must be done over a low heat so that the steam is just puffing gently out of the open vent, which ensures that the pan is full of steam and the water only simmering. If, during this preliminary steaming time, the heat is left unnecessarily high, then too much water will be driven off as steam and the pan will boil dry before the full pressure-cooking time is up.

The recommended pressure for all steamed mixtures is L which will give the perfect result of a light, open texture with the mixture risen to the fullest extent. If your pressure cooker is fitted with a fixed pressure, then it would be worth while to apply to the manufacturer to see if it is possible to buy and fit a variable pressure control, particularly as you will certainly want to use your cooker for this purpose now you can see all the advantages.

However, if you have only the fixed pressure, excellent results can still be obtained if the quantity given in the following pudding recipes is divided into four and is cooked in individual bowls or ordinary teacups. This cuts down the cooking time so that the extra pressure does not have too much chance to affect the desired result.

When the cooking time is up, the pressure should be allowed to reduce at room temperature. If you are then not quite ready to serve the pudding, just remove the weight or open the valve but leave the lid on and the pudding will remain hot for at least 10–15 minutes.

If some pudding is left over and is to be served again, just put 3 dl ($\frac{1}{2}$ pt) of hot water in the cooker, then the pudding, covered as before; bring to pressure and allow the pressure to reduce at room temperature. This will be sufficient to heat it through.

It is not advisable to pressure cook steamed mixtures with other foods. This is because they require a lot of water which would swamp meat, fish, vegetables and so on, and because they do not take kindly to being disturbed during the cooking or having the water taken off the boil (this would have to be done to open the cooker as they have a longer cooking time than most other foods which would be served for the same meal). If the pressure cooker is needed, as it probably will be, to prepare part of the first course, then the pudding should be cooked first and kept hot, either with the serving dishes or by being stood in a pan of boiling water over a low heat on the back of the stove.

If you want to adapt your favourite recipes to pressure cooking or are using packet mixes, then between half and one-third of the normal cooking time would be about the average, for example:

Normal cooking time	Presteaming time	Pressure-cooking time at L
30 minutes	3 minutes	5 minutes
45 minutes	5 minutes	10 minutes
1–1¼ hours	15 minutes	25 minutes
1¼–2 hours	15 minutes	35 minutes
2–3 hours	20 minutes	50–60 minutes

If increasing the quantities given in the following recipes, then a general rule is to increase the pressure cooking time by 10 minutes for every 50 g (2 oz) extra flour, the other ingredients being increased in proportion.

These times do not apply to Christmas Puddings, for which a special table is given on p 157.

The recipes in this section are to serve four people. The quantities for these recipes, where accuracy is important, are given by weight, but if you have no scales you can refer to the table of measurements in spoonfuls given on p 17.

General instructions

Have ready in the cooker the right amount of boiling water with a little lemon juice or vinegar added and the trivet.

Always grease the bowl well.

Always leave a little space in the bowl or container for the pudding to rise.

Tie a double thickness of greased greaseproof paper securely down over the bowl; pleat the paper to allow for expansion during cooking.

When the pudding is in the cooker, put on the cover, turn the heat high and wait until the steam escapes freely through the open vent. Next, lower the heat and cook gently with the vent open and the steam just puffing out for the steaming time as given in the recipe.

When this time is up, raise the heat again to high, put on the L or fixed weight as recommended – and wait for the hissing sound and the second escape of steam to show that pressure has been reached. Lower the heat again and pressure cook in the usual way for the required time.

Remove the cooker from the heat and allow the pressure to reduce at room temperature.

Lift out the bowl, take off the paper, loosen round the edges, put the hot serving dish over the top, turn upside down, give the container a good shake and lift off.

Basic rich pudding mixture

Canary pudding

Cooking time (in one bowl): 15 minutes' steaming, 25 minutes at L; (in 4 individual bowls): 5 minutes' steaming, 10 minutes at H.

7·5 dl (1¼ pt) water for the cooker
75 g (3 oz) margarine or butter
grated rind of 1 lemon
75 g (3 oz) caster sugar
1 large or 2 small eggs

150 g (6 oz) self-raising flour
pinch of salt
little milk if necessary
custard*, jam sauce* or a fruit sauce* to hand separately

Grease a 9-dl (1½-pt) bowl or container and the greaseproof paper for covering. Put the cooker with the trivet and water on a low heat to boil. Cream the fat with the grated lemon rind until quite soft, add the sugar and continue beating until creamy and white. Add the lightly beaten egg, a little at a time, beating well between each addition so that the mixture does not curdle. Fold in the sieved flour and salt, then add a little milk if necessary to give a soft, dropping consistency. Put into the container, smooth the top and tie down securely with the greased and pleated greaseproof paper. Continue as given in the instructions on p 152. Serve the sauce separately or, if a lemon sauce*, a little may be poured over the pudding before being taken to table.

Variations

CHOCOLATE: 50–75 g (2–3 oz) cocoa or drinking chocolate sieved with 100 g (4 oz) flour, or 75 g (3 oz) grated chocolate added with milk and vanilla essence to taste. Serve with a chocolate sauce*.

COCONUT: 50 g (2 oz) desiccated coconut folded in with the flour. Serve with a jam sauce*.

COLLEGE: Put 2 tablespoons raspberry jam into the bottom of the container before the mixture. Serve with a raspberry jam* or redcurrant jelly* sauce.

FRUIT: 75–100 g (3–4 oz) dried fruit such as raisins, sultanas, currants, with 1 teaspoon mixed spice, added with the flour.

GINGER: 2 teaspoons ground ginger sieved with the flour. Serve with a white sauce* in which can be stirred some finely chopped crystallized ginger, or with a thin custard*.

Cherry cup puddings
Cooking time (4 individual): 5 minutes' steaming, 10 minutes at **H**.

100 g (4 oz) margarine or butter	1 small tin of red cherries
125 g (5 oz) caster sugar	4·5 dl (¾ pt) water for the cooker
2 small eggs	*for the sauce:*
100 g (4 oz) self-raising flour	1 teaspoon cornflour
2 tablespoons milk	a little cochineal to colour and maraschino essence to flavour

Grease 4 large cups and a double sheet of greaseproof paper. Make the pudding as given in the previous recipe, adding the strained, chopped cherries with the milk. Put the cooker on a high heat with the trivet and water to bring to the boil. Divide the mixture into the cups, smoothing the tops. Put the cups on the trivet, lay the piece of greaseproof paper over the top and continue as given in the instructions on p 152. Make the sauce, using the juice from the

cherries and adding the colouring and flavouring as required.
Hand separately.

For a special occasion, the Compote of Cherries* could be
handed as an accompaniment, with pouring or whipped cream.

Orange castles
Cooking time (4 individual): 5 minutes' steaming, 10 minutes at L.

halved cherries and small pieces
of angelica to decorate
2 eggs and their weight in butter,
sugar, self-raising flour
1 tablespoon orange juice

4·5 dl (¾ pt) water for the cooker
for the marmalade sauce:
1 tablespoon water
1 tablespoon sugar
1 tablespoon orange marmalade
rest of juice of orange

Grease 4 large cups very well and put a halved cherry and a small
diamond of angelica as a leaf, in the bottom of each. Make the
pudding as given for Canary Pudding, using the orange juice instead of the milk, and cook as given in the instructions on p 152.

MARMALADE SAUCE: Melt the sugar in the water, being careful to
stir until dissolved, boil with the marmalade and add the orange
juice to give a pouring consistency. These orange castles should be
served on individual dishes with the sauce poured round.

Caramel pudding
Cooking time: 15 minutes' steaming, 35 minutes at L.

for the caramel:
50 g (2 oz) granulated sugar
2 tablespoons water

for the pudding:
75 g (3 oz) margarine or butter
75 g (3 oz) caster sugar
2 large, separated eggs
150 g (6 oz) self-raising flour
4 tablespoons milk
9 dl (1½ pt) water for the cooker
single cream to hand separately

To make the caramel: put the sugar and water in a small saucepan
over a low heat, stir and do not allow to boil until the sugar has
dissolved. Stop stirring and continue boiling rapidly until the syrup
begins to turn golden-brown. Quickly pour into the warmed bowl
and turn it round and round, coating the sides right up to the top.
Make the pudding by creaming together the butter and sugar;

beat in the yolks only, then fold in the flour and milk alternately, a little at a time. Put the cooker on with the water and trivet and bring to the boil. Whisk the egg whites until stiff and fold into the mixture. Put into the bowl, smooth the top and tie down with a double sheet of greased greaseproof paper, pleated down the centre to allow for the pudding to rise. Continue as given in the instructions on p 152. Turn the pudding on to the serving dish when the pressure has reduced, but leave the bowl in position over the pudding until ready to serve so that all the caramel will run out. Hand the cream separately.

(If any caramel should be left in the bottom of the bowl, just leave it to soak overnight with a little water. The syrup thus made can be used for stewing fruit.)

Pineapple sponge
Cooking time: 15 minutes' steaming, 25 minutes at **L**.

2 eggs with their weight in butter, sugar and self-raising flour
pinch of salt
1 tablespoon finely chopped pineapple
1 tablespoon pineapple syrup
7·5 dl (1½ pt) water for the cooker
pieces of pineapple and angelica for decoration

for the sauce:
pineapple juice
a little chopped pineapple
a squeeze of lemon juice
1 tablespoon sherry
1 teaspoon arrowroot
a little sugar to taste

This pudding would make an attractive dinner-party sweet if cooked in a seamless ring mould. Cut a piece of greased greaseproof paper to fit the bottom and on this put a decoration of pieces of pineapple and angelica. Put the cooker with the water and trivet on to boil. Make the mixture as given for **Canary Pudding**, gently fill the mixture into the mould, smooth the surface, cover and cook as given in the instructions on p 152.

To make the sauce, blend the arrowroot with a little of the pineapple juice, boil the rest, add to the arrowroot and then reboil until clear. Just before serving, add the chopped pineapple, the lemon juice, a little sugar if necessary and the sherry.

Turn the pudding out carefully, lift off the paper and pour the sauce around it.

Christmas pudding

To give them a chance to mature so that they are in perfect condition for serving on Christmas Day, Christmas Puddings should be made at least 6 to 8 weeks ahead, in fact, any time from September onwards when the new crop of dried fruit is fresh in the shops. Once cooked, Christmas Puddings will last from one year to the next quite happily. With ordinary steaming or boiling at least 6 to 8 hours is necessary to give thorough cooking and the darkness and richness which is essential for this type of pudding, but with a pressure cooker this time can be cut down to as little as 2 hours.

Christmas Puddings should be made in china, earthenware, oven glass, stainless steel or boilable plastic bowls; if aluminium bowls or foil containers are used they must first be lined with greaseproof paper, otherwise a reaction with the acid content in the fruit can give a bitter flavour.

The covering should be a triple thickness of greaseproof paper securely tied down for the cooking. When the pudding is cold this should be replaced with a clean double sheet of greaseproof and a piece of cloth again tied down (or the covers of plastic bowls), to prevent loss of moisture by evaporation.

The recipe which follows is a rich one and easy to make, but if you have your own favourite then make that and refer to the timetable for the steaming and pressure-cooking times. An explanation of the steaming process is given on pp 149–50.

To find the correct cooking time, the weight of the actual pudding itself must be known. To do this weigh the basin, fill it with the mixture, weigh again and deduct the weight of the basin from the total. A little room should be left in the basin for the pudding to rise.

The number of puddings that can be cooked at one time will depend on the size of your cooker and the height of the basins you are using. If there is room you can stand one basin on top of the other with the trivet in between, but make sure that there is enough space between the top of the top basin and the vent so that if the pudding rises above the basin this vent will not become blocked and bring the safety plug into action through excess pressure being built up. If the amount of water necessary for the pressure cooking comes above the top of the basin, there is no need to worry as it will not harm the pudding provided it is covered with a cloth as well as the greaseproof paper. In the old days before basins were thought of, Christmas Puddings were always cooked only in cloths and were plunged into a depth of boiling water – usually the clothes boiler or copper.

The following recipe will make approximately 4 × 450-g (1-lb) puddings, but times for other weights would be as follows:

Weight of mixture	Water for cooker	Steaming time	Pressure-cooking time at H
150 g (6 oz) individual	9 dl (1½ pt)	10 minutes	50 minutes
450 g (1 lb)	1·3 litres (2¼ pt)	15 minutes	1¾ hours
675 g (1½ lb)	1·8 litres (3 pt)	20 minutes	2½ hours
900 g (2 lb)	2 litres (3½ pt)	30 minutes	3 hours

A little lemon juice or vinegar should be added to the water in the cooker unless the water will come over the top of the pudding.

The trivet should be used under the pudding, or between two puddings if one is stood on top of the other.

100 g (4 oz) flour
225 g (8 oz) raisins
225 g (8 oz) sultanas
325 g (12 oz) currants
100 g (4 oz) mixed peel
50 g (2 oz) almonds
grated rind and juice of 1 lemon
2 tablespoons treacle
2–3 eggs
½ teaspoon salt

1 teaspoon mixed spice
1 teaspoon grated nutmeg
½ teaspoon cinnamon
225 g (8 oz) shredded suet
225 g (8 oz) fine white breadcrumbs
375 g (12 oz) brown sugar
2 tablespoons brandy
1 tablespoon rum
about 3 dl (½ pt) stout, old ale or milk

Grease the basins well. Take 2–3 spoonfuls of the weighed flour and toss the dried fruit in it. Leave the almonds to stand in boiling water for 2–3 minutes, remove the skins and shred nuts finely. Chop the peel; warm the treacle and add the lemon juice; beat the eggs.

Into a large bowl, sieve the flour, salt and spices; stir in the suet, breadcrumbs, sugar, almonds and fruit, beat in the eggs, treacle, brandy, rum and lastly the stout (ale or milk) to give a firm, holding consistency. This pudding requires a great deal of stirring so that all the ingredients are thoroughly mixed, so you can allow all the family to take their turn and keep up a very old tradition of ensuring good luck for the year ahead.

Put the mixture into the prepared basins, cover and tie securely and continue as given in the instructions, putting the puddings into boiling water in the pressure cooker. If liked, the mixture can be prepared and left covered overnight; next day give a final stir before continuing as above.

After the pressure has been allowed to reduce at room temperature, leave the pudding to cool. If more spirit is to be added, uncover, prick the pudding well with a skewer and pour over it 2 tablespoons brandy, whisky or rum, re-cover and store in a cool place until required. This process can be repeated at least once more, if liked, before reheating on Christmas Day.

To reheat, have the trivet and 6 dl (1 pt) boiling water (with a little lemon juice or vinegar) ready and pressure cook for 20 minutes at H, allowing the pressure to reduce at room temperature.

The simplest way to get brandy to light around the pudding so that you can take it to the table 'flaming' is to warm the brandy in a small saucepan, pour it over the pudding (turned on to a hot serving dish) and then put a match to it. A sprig of holly on top will then complete the picture.

If you have not made your own Christmas Pudding, you can still use the pressure cooker for reheating the bought one. For a pudding in a container with an airtight cover, have 6 dl (1 pt) boiling water in the cooker and reheat for 40 minutes at H: if the cover is taken off and the pudding covered with a double thickness of greased greaseproof paper, only 30 minutes is required.

Basic plain pudding mixture

Spiced sultana pudding
Cooking time: 15 minutes' steaming, 30 minutes at L;
(4 individual): 5 minutes' steaming, 10 minutes at H.

7·5 dl (1½ pt) water for the cooker	pinch of salt
150 g (6 oz) self-raising flour	75 g (3 oz) margarine

75–100 g (3–4 oz) sultanas
50g (2oz) sugar
1 level teaspoon mixed spice
1 egg

2–3 tablespoons milk
melted golden syrup to hand
  separately

Grease the bowl and a double sheet of greaseproof paper. Put the cooker on with the water and trivet to boil. Sieve the flour with the pinch of salt, rub in the fat until the texture of fine breadcrumbs, add the sultanas, the sugar and spice and mix to a soft dropping consistency with the beaten egg and milk. Put into the bowl, smooth the surface, tie down securely with the paper and cook as given in the instructions on p 152 for the required time. Serve with warmed golden syrup, handed separately.

Variations

MARMALADE: Leave out the fruit and spices. Put 2 tablespoons marmalade in the bottom of the bowl before putting in the mixture, or stir 3 tablespoons marmalade into a little less milk to mix the pudding. Serve with a fruit* or marmalade* sauce.

GINGER: Leave out the fruit and spices. Add 1 teaspoon ground ginger and mix 2 tablespoons golden syrup or treacle into a little less milk to mix the pudding. Serve with warmed syrup or custard*.

BLACK CAP PUDDING: Leave out the fruit and spices. Put 2 tablespoons blackberry jelly in the bottom of the bowl first; add ½ teaspoon almond essence with the beaten egg. Serve a matching jam sauce*.

Summer currant pudding
Cooking time: 15 minutes' steaming, 40 minutes at L.

450 g (1 lb) prepared stewed
  black- or redcurrants
100 g (4 oz) self-raising flour
pinch of salt
150 g (6 oz) melted margarine or
  butter
100 g (4 oz) fine breadcrumbs

1 large egg
sugar for sweetening
juice of 1 lemon
milk to mix
a little arrowroot or cornflour
  to thicken the sauce

Grease a bowl and a double thickness of greaseproof paper. Strain the blackcurrants, keeping the juice. Sieve the flour and salt, mix in the melted margarine, stir in the breadcrumbs and mix to a stiff dough with the beaten egg and milk as required. Roll two-thirds of the dough into a circle, flour well, fold in quarters, lift into the basin and spread it out to line it evenly, pressing it firmly against the base and sides. Put in the currants, adding sugar as necessary and a little lemon juice. Trim the pastry and damp the edges. Add the trimmings to the one-third of pastry left, roll into a circle to cover the top of the pudding and squeeze the edges together. Tie down securely with the greaseproof paper and continue the cooking as given in the instructions on p 152.

Boil the juice from the fruit with 1 tablespoon of sugar and thicken with blended cornflour or arrowroot. A tablespoon of sherry added to this sauce will make it even more delicious.

Fruity dumpling
Cooking time: 15 minutes' steaming, 45 minutes at **L**.

1 litre (1¾ pt) water for the cooker	½ teaspoon each ground ginger,
225 g (8 oz) self-raising flour	mixed spice, cinnamon
pinch of salt	1 tablespoon treacle
100 g (4 oz) margarine	½ tablespoon golden syrup
2 tablespoons sugar	a little milk
50 g (2 oz) mixed dried fruit	custard* to hand separately

Put the cooker on to boil with the water and trivet. Line a pudding cloth with a piece of greased greaseproof paper. Sieve the flour and salt, rub in the margarine, stir in the sugar, fruit and spices and mix to a soft but not sloppy dough with the warmed treacle, syrup and a little milk. Form into a dumpling, tie loosely but securely in the cloth, put in the cooker and continue as given in the instructions on p 152. When the dumpling is lifted out it should be left on a deep plate for a few minutes to drain before being opened and lifted out. Serve with a custard* handed separately.

Cinnamon pudding
Cooking time: 10 minutes' steaming, 45 minutes at **H**.

9 dl (1½ pt) water for the cooker	100 g (4 oz) self-raising flour
75 g (3 oz) margarine	sieved with a pinch of salt

75 g (3 oz) granulated sugar
  (brown if using white bread)
100 g (4 oz) breadcrumbs,
  preferably brown
1 level tablespoon cinnamon

100 g (4 oz) sultanas
1 large egg
milk to mix
warmed syrup or custard* to
  hand separately

Grease a 9-dl (1½-pt) bowl and a double thickness of greaseproof paper. Put the cooker on to boil with the water and trivet. Rub the margarine into the flour, stir in the dry ingredients and the fruit and mix to a dropping consistency with the beaten egg and a little milk. Continue as given in the instructions on p 152. Serve with a warmed syrup or custard.

Fluffy bread pudding
Cooking time: 5 minutes' steaming, 10 minutes at H.

This pudding is best made in a small seamless loaf pan and should be made in time to leave in the oven for 10 minutes before serving.

6 dl (1 pt) water for the cooker
4 teacups (4–6 thick slices) of
  stale bread soaked for 20–30
  minutes in hot water
2 tablespoons margarine or butter
3 tablespoons brown sugar
75 g (3 oz) dried fruit: currants,
  raisins, sultanas or mixture

1 teaspoon mixed spice or nutmeg
1 large egg
milk to mix
custard* or vanilla white sauce*
  to hand separately

Grease a loaf pan and a double thickness of greaseproof paper. Put the cooker on to boil with the water and trivet. Squeeze all the water out of the bread and beat with a fork until broken up and smooth. Melt the fat with the sugar, pour over the bread, add in the dried fruit and spice, mix with the beaten egg and sufficient milk to give a soft mixture. Fill into the pan, leaving at least 2-cm (1-in) space at the top. Tie down securely and cook as given in the instructions on p 152. During the cooking, preheat the oven to Gas No 4, 180°C (350°F). Lift off the paper and leave in the oven, as near the top as possible, while the first course is being eaten. Serve with a sauce to choice.

Suet puddings

The basic **suet mixture** from which these recipes are made is in the proportion of twice as much flour as shredded suet, a pinch of salt and sufficient cold water to mix to an elastic dough with sugar and flavourings added according to the recipe. The quantity is always referred to by the weight of flour, e.g. 150 g (6 oz) suet crust would be 150 g (6 oz) self-raising flour sieved with a pinch of salt, mixed with 75 g (3 oz) shredded suet and any sweetening or flavouring required, with sufficient water added to give a stretchy dough – neither sticky so that it cannot be easily handled with floured hands or rolled on a floured board, nor so stiff that it will break up when shaped or rolled.

Boiled fruit pudding

Cooking time: 15 minutes' steaming, 30 minutes at **L** or **H**.

225 g (8 oz) suet crust (see above)	4 tablespoons sugar to taste
675–900 g (1½–2 lb) prepared stewed fruit such as apples, plums, damsons	9 dl (1½ pt) boiling water for the cooker
1 tablespoon water	custard* or cream to hand separately

Make the suet crust, roll two-thirds into a circle, flour well, fold in flour, lift carefully and line the greased basin with it, pressing the crust firmly against the basin at the bottom and round the sides. Put in half the prepared fruit, 1 tablespoon water and the sugar, then fill in the rest of the fruit. Trim the edges, add these to the one-third of pastry left and roll this into a circle the size of the top of the basin. Damp the edges of the pastry lining the basin, put on the circle and press the edges together well all round. Cover with a double thickness of greased greaseproof paper. Put into the cooker and continue as given in the instructions on p 152 for the required time. Turn carefully on to a hot dish and hand custard or cream separately.

Variations

APPLE: Slice the apples finely, flavour with lemon rind, cloves or cinnamon; golden syrup could be used for sweetening instead of the sugar.

PLUMS: If small these may be cooked whole, but prick each once or twice with a fork. If large, halve and stone.

DAMSONS: If very hard these should be brought to pressure in the cooker first, as they may not cook completely inside the suet crust.

BLACKCURRANTS: These must be packed very tightly or the pudding will collapse when turned out, as this fruit shrinks a lot when cooked.

BLACKBERRY AND APPLE: Put a layer of each alternately and a little extra sugar, as blackberries are very tart.

Jam layer pudding

Cooking time: 15 minutes' steaming, 40 minutes at **L**;
10 minutes' steaming, 30 minutes at **H**.

150 g (6 oz) self-raising flour	3 tablespoons milk
pinch of salt	3–4 tablespoons jam
75 g (3 oz) sugar	9 dl (1½ pt) water for the cooker
75 g (3 oz) shredded suet	jam sauce* to hand separately

Sieve the flour and salt, mix in the sugar and suet. Make a well in the centre, put in the milk and stir until well mixed. Roll out the pastry thinly, cut into four or five rounds and spread all but one with jam. Put the cooker on to boil with the water and trivet. Put a little jam in the bottom of the basin, then pile the rounds one on top of the other with the plain round on the top, leaving at least 2·5 cm (1 in) space for the pudding to rise. Tie down securely with a double thickness of greased greaseproof paper and continue the cooking as given in the instructions on p 152. Turn carefully on to the hot serving dish and hand the jam sauce* separately.

This recipe may be used as a simple Jam, Golden Syrup or Lemon Curd Pudding, putting the jam or syrup into the bottom of the bowl, then the suet mixture flattened to fill it. Golden syrup or a lemon* or jam* sauce should be handed separately.

Golden crumb pudding

Substitute for the jam in the preceding recipe 3 tablespoons breadcrumbs mixed with 4 tablespoons syrup and a squeeze of lemon juice.

Jam roly-poly

Cooking time: 10 minutes' steaming, 25 minutes at **L**.

225 g (8 oz) suet crust (see p 162)
jam
9 dl (1½ pt) water for the cooker
custard* to hand separately

Put the cooker on to boil with the water and trivet. Make the suet crust and roll out thinly to a width at least 2·5 cm (1 in) less than that of the cooker. Spread with jam, moisten round the edges with water or milk and roll up. Wrap in a double thickness of greaseproof paper, or in aluminium foil or a pudding cloth lined with greaseproof paper, and make the ends secure. Put the roll in the cooker and continue as given in the instructions on p 152. Serve with custard*, handed separately.

Variations

ORANGE DELIGHT: Spread the roll with marmalade instead of jam and put a layer of thinly sliced, peeled oranges with all pips removed. Serve with marmalade sauce*.

SPICED APPLE: Spread the roll with finely chopped cooking apples mixed with 50 g (2 oz) currants, 1 teaspoon mixed spice and 50 g (2 oz) brown sugar.

SPOTTED DOG: Spread the roll with 75 g (3 oz) mixed dried fruit, chopped peel and a little grated lemon rind.

Milk and egg puddings

To many people this heading will simply mean memories of rice puddings from childhood – and not very happy memories at that. But this is where you can really score with your pressure cooker; rice puddings can come in many guises and so can all the delicious hot and cold sweets made with a basis of milk and eggs, with an endless choice of fruits, flavourings and additions to give both winter and summer dishes – and for you, minutes instead of hours of slow oven cooking.

Milk puddings, on their own, should be cooked directly in the pressure cooker, without the trivet so that the milk is then the liquid supplying the steam to build up pressure. Cooked this way the puddings will be thick, creamy and delicious. As they will usually fit best into the cooking time-table for the meal if they are prepared first, they can be left to brown off either under a grill or in the oven while the first course is being cooked and eaten. Use H pressure.

Creamy rice pudding
Pressure-cooking time: 12 minutes

a good knob of margarine or butter	2–3 tablespoons sugar
6 dl (1 pt) milk (less 2 tablespoons)	a slice of lemon rind for the cooking, if liked
2 heaped tablespoons pudding rice	nutmeg and a little butter

Lift the trivet from the cooker, put in the margarine or butter and let it melt to grease the bottom of the pan. Pour in the milk and bring to the boil on a high heat. Do not go away and leave the cooker for, as soon as the milk boils and begins to rise in the pan, you must put in the rice and sugar, stir until the milk reboils, then straight away lower the heat to between medium and low until the milk is simmering well but not rushing up to the top, and put on the cover. The steam will now be seen to be escaping straight away, so put on the weight or close the valve and bring the cooker to pressure, but without altering the heat. This will take a little longer than usual but after no more than 2–3 minutes you should hear the hissing sound to tell you that pressure is up, so start the cooking time then and lower the heat further if the cooker is hissing unnecessarily loudly. When the cooking time is up, allow the pressure to reduce at room temperature for at least 5 minutes. Stir the pudding well, put into a dish, sprinkle with nutmeg, dot with a little butter and set to brown under a low grill or at the top of a warming oven, or put on one side to cool if required as the basis for another sweet.

Variations

VANILLA: Flavour with a vanilla pod put in for the cooking and removed before serving.

SULTANA: 25–50 g (1–2 oz) sultanas added for the cooking.

COCONUT: 1 dessertspoon desiccated coconut added with the rice.
The rice for the following recipes can be cooked at any time when
the cooker is not in use for a meal and kept in a cool place until
required.

Hot fruit condé

Pressure-cooking time: 12 minutes; oven time: 20 minutes

rice pudding as in previous recipe
6–8 fruits such as cooked pears,
   halved, tinned halved apricots or
   peaches, pineapple slices
2 small eggs
a little vanilla essence
1½ tablespoons caster sugar

to decorate:
halved glacé cherries
small pieces of angelica
1 tablespoon granulated sugar

Preheat the oven to Gas No 3, 170°C (325°F). While the rice pudding is cooking, strain the fruit but leave whole; butter a pie-dish
well; separate the yolks and whites of the eggs. Flavour the rice
pudding with vanilla essence to taste, beat in the egg yolks and
pour into the dish. Lay the fruit on top. Beat the whites until stiff,
fold in the caster sugar and pile on top of the fruit. Bake on the
middle shelf of the oven for 20 minutes or until pale golden.
Arrange five or six halved cherries, each with a leaf of angelica,
on the meringue, sprinkle with the granulated sugar and serve
quickly.

Rice custard

Pressure-cooking time: 5 minutes and 5 minutes

1 cup rice with 2 cups water
2 eggs
1 teaspoon vanilla essence
4 tablespoons sugar

3 dl (½ pt) hot milk
50 g (2 oz) seedless raisins
3 dl (½ pt) water for the cooker
a little nutmeg

Cook the rice as given in the instructions on p 142. During the
cooking, beat the eggs with the vanilla essence and sugar, heat the
milk and pour over, stirring all the time. Butter a soufflé or casserole dish that will fit in the cooker. Stir the raisins into the rice,
then mix thoroughly with the custard and put into the dish, stand
on the trivet and cover with a double thickness of greaseproof

paper. Bring to pressure, cook for 5 minutes and allow the pressure to reduce at room temperature. Sprinkle with nutmeg and brown lightly under the grill.

Lemon rice
Pressure-cooking time: 5 minutes and 5 minutes

1 cup rice with 2 cups water	3 dl ($\frac{1}{2}$ pt) water with a little lemon
1 large egg	juice or vinegar for the cooker
juice and grated rind of 1 lemon	3–4 tablespoons lemon curd*
4 tablespoons sugar	a handful of chopped nuts

Cook the rice as given in the instructions on p 142. During the cooking, separate the yolk and white of egg; grate the lemon rind and strain the lemon juice. Beat the egg yolk, sugar and lemon juice and rind into the cooked rice. Whip the egg white very stiffly and fold into the rice lightly and carefully. Put into a buttered soufflé or casserole dish, stand in the cooker on the trivet and cover with a double piece of greaseproof paper. Bring to pressure, cook for 5 minutes and allow the pressure to reduce at room temperature. During this cooking, warm the lemon curd and chop the nuts. Lightly spread the curd over the pudding and just before serving sprinkle with the chopped nuts.

Lemon snow
Pressure-cooking time: 7 minutes

6 dl (1 pt) water	*for decoration:*
2 tablespoons golden syrup	a little whipped cream
grated rind and juice of 2 lemons	a few cherries
2 good tablespoons sago	pieces of angelica or small
a little sugar if necessary	ratafias
2 egg whites	

Lift the trivet from the cooker, put in the water and syrup and stir in the open pan until boiling. Add the lemon rind and juice, reboil, throw in the sago. Continue as in the instructions for **Rice Pudding** (p 165). Stir the sago well, put into a large bowl and leave until cold. Taste and add more sugar if liked, then gently fold in the stiffly beaten egg whites. Pile into a large dish or individual serving dishes, decorate with the whipped cream, cut cherries and angelica or ratafias.

Other cereals for milk puddings should be made following the instructions for **Rice Pudding** (p 165), in the proportion of 2 large tablespoons (50 g or 2 oz) cereal, 3 tablespoons sugar, to 6 dl (1 pt) milk. Flavourings such as vanilla, a piece of lemon rind or a bay leaf can be added as required.

Large-grain cereal (rice, pearl barley): 12 minutes.
Small-grain cereal (tapioca, sago, semolina): 7 minutes.

Egg puddings

Do not be surprised to find these puddings and those given in the following recipes in a book on pressure cooking. Steaming has always been an accepted method of cooking these sweets and all that has to be done to achieve perfect results is to cut down by at least two-thirds the normal cooking time. Eggs are plentiful, not expensive and can provide easily digested, concentrated protein while pleasing the young and old who have a sweet tooth.

In all these custards and crèmes a more extravagant and rich sweet can be served by increasing the proportion of eggs to milk to 1 egg for each 1·5 dl ($\frac{1}{4}$ pt) milk; even more so if 2 yolks are taken as 1 egg. Use **H** pressure.

Basic egg custard
Pressure-cooking time: 5 minutes

2 large eggs
2 tablespoons sugar or to taste
vanilla essence to taste
4·5 dl ($\frac{3}{4}$ pt) milk

3 dl ($\frac{1}{2}$ pt) water with a little lemon juice or vinegar for the cooker
nutmeg for the top

Butter a soufflé dish or casserole in which the custard can be taken to table. Beat the eggs, sugar and vanilla gently but not to a froth; warm the milk but do not allow to boil. Pour on the eggs, stirring all the time, then turn into the prepared dish. Have the water and trivet ready in the cooker, put in the dish covered with a double thickness of greaseproof paper, bring to pressure, cook for 5 minutes and allow the pressure to reduce at room temperature. Carefully lift off the paper, sprinkle nutmeg over the top.

This egg custard may be served hot or cold with any stewed, bottled or tinned fruit.

It may be cooked with the stewed fruit as a complete dessert, see p 176.

When cold, it may be whisked well, either plain or with a little half-whisked cream stirred in, and be used as a base in sponge flans, fruit pastry flans and tartlets or for trifles; alternatively it may be beaten and sieved to make fruit fools.

Variations

HONEY: Replace sugar with 2 good tablespoons thin honey, heating it with the milk.

COFFEE: Add 2 tablespoons strong coffee or 1 tablespoon coffee essence in place of 2 tablespoons milk. Sprinkle top of custard with chopped nuts.

Chocolate cream
Pressure-cooking time: 5 minutes

small bar of plain chocolate or 2 tablespoons cocoa
2 eggs plus 1 yolk
3 dessertspoons sugar
vanilla essence to taste

4·5 dl (¾ pt) milk
chocolate sauce to hand separately
to garnish:
  a little sweetened whipped cream
  pieces of glacé cherry and angelica

Butter a china or earthenware bowl; grate the chocolate and take a little to sprinkle in the bowl and turn it around to coat the sides. Beat the eggs, sugar, essence and grated chocolate lightly, pour on the heated milk, turn into the prepared bowl. Continue as for **Egg Custard** (p 168). Chill thoroughly.

Make the chocolate sauce and allow to get cold (an excellent chocolate sauce can be made from chocolate Instant Whip. Use half the packet and add 1 tablespoon strong sweetened coffee to give it extra flavour and a pouring consistency). Turn out the cream, decorate with whirls of sweetened whipped cream, each with a small piece of cherry and angelica, and hand the sauce separately.

7 Fruits and desserts

Fresh fruits

As it is difficult not to overcook soft fruits if they are put loose into a pressure cooker (as in an ordinary saucepan), the recommended method is to cook them in a heatproof container such as a soufflé or casserole dish so that they can be taken straight to table. This must, of course, be of a size which can be easily put into and taken out of the cooker and it should be covered with a double thickness of greaseproof paper. When cooked on their own, pressure can be reduced in cold water; but if an accompanying sweet, such as an egg custard, is being done at the same time, as is explained in the recipe section, the pressure must be allowed to reduce at room temperature.

For large, hard fruits, pressure cooking is an easy and quick way, ensuring good colour and flavour and a delicious, concentrated syrup, as only a minimum amount of water need be put in for the short cooking time. In fact, as will be seen from the following recipes, many can be cooked in their own juice with sugar and flavouring added. The trivet is not required and the pressure can be reduced with water or allowed to reduce at room temperature, depending on the particular result required or the recipe being followed. Use **H** pressure.

Crème caramel
Pressure-cooking time (4 individual): 3 minutes

for the caramel:
3 tablespoons water
3 tablespoons sugar

3 dl ($\frac{1}{2}$ pt) water with a little lemon juice or vinegar for the cooker

for the crème:
2 eggs plus 1 yolk
2 tablespoons sugar
vanilla essence to taste
4·5 dl ($\frac{3}{4}$ pt) milk
pouring cream to hand separately

Put 4 teacups to warm, or use 4 individual boilable plastic bowls. To make the caramel: put the water and sugar in a small saucepan, stir over a very low heat without boiling until the sugar is dissolved. Boil rapidly, without stirring but shaking the saucepan occasionally, until the sugar begins to turn a deep gold. Carefully but quickly divide into the cups or bowls and smartly turn each around to coat the sides. With cups, butter any parts which do not get coated, once the caramel has cooled.

Beat the eggs, sugar and essence, heat the milk in the saucepan used to make the caramel and pour over the eggs, stirring all the time. Fill into the cups or bowls. Continue as for **Egg Custard** (p 168), using just one big piece of doubled greaseproof paper to cover all the cups. Chill the crèmes, and when ready to serve, gently loosen round the edge of each and turn into an individual dish. Hand the cream separately.

If there is room in your cooker, you can double this recipe and cook the crèmes, standing 4 directly in the water in the cooker covered with greaseproof, then the trivet and 4 more covered on the top again.

Crème brûlée
See recipe on p 190.

Preparing fresh fruits Pressure-cooking time: 5 minutes

Fruit	Preparation	Method of cooking
Apples	Peel, core, slice, rinse under cold water, do not drain	Pack in layers in container, sprinkling each with brown sugar, a strip of lemon peel, a little nutmeg or cloves to taste
Apricots	Halve and stone. Some of the stones can be cracked, the kernels blanched and cooked with the fruit for extra flavour	Basic sugar syrup in container
Blackberries	Alone; with sliced apples	Basic sugar syrup, in container; pack in layers in container, sprinkling each with a little water and a spoonful of sugar
Cherries	Whole or stoned	Basic sugar syrup in container with a little red colouring to improve the appearance
Currants	String and wash, do not drain	Pack in layers in container, sprinkling each with sugar

Gooseberries	Top and tail, wash	Use only 2 tablespoons water when making syrup, in container
Greengages, plums, damsons	Cook whole, prick each once or twice with fork, or halve and stone	Basic sugar syrup, in container
Peaches	Plunge for 1–2 minutes in boiling water, peel, stone and slice	Basic sugar syrup, in container
Pears (hard, stewing)	Peeled, halved, cored	Basic sugar syrup, in container or in cooker without trivet: 8 minutes
(dessert)	Peeled, halved, cored	Basic sugar syrup, in container, using 3 dl ($\frac{1}{2}$ pt) and coloured with a little cochineal sometimes for variety
Raspberries	Rinse in cold water, do not drain	Sprinkle each layer with sugar, in container
Rhubarb	Cut in lengths, rinse in cold water, do not drain	Sprinkle each layer in container with sugar, a little cinnamon or piece of lemon peel to taste

Golden crumble
Pressure-cooking time: 10 minutes

6 dl (1 pt) milk
225 g (8 oz) fine bread or stale
cake crumbs
2 large eggs
50 g (2 oz) currants

1 teaspoon almond flavouring
3 tablespoons sugar
3 dl (½ pt) water with a little lemon
juice or vinegar for the cooker
warmed golden syrup

Warm the milk, pour over the crumbs and allow to stand for 15 minutes. Stir in the beaten eggs, currants, flavouring and sugar, and put into a greased bowl. Continue as for **Egg Custard** (p 168). Allow to stand a moment or two on lifting out of the cooker, turn on to a hot serving dish and coat with the warmed syrup.

Bread and butter pudding
Pressure-cooking time: 6 minutes

3–4 thin slices buttered bread
pinch of cinnamon or nutmeg
3 tablespoons mixed dried fruit
2 large eggs
2 tablespoons sugar

4·5 dl (¾ pt) milk
3 dl (½ pt) water with a little lemon
juice or vinegar for the cooker
a little brown sugar for the top
pouring cream to hand separately

Fill a soufflé dish or casserole with alternate layers of bread (cut into 4, sprinkled with nutmeg or cinnamon and put in buttered side down), and the fruit. Continue as for **Egg Custard** (p 168) and when the dish has been lifted from the cooker, sprinkle lightly with brown sugar and crisp up the top by browning carefully under a hot grill.

Apple charlotte
Pressure-cooking time: 12 minutes

2 large cooking apples
8–10 slices thinly cut white bread
2–3 tablespoons margarine or
butter
1 teaspoon cinnamon

4 tablespoons demerara sugar
3 dl (½ pt) water with a little lemon
juice or vinegar for the cooker
custard* or pouring cream to
hand separately

Butter a soufflé dish or bowl. Peel, core and slice the apples. Cut 2 circles of bread to fit the top and bottom of the dish and trim enough slices to line it. Heat the butter, stir in the cinnamon and lightly fry the slices, except the one for the top, on both sides until golden brown. Line the basin with them, fill it with alternate layers of apple, sugar and the rest of the bread, finishing with the large circle. Continue as for **Egg Custard** (p 168), allow to stand for a minute or two after lifting out of the cooker, then turn on to a hot serving dish.

Hand the custard or cream separately.

Cabinet pudding

Pressure-cooking time: 7 minutes

a little sherry or liqueur
4 sponge cakes
chopped crystallized fruit
(cherries, angelica, pineapple,
orange and lemon slices as
available)

2 large eggs plus 2 yolks
2 tablespoons sugar
4·5 dl (¾ pt) milk
3 dl (½ pt) water with a little lemon
juice or vinegar for the cooker
apricot sauce*

Put a little liqueur or sherry into a shallow dish, put in the broken up sponge cakes, leave a little, then turn over until all has been absorbed. Pile into a buttered bowl with the chopped crystallized fruit. Continue as for **Egg Custard** (p 168). Make a thick apricot sauce during the cooking. Allow the pudding to stand for a minute or two when lifted out of the cooker, turn gently on to the hot serving dish and coat with the sauce.

This really special pudding is even more delicious for a summer meal if, at the very last moment, thin slices of ice-cream are laid over it.

Where fresh fruit of any kind is being cooked for pulping or purée, the trivet is not required and the fruit can be put directly into the cooker with a little water, with the sugar added or not – again depending on the recipe being followed.

It is difficult to give any hard-and-fast rule as to the amount of water and sugar required to make the syrup, as this will depend on the ripeness and sweetness of any particular fruit. A basic syrup would be 1·5 dl (¼ pt) water boiled rapidly in a small saucepan with 3–4 tablespoons sugar until beginning to thicken, then poured over the fruit.

To save time, the water can be put first in the bottom of the container and the sugar sprinkled over the fruit as it is packed in layers.

Stewed fruit and egg custard
Pressure-cooking time: 5 minutes

For this easy dessert 2 heatproof containers such as soufflé or casserole dishes are the best, but they must be chosen so that they will stand one on the other without interfering with the vent or with the closure of the cover.

STEWED FRUIT: Plums, gooseberries, apricots, apples, rhubarb prepared and sliced, halved or cut into lengths, layered in the dish with plenty of sugar. No water need be added except for fruits such as pears which do not make much juice of their own.

EGG CUSTARD: As given in recipe on p 168.
Lift the trivet out of the cooker, put in 3 dl ($\frac{1}{2}$ pt) water with a little lemon or vinegar, then the dish with the stewed fruit covered with a double thickness of greaseproof paper, then the trivet and on top the dish with the egg custard, also with a double thickness of greaseproof paper laid on top. Bring to pressure, cook for 5 minutes, allow the pressure to reduce at room temperature. Lift out and serve at once or allow to chill thoroughly.

As this sweet does not mind being kept waiting, it can always be prepared before the meat course and be put on one side until required.

Apple cloud
Pressure-cooking time: 2 minutes

450 g (1 lb) cooking apples
a squeeze of lemon juice
3–4 tablespoons sugar

2 good tablespoons condensed milk
2 egg whites
a little cochineal if available

Peel, core and slice the apples, dip in cold water, then strain. Lift the trivet from the cooker, put in the apples, lemon juice, and sugar and cook on a low heat until the bottom is covered with juice and the sugar dissolved. Bring to pressure, cook for 2 minutes and allow the pressure to reduce at room temperature. Take out the apples, stir in the condensed milk, add a little colouring if liked, taste to see if more sugar is needed, and leave until cold. In a large bowl, beat the egg whites until stiff, then gently fold in the apple mixture and pile into the serving dish.

Spiced caramel apples
Pressure-cooking time: 2–3 minutes

4 medium eating apples
for the syrup:
  1·5 dl (¼ pt) water
  150 g (6 oz) loaf sugar
  1 clove
  a pinch of cinnamon
  juice of 1 lemon

3 dl (½ pt) water with a piece of
  lemon for the cooker
1·5 dl (¼ pt) double cream
1 teaspoon caster sugar
pieces of cherry and angelica
4 slices pineapple
chopped nuts

Peel the apples very thinly and core. Put into a shallow plate or
dish which will fit into the cooker. Put the ingredients for the syrup
into a small saucepan, stir over a low heat until the sugar has dissolved, then boil rapidly until thick and turning golden-brown.
Pour immediately over the apples. Put the water, trivet and dish
into the cooker and cover with a piece of buttered greaseproof
paper. Bring to pressure, cook for the required time and allow the
pressure to reduce at room temperature. Lift out the dish, strain off
the juice and immediately spoon it back over the apples to coat
them evenly. Chill in the refrigerator or leave until quite cold.
Whip the cream until stiff, fold in the sugar and the small pieces of
cherry and angelica. Put a slice of pineapple in 4 individual dishes,
stand an apple on each, fill the centre with the cream mixture and
sprinkle with the chopped nuts.

Stewed apples
Pressure-cooking time: 2 minutes

Do not fill the cooker more than one-third full as apples tend to
froth up.

cooking apples
a piece of lemon peel or unusual flavourings such as rose petals,
  rosemary, a sprig of elderflower or a tablespoon of orange-flower water
white or brown sugar to taste
knob of butter

Peel, core and slice the apples or cut up roughly. If adding any of
the unusual flavourings suggested, lift the trivet from the cooker,
put in 1·5 dl (¼ pt) water and the flavourings, boil in the open pan
for 3–4 minutes, then lift out the flavourings before putting in the

sugar and allowing it to dissolve. If using orange-flower water, put into the cooker with the sugar, stir until dissolved and boil for 2–3 minutes. Otherwise, rinse the apples with cold water, put into the cooker with the sugar and lemon, bring to the boil slowly in the open pan until sufficient juice has run out to cover the bottom of the pan. Bring the apples to pressure, cook for 2 minutes and allow the pressure to reduce at room temperature. If there is too much juice with the apples, strain them; beat thoroughly with a potato masher or wooden spoon, taste to see if more sugar is needed, add a good knob of butter and stir until melted.

This method should be used for all fruits which are to be pulped or puréed for use as tart fillings, for sweet omelettes or fruit fools.

Compote of cherries
Pressure-cooking time: 1 minute

225 g (8 oz) bright red cherries
2 tablespoons water
a squeeze of lemon juice
100 g (4 oz) white sugar

1 big teaspoon redcurrant jelly
cochineal
1 tablespoon Kirsch
whipped cream, flavoured with Kirsch

Wash and stone the cherries. Lift the trivet from the cooker, put in the water, lemon juice and sugar, stir until dissolved and boil rapidly until beginning to thicken, put in the cherries, bring to pressure, cook for 1 minute and allow the pressure to reduce at room temperature. Lift the cherries with a straining spoon into a deep bowl. Pour the syrup into a small saucepan, add the jam and colouring and boil until really syrupy, skimming from time to time to keep the syrup clear. Remove from the heat, stir in the Kirsch, pour over the cherries and put to chill thoroughly. About 5 minutes before serving, put stemmed glasses in the refrigerator, serve the cherries into them, decorating with a swirl of the flavoured whipped cream.

Any suitable fruits prepared this way are excellent for serving over ice-cream, or for filling meringue cases.

Gooseberry fool
Pressure-cooking time: 2 minutes

450 g (1 lb) gooseberries (3 dl or
½ pt purée) with a little extra

sugar and a little green
colouring added after sieving

for the custard:
 3 dl (½ pt) milk
 1 dessertspoon cornflour
 1 egg
 sugar to taste
 (or 3 dl/½ pt custard made from
  custard powder)

to decorate:
 whipped cream
 cherries, angelica and small
  ratafias

Prepare the gooseberry purée as in preceding recipe, adding the extra sweetening and a little green colouring, if necessary. To make the custard, mix a spoonful of the milk with the cornflour, boil the rest, add the blended cornflour, return to the heat and reboil. Stir in the yolk of egg and cook for a minute or two but without boiling. Add sugar to taste and allow to cool. Beat the white of egg and fold in, alternately with the gooseberry purée. Put into a serving dish or individual dishes and, at the last moment, decorate with whipped cream, cherries, angelica or baby ratafias as desired.

Orange delights
Pressure-cooking time: 5 minutes

3 dl (½ pt) water for the cooker
4 seedless oranges

for the syrup:
 1 tablespoon hot water
 4 tablespoons brown sugar
 pinch of cinnamon
 pinch of nutmeg
 2 tablespoons golden syrup
 a few chopped dates and nuts

Lift the trivet from the cooker, put in the water and the whole, washed, unpeeled oranges. Bring to pressure, cook for 3 minutes and reduce the pressure in cold water. When cool, peel the oranges, put in a shallow dish that will fit easily into the cooker and pour over the mixed ingredients for the syrup. Bring to pressure again, cook for 2 minutes and reduce the pressure with cold water. Strain off the syrup and boil rapidly until thick in a small saucepan. Serve the oranges with the syrup poured over.

These orange delights may be served sliced with cream as a dessert, or with cottage or cream cheese in a salad.

Peach royal
Pressure-cooking time: 2–3 minutes

1·5 dl ($\frac{1}{4}$ pt) water
4 tablespoons sugar
4 whole peaches
juice of $\frac{1}{2}$ lemon
1·5 dl ($\frac{1}{4}$ pt) double cream
1 tablespoon brandy if liked

caster sugar to taste
1 small punnet of firm, small
 strawberries
finely chopped or shredded
 almonds to decorate

Lift the trivet from the cooker. Put in the water and sugar and bring to the boil, stirring to make sure the sugar dissolves. Boil for 2–3 minutes, put in the washed peaches, bring to pressure, cook for 3 minutes and allow the pressure to reduce at room temperature. When cool, skin, halve, stone, put in a shallow dish, sprinkle with the lemon juice and chill in the refrigerator. For serving, whip the cream, fold in the brandy, a little caster sugar and lastly the halved strawberries. Pile this on to the cut side of the peach halves, decorate with the nuts and serve in individual dishes.

Golden pears
Pressure-cooking time: 4–8 minutes

1 or 2 pears per person
100 g (4 oz) soft brown sugar
thinly peeled rind of orange
small bottle or tin of apple juice

to decorate:
double cream
sugar to sweeten
cherries, angelica and chopped
 nuts

Peel the pears very thinly, leave whole and with the stalk on. Lift the trivet out of the cooker, put in the sugar, orange rind and apple juice, stir until the sugar is dissolved and boil rapidly for 5 minutes. Put in the pears standing upright and lay the trivet on top to keep them in position. Bring to pressure, cook 4 minutes for dessert pears, 8 minutes for hard, cooking pears, and leave the pressure to reduce with the cover on for 20 minutes or longer if possible. Lift out the pears and again stand upright in a large serving dish. Put the syrup into a small saucepan, boil until syrupy, then coat each pear. Chill, and just before serving, whip the cream, sweeten, stir in small pieces of cherries and angelica and the chopped nuts, put into a small dish and stand in the centre of the pears.

Pineapple carmelite
Pressure-cooking time: 1 minute

1 pineapple giving 5–6 slices
for the syrup:
  1·5 dl (¼ pt) water
  100 g (4 oz) white sugar

1 layer 17-cm (7-in) sponge cake
  topped with vanilla glacé icing
1 large tub vanilla ice-cream

Cut the pineapple into even slices (saving the top with the green leaves); trim off the outside, cut away any black pieces, remove the centres with an apple corer. Lift the trivet from the cooker, put in the pineapple and syrup, bring to pressure, cook for 1 minute and allow the pressure to reduce at room temperature. Lift out the slices and leave to drain thoroughly. In a small saucepan, boil the syrup until thick, and put to cool. When ready to serve, lay the slices around the top of the sponge cake leaving a space in the centre. Beat the ice-cream, fill into the centre and cap with the pineapple top. Hand the syrup separately.

Dried fruits

In a pressure cooker the super-heated steam quickly softens and swells dried fruit while bringing out all the sweetness and flavours in a matter of minutes.

Wash the dried fruits with hot water, put into a bowl, pour over boiling water in the proportion of 6 dl (1 pt) to 450 g (1 lb) fruit, making sure that all the fruit is under water, cover with a plate and leave for 10 minutes.

The trivet is not required.

Fruit	For cooking	Pressure-cooking time
Apple rings	Shreds of lemon peel, or cloves	6 minutes
Apricots	Add a little orange juice to 4·5 dl (¾ pt) water	3 minutes
Figs	Cut off dried stalks	10 minutes
Peaches	Add a little orange juice	5 minutes
Pears	Add 1 or 2 cloves to 4·5 dl (¾ pt) water	10 minutes
Prunes	Add a shred of lemon or orange peel	10 minutes
Fruit salad	Add a shred of lemon or orange peel	10 minutes

Add 2 to 3 tablespoons sugar per 450 g (1 lb) fruit and use the soaking water for the cooking.

Use **H** pressure and reduce at room temperature.

Apricot mallow
Pressure-cooking time: 2 minutes

150 g (6 oz) dried apricots
1·5 dl (¼ pt) water
2 tablespoons orange juice
18 marshmallows
2 egg whites

3 tablespoons sugar
to decorate:
  sliced marshmallows
  shredded almonds

Presoak the apricots using only 1·5 dl (¼ pt) boiling water, as directed. Lift the trivet from the cooker, put in the apricots, soaking water and orange juice, bring to pressure, cook for 2 minutes and allow the pressure to reduce at room temperature. Strain off the juice, chop the apricots and put them with 2 tablespoons juice and 16 of the marshmallows into a saucepan. Fold the mixture over and over on a low heat until the marshmallows are beginning to melt, remove from the heat, continue folding until the mixture is smooth and spongy and allow to cool. Beat the egg whites stiffly, fold in the sugar, then fold this into the apricot mixture. Serve in a deep dish or pile into individual dishes and when cool, decorate with sliced marshmallows and shredded almonds.

Apricot snow
Pressure-cooking time: 3 minutes

150 g (6 oz) dried apricots
3 dl (½ pt) water
3 egg whites

sugar to sweeten
browned almonds to decorate

Wash, presoak and cook the dried apricots as given in the instructions. During this cooking, preheat the oven to Gas No 5, 190°C (375°F). Sieve the apricots and add about 1 dessertspoon juice to the purée. Taste and add sweetening if thought necessary. Fold in the stiffly beaten egg whites and put into a buttered, sugared heatproof serving dish. Bake until golden for 15–20 minutes.

To brown the almonds, blanch and shred them, then put on a baking tray and leave on the bottom of the oven while the pudding is cooking, until golden-brown. Sprinkle over the pudding just before serving. Boil the syrup in an open saucepan until thick and hand separately. It may be sharpened, if preferred, with a little lemon juice.

Prune whip
Pressure-cooking time: 10 minutes

225 g (8 oz) prunes
3 dl (½ pt) water
strip of lemon peel
squeeze of lemon juice
2 large tablespoons marmalade
2 egg whites

2 tablespoons sugar
to decorate:
  crushed crystallized violets or
  roses, sugar strands or
  hundreds and thousands

Wash, presoak and cook the prunes with the lemon rind according to the instructions (p 181). Strain the prunes, stone and mash to pulp. Add the lemon juice and marmalade and allow to cool. Beat the egg whites stiffly, fold in the sugar, then fold into the prune mixture. Pile into individual glasses and just before serving decorate to give a touch of colour.

For a children's sweet, use the prune juice made up to 6 dl (1 pt) with cold water to dissolve a lemon jelly. Stir in the mashed prunes and marmalade and, when cool, add a little sugar if necessary; fold in the stiffly beaten whites and put into a serving dish. Decorate as for **Prune Whip**.

8 International dishes

Nowadays when people have many more opportunities to travel abroad, everyone is becoming more familiar with the regional and national dishes of other countries. Many of them can be adapted to pressure cooking and it is a pleasant reminder to make these in your own home, for they can add variety and spice to the family menus and serve as excellent conversation pieces for your dinner parties.

Ireland

Crubeens
Pressure-cooking time: 30 minutes

2 fresh pig's trotters
3 dl (½ pt) water
potatoes for 4 if liked

1 large crisp cabbage
salt and pepper

Wash and scrub the trotters thoroughly, lift the trivet from the cooker, put in the water and trotters, bring to pressure, cook for 25 minutes and reduce the pressure with cold water. During this cooking, peel the potatoes if they are to be served as well, wash the cabbage and shred roughly, tossing it well in plenty of salt and pepper. Pack the cabbage down into the liquid, put the trivet on top and the potatoes, cut to cook in 5 minutes. Bring to pressure again, cook for the last 5 minutes and reduce the pressure with cold water. Serve the potatoes, and the trotters dished on the strained cabbage. Taste and correct seasoning, boil the liquor in the open pan for 2–3 minutes to reduce it, then pour into the dish.

Scotland

Potted haugh
Pressure-cooking time: 1 hour

9 dl (1½ pt) water
900 g (2 lb) nap bone (foot or
  marrow bone)
½ teaspoon peppercorns,
  ¼ teaspoon mixed spice, blade of
  mace tied in a piece of muslin

450 g (1 lb) haugh (shin of beef)
salt and pepper

Lift the trivet from the cooker, put in the water, the nap bone and the bag of spices, bring to the boil, skim well, bring to pressure, cook for 40 minutes and allow the pressure to reduce at room temperature. Leave to stand a while, then remove as much fat as possible. Bring to the boil again in the open cooker, add the well-seasoned meat, bring to pressure again, cook for a further 20 minutes and allow the pressure to reduce at room temperature. Lift out the meat and strain the stock. Shred the meat, cut small or put through a mincer, and fill into bowls or moulds rinsed in cold water. Remove the fat again from the stock, return to the cooker, taste and correct seasoning, boil rapidly for 5 minutes and fill the bowls. Put on one side, stirring occasionally as the stock sets to make sure the meat is evenly distributed. Leave until set, then turn out by dipping quickly in hot water. Serve with a green or mixed salad.

Wales

Cawl mamgu
Pressure-cooking time: 20 minutes

It is recommended to scald the meat the night before so that the fat can be removed.

900 g (2 lb) best end of neck of
  Welsh lamb
4·5 dl (¾ pt) water
225 g (8 oz) carrots
1 small swede
2 large leeks

450 g (1 lb) medium potatoes
1 tablespoon chopped parsley
salt and pepper
a little blended flour for
  thickening

Wipe the meat, lift the trivet from the cooker, put in the joint and the water, bring slowly to the boil in the open pan and skim carefully or allow to stand overnight and remove the fat just before starting the cooking. Bring to pressure, cook for 15 minutes and reduce the pressure with cold water. During this cooking, prepare the vegetables, cutting the carrots in half, the swede and leeks in slices and the potatoes in quarters; add with the parsley to the cawl. Bring to pressure again, cook for the last 5 minutes and reduce the pressure with cold water. Lift out the meat, divide into portions and serve into individual bowls or plates with a selection of the strained vegetables. Taste the cawl and correct the seasoning, add the blended flour, allow to cook for a minute or two while stirring, and pour into the dishes.

America

Chicken paprika
Pressure-cooking time: 7 minutes

1 young roasting chicken about
  1 kg (2¼ lb)
4 medium onions
4 tablespoons butter
1–1½ tablespoons paprika

2 medium tomatoes
1·5 dl (¼ pt) water
1 cup rice with 2 cups water in a
  solid container

for thickening:
  1 tablespoon flour
  2 tablespoons soured cream*
salt and pepper

to garnish:
  a little extra paprika

Joint the chicken into portions; chop the onions finely, quarter the tomatoes. Lift the trivet from the cooker, heat the butter and gently fry the onions until just turning colour but not brown. Add the paprika, stir until well mixed, then put in the tomatoes, the water and the chicken. Put the trivet on top and the covered container of rice. Bring to pressure, cook for 7 minutes and allow the pressure to reduce at room temperature. During this cooking, boil a kettle of water to strain the rice and heat the oven. Blend the flour and cream. Lift out the rice and finish as instructed. Serve the chicken and vegetables and keep hot. Gradually add the strained stock to the cream, taste and correct seasoning, reheat but do not allow to reboil, and pour over the chicken. Hand the rice separately, sprinkled with a little paprika.

Brown apple betty
Pressure-cooking time: 10 minutes

150 g (6 oz) soft white
  breadcrumbs
2–3 tablespoons melted butter
100 g (4 oz) brown sugar
1 teaspoon grated lemon rind
½ teaspoon each nutmeg and
  cinnamon
4–5 large cooking apples

a little lemon juice if apples are
  not of the sour variety
3 dl (½ pt) water with a little
  lemon juice or vinegar for the
  cooker
pouring or whipping cream to
  hand separately

Butter a soufflé dish or suitable-sized heatproof bowl. Combine the crumbs with the melted butter, sugar, peel and spices; peel, core and slice the apples (and sprinkle with lemon juice if not using sour apples). Put in alternate layers of the crumb mixture and apples, starting and finishing with the crumbs and leaving at least 2-cm (1-in) space at the top as the crumbs will swell during the cooking. Put the water into the cooker with a trivet and the dish covered with a double thickness of greased greaseproof paper. Bring to pressure, cook for 10 minutes and allow the pressure to reduce at room temperature. Serve in the dish or allow to stand for 2–3 minutes and unmould.

Serve with cream.

Belgium

Carbonnades à la flamande
Pressure-cooking time: 20 minutes

675 g (1½ lb) good stewing steak
2 large onions
2 tablespoons dripping
3 dl (½ pt) beer or brown ale
1·5 dl (¼ pt) brown stock*

salt and pepper
pinch each of sugar and nutmeg
bay leaf
to garnish:
    chopped parsley

Cut the meat into large squares and season well; chop the onions. Lift the trivet from the cooker, heat the fat and quickly sear the meat all over, keeping it on the move. Brown the onions, drain off any surplus fat, take the cooker away from the heat and allow it to cool. Add the liquids, the seasonings and the bay leaf, bring to pressure in the usual way, cook for 20 minutes and reduce the pressure with cold water. Lift out the bay leaf, serve the meat and onions and keep hot. Boil the liquid in the open pan until thick, taste and correct seasoning and pour over the meat. Sprinkle thickly with chopped parsley.

To give a sharp taste 1 teaspoon wine vinegar can be stirred into the sauce just before serving.

If a lot of sauce is preferred, thicken in the usual way with a little blended flour instead of reducing by rapid boiling.

Chicorée à la royale
Pressure-cooking time: 3 minutes and 5 minutes

4 heads of chicory
2 tablespoons butter
2 tablespoons water
3 dl (½ pt) milk
2 eggs

salt and pepper
pinch of nutmeg
a little butter
3 dl (½ pt) water with a little lemon
    juice or vinegar for the cooker

Wash the chicory well but do not cut it in any way. Lift the trivet from the cooker, put in the butter, allow to melt, add the water and chicory, bring to pressure in the usual way, cook for 3 minutes and reduce the pressure with cold water. During this cooking, warm the milk and pour on to the seasoned beaten eggs. Lift the chicory into a greased soufflé or heatproof dish, pour over the custard and dot with butter. Rinse the cooker, put in the water, the trivet and the dish covered with a double thickness of greased greaseproof paper. Bring to pressure, cook for 5 minutes and allow the pressure to reduce at room temperature. Serve garnished with sprigs of watercress, or the top may be sprinkled with grated cheese and lightly browned under a hot grill.

France

Pot au feu
Pressure-cooking time: 20–25 minutes

900 g (2 lb) topside of beef	1 clove garlic, chopped
a large piece of marrow, shin bone or knuckle of veal	bay leaf
1·2 litres (2 pt) water	sprig each of parsley and thyme
2 legs and 2 wings of chicken	salt and pepper
4 small onions	crisp french bread as
4 medium carrots	accompaniment
2 small turnips, halved	mustard* or horseradish* sauce
4 leeks (white part only)	handed separately

Lift the trivet from the cooker, put in the meat, the bone and the water. Bring to the boil in the open pan, skim well. Bring to pressure, give all but 8 minutes of the cooking time and reduce the pressure with cold water. Skim again if necessary, put in the chicken, vegetables and seasonings, bring to pressure again, give the rest of the cooking time and allow the pressure to reduce at room temperature. Lift out the meat and serve, with the skinned chicken, on a hot dish. Strain the broth, lift out the vegetables, arrange round the serving dish and keep hot. Skim the fat from the broth with kitchen paper, return to the pan, taste and correct seasoning, reheat and serve in individual bowls, with the crisped french bread handed separately. The meat may be carved before being taken to table; lay out in slices with a chicken piece to form a portion, each being accompanied by a selection of the vegetables. Hand the mustard* or horseradish* sauce (which would be delicious made with soured cream), separately.

Crème brûlée
Pressure-cooking time: 4 minutes

1 tablespoon milk	1 teaspoon vanilla essence or to
4·5 dl (¾ pt) double cream	taste
yolks of 3 large eggs	3 dl (½ pt) water with a little lemon
3 tablespoons sugar	juice or vinegar for the cooker
	3 tablespoons light brown sugar

Put the milk and then the cream into a small saucepan and warm very gently over a low heat, stirring all the time. Pour over the beaten yolks and sugar and stir again. Add the vanilla to taste, then pour the cream into a buttered soufflé dish. Have ready in the cooker the water and the trivet, put in the cream and lay on top a double piece of greaseproof paper. Bring to pressure, cook for 5 minutes and allow the pressure to reduce at room temperature. Allow to cool first and then chill thoroughly. When ready to serve, light the grill, half fill the grill pan with crushed ice (to do this, take the cubes from the ice-box, put in a tea-towel and crush with a hammer or the heavy weight from a set of scales), put the cream in the middle and cover with the brown sugar. Set the cream under the grill and watch it all the time until the sugar melts and turns brown. Be very careful here or the sugar will burn. Serve at once or chill again and serve ice-cold.

Germany

Sauerbraten
Pressure-cooking time: 20–25 minutes

Correctly the meat should be left to marinate for seven days, turning it over every day.

1 large onion	4 thin slices of fat pork belly
1·5 dl (¼ pt) water	900-g (2-lb) piece of topside of
1·5 dl (¼ pt) vinegar	beef

bouquet garni*
2 tablespoons dripping or fat
1 teaspoon flour

1 teaspoon sugar
1·5 dl (¼ pt) soured cream*
salt and pepper

To make the marinade, boil together for 5 minutes the chopped onion, the water and vinegar. Tie strips of the pork right round the joint, put it in a deep bowl with the bouquet garni and pour the marinade over. To keep the meat down in the liquid put a weighted saucer or plate on top. Leave as long as possible, but turn the meat at least once during the soaking. When ready, lift the trivet from the cooker, heat the fat and brown the well-dried meat on all sides. Lift out and dust lightly with flour. When the cooker has cooled slightly, pour in half the strained marinade liquid, the sugar and the cream, put back the meat, bring to pressure, cook for the required time and reduce the pressure with cold water. Lift out the meat and carve it; lay the overlapping slices on the serving dish and keep hot. Taste and correct the seasoning, reboil the sauce, pour a little over the meat and hand the rest separately.

Hühner frikassee
Pressure-cooking time: 15–20 minutes

1 roasting chicken
salt and pepper
a little lemon juice
12 button onions or shallots
6 large field mushrooms
2 tablespoons butter
1·5 dl (¼ pt) dry white wine

1 tablespoon flour blended with a
    little milk for thickening
1·5 dl (¼ pt) single cream
to garnish:
    bacon rolls*
    chopped parsley

Wipe the chicken, cut into joints and season well with salt, pepper and a sprinkling of lemon juice. Prepare the onions, leaving whole, cut the mushrooms into 4. Lift the trivet from the cooker, heat the butter, fry the chicken pieces evenly until golden-brown and lift out. Add the onions and mushrooms and cook gently for 2–3 minutes. Lift the cooker from the heat, allow to cool, add the wine and put back the chicken portions. Bring to pressure, cook for the required time and reduce the pressure with cold water. During this cooking, prepare the blended flour and make and grill the bacon rolls. Lift the chicken on to the serving dish and keep hot. Add blended flour to the liquid, bring to the boil and cook for 2–3 minutes, stirring all the time. Taste and correct seasoning, stir in the cream, reheat without boiling and pour over the chicken. Garnish with chopped parsley and the bacon rolls. This dish is at its best when soured, rather than fresh cream is used.

Greece

Psari me kolokythia
Pressure-cooking time: 5–10 minutes

2 tablespoons olive oil
2 medium onions, sliced
1 clove garlic, crushed
herbs to taste (including dill, mint and chopped parsley)
4 ripe tomatoes
1 teaspoon sugar
seasoning and a pinch of cinnamon

1·5 dl ($\frac{1}{4}$ pt) water
5 or 6 courgettes, or 2 very young marrows
4 whole fish (such as small, fresh haddock) or 4 steaks of cod, turbot, halibut etc
strained lemon juice to taste

Lift the trivet from the cooker, heat the olive oil, put in the sliced onions, garlic, herbs and seasonings and the tomatoes, and cook for 2–3 minutes without allowing to colour. Add the water and stir well. Put the unpeeled whole courgettes or the young marrows cut in half lengthways and with the seeds removed, on top of the vegetables, and on this bed lay the fish. Cover with a piece of buttered greaseproof paper, bring to pressure, cook for the required time and allow the pressure to reduce at room temperature. Lift the fish out carefully, put the courgettes on a deep serving dish, then the fish back on top and keep hot. Reheat the sauce, add a little lemon juice, taste and correct seasoning, reboil rapidly in the open cooker to reduce to a coating consistency, then pour over the fish.

In Greece this dish is served either hot or cold.

Holland

Zuurkool stampot
Pressure-cooking time: 9 minutes

4 slices streaky bacon
1·5 dl (¼ pt) water
900 g (2 lb) potatoes
salt and pepper

450 g (1 lb) sauerkraut
1 large onion
150–225 g (6–8 oz) continental
   sausage

Lift the trivet from the cooker, put in the chopped bacon and allow to fry until golden-crisp but not brown; lift out. Add the hot water (if cold, allow cooker to cool), the sliced potatoes in layers, well sprinkled with salt and pepper, then a layer of sauerkraut and onion. Sprinkle with the fried bacon and lastly add the piece of sausage. Bring to pressure, cook for 9 minutes and allow the pressure to reduce at room temperature. Lift out the sausage, slice and keep hot. Mash the vegetables or cut through roughly with a knife; taste and correct seasoning, reheat, serve into a deep dish and lay the sliced sausage on top.

Kabeljauw en garnalenragout
Pressure-cooking time: 6 minutes

4·5 dl (¾ pt) water
2 small cod or 4 steaks
a little lemon juice
salt and pepper

for thickening:
1 tablespoon butter
1 tablespoon flour
100 g (4 oz) shrimps (fresh or
   frozen)
to garnish:
2 tablespoons chopped parsley

Lift the trivet from the cooker, put in the water, the fish and the lemon juice and seasoning, bring to pressure, cook for 6 minutes and reduce the pressure with cold water. During this cooking melt the butter in a small saucepan, add the flour and allow to cook without browning. Lift out the fish, add the stock to the flour in the saucepan, stirring all the time, put in the shrimps, bring to the boil, taste and correct seasoning and cook for 2–3 minutes. Divide the fish into large pieces, removing all skin and bone, put back in the cooker, pour over the sauce and reheat. Serve in a deep dish, sprinkled thickly with parsley.

Italy

Minestrone milanese
Pressure-cooking time: 10 minutes

2 thick slices streaky bacon
1 medium onion
1 celery heart
1 potato
¼ large green cabbage
100 g (¼ lb) french or runner beans
3 tomatoes
2 courgettes or 1 small marrow

2 tablespoons olive oil or butter
2 tablespoons peas
9 dl (1½ pt) stock
1 tablespoon chopped parsley
salt and pepper
100 g (4 oz) rice
grated parmesan cheese can be
   handed separately

Chop the bacon finely, saving the rinds; slice the onions into strips, the celery and potato into strips 5 cm (2 in) long, shred the cabbage, cut the beans into thin diagonal slices and peel and chop the tomatoes. If courgettes are used, do not peel but slice, remove the seeds and cut into 5-cm (2-in) strips; for a marrow, skin and cut as before. Lift the trivet from the cooker, heat the oil and gently fry the bacon, onions and celery until just turning brown. Add all the rest of the vegetables, the bacon rinds, the stock and seasoning and bring to the boil. Throw in the rice, bring to pressure, cook for 10 minutes and allow the pressure to reduce at room temperature. Taste and correct the seasoning, reheat and serve in individual soup bowls, handing the cheese separately if liked.

Ossobuco
This recipe should be made well in advance of the meal as it requires to stand for 2–3 hours.
Pressure-cooking time: 20 minutes

1·35 kg (3 lb) veal shank or shin,
   sawn by the butcher into
   6-cm (2½-in) pieces
2 tablespoons butter
3 dl (½ pt) marsala
salt and pepper
1 teaspoon flour
1 beef or chicken stock cube
water

risotto* to hand separately
1 clove garlic
2 or 3 strips of lemon rind
1 tablespoon chopped parsley
to garnish:
   1 tablespoon grated lemon rind,
   1 tablespoon chopped parsley
   and 1 small teaspoon chopped
   garlic

Tie each piece of veal with thin string so that it will hold together. Lift the trivet from the cooker, heat the butter and brown the pieces until golden; lift out. Pour in the wine, add the seasoning, bring to the boil; put back the veal and boil, turning the pieces at least once, until the wine is well reduced. Sprinkle in the flour, put in the stock cube and sufficient water almost to cover the pieces. Bring to pressure, cook for 20 minutes and allow the pressure to reduce at room temperature. Turn into a covered dish and leave to stand for 2–3 hours.

About three-quarters of an hour before the meal, use the pressure cooker to cook the risotto, p 144, and keep hot in the oven. Put the *ossobuco* back in the cooker, add the garlic, lemon peel and anchovies and warm through gently until bubbling. Lift the pieces on to a hot serving dish, remove the clove of garlic and the lemon peel and boil the sauce until a thick, coating consistency. Pour over the meat, garnish with the mixed lemon rind, parsley and garlic and hand the risotto separately.

Mexico

Chili con carne
Pressure-cooking time: 20 minutes and 10 minutes

225 g (8 oz) small kidney beans (use the red ones if available)	450 g (1 lb) finely minced lean steak
1·2 litres (2 pt) water	4·5 dl (¾ pt) brown stock*
2 tablespoons butter	salt
2–3 teaspoons chilli powder	cream crackers and pickled
2 tablespoons bacon fat	cucumbers to hand separately
1 large onion, chopped	

Wash, soak and cook the beans according to the instructions on p 64. After straining, put back in the cooker and reheat with the butter and 1 teaspoon of the chilli powder. Lift out, take one-third of the beans and mash thoroughly. Rinse the cooker, heat the bacon fat and fry the onion until transparent. Add the meat, brown quickly, stirring all the time; put in the hot stock (if cold, allow cooker to cool), the mashed beans, salt and the rest of the chilli powder, stirring all together well. Bring to pressure, cook for 10 minutes and reduce the pressure with cold water. Add the rest of the beans, taste and correct seasoning, and allow to boil until the consistency is that of a thick stew. Hand the crackers and cucumbers separately.

This dish is often preferred flavoured with tomatoes: for this, use a tin of tomatoes with the juice and only 3 dl (½ pt) water. For quickness, a large tin of baked beans in tomato sauce could be used instead, with a little extra tomato purée or sauce.

Spain

Gazpacho
Pressure-cooking time: 5 minutes
This is served as an iced soup and must be prepared well in advance to allow plenty of time for it to be thoroughly chilled.

8 fresh tomatoes	1·5 dl (¼ pt) white stock* or water
1 large onion	1·5 dl (¼ pt) red wine
1 cucumber	2 tablespoons lemon juice
1 green pepper	cayenne pepper
1 tablespoon butter	1·5 dl (¼ pt) tomato juice
1 clove garlic, crushed	2–3 tablespoons olive oil
1 teaspoon sugar	1 tablespoon butter, 1 clove garlic
salt and pepper	and diced bread for croûtons*

Skin the tomatoes, put 2 on one side and cut the rest up roughly; chop the onion; wash the cucumber, put half on one side, cut the other half into cubes; wash the pepper, remove seeds, put half on one side and chop the other roughly. Lift the trivet from the cooker, heat the butter, put in the onions and tomatoes and cook until the onions are transparent but not coloured. Add the cucumber, pepper, garlic, sugar, seasoning and liquids, bring to pressure, cook for 5 minutes and reduce the pressure with cold water. Strain the soup through a fine sieve and put the liquid to one side. Sieve the soup and add just sufficient liquid to give a thick consistency to the soup. Put in the refrigerator and chill thoroughly. Just before serving, put the lemon juice and seasoning into a small bowl; stir in the tomato juice and the olive oil drop by drop until well blended and stir gently into the soup. Prepare the following and serve each in separate dishes to be handed round separately: the half cucumber, unpeeled, cut into cubes and tossed with the half green pepper cut into thin strips; the 2 tomatoes each cut into eight pieces; the croûtons of bread fried golden-brown in the butter heated with the garlic.

At the last moment, serve the soup into individual bowls and add a small ice cube to each.

Hungary

Goulash
Pressure-cooking time: 15–20 minutes

450–600 g (1–1½ lb) good stewing
  steak such as chuck, rump
seasoned flour
2 tablespoons dripping or butter
2 large onions, sliced
1·5 dl (¼ pt) stock or water
1·5 dl (¼ pt) tomato juice
1 clove garlic, minced or crushed
  (optional)

about 2 tablespoons paprika
salt
bay leaf
4 potatoes, thickly sliced
a little red wine
to garnish:
  chopped parsley

Wipe and trim the meat, cut into large cubes and toss in seasoned flour, shaking well to remove any surplus. Lift the trivet out of the cooker, heat the fat and fry the onions until golden-brown; lift out. Fry the meat, keeping it moving to colour evenly all over; lift out. Away from the heat, add the hot liquids (if cold, allow the cooker to cool), stirring until all the brown bits have been lifted from the bottom. Put back the onions and the meat, then the garlic, bay leaf and paprika, bring to pressure, cook for all but 4 minutes of the cooking time, and reduce the pressure with cold water. Check that there is still sufficient liquid, remembering that the potatoes will take up about one-third of what there is; if necessary, add a little more. Put in the potatoes, stir the goulash well, taste to correct seasoning (which should be on the peppery side), bring to pressure again and cook for the last 4 minutes, reducing the pressure with cold water. Lift out the bay leaf, stir in a little red wine to taste and serve garnished with chopped parsley.

West Africa

Joliff rice
Pressure-cooking time: 5 minutes

1 chicken weighing about 1–1·5 kg
  (2½–3 lb)
salt and pepper
4 small onions
1 green pepper
2 tablespoons butter
1 clove garlic, chopped
4·5 dl (¾ pt) chicken stock

1·5 dl (¼ pt) beer
bay leaf
pinch of turmeric
150 g (6 oz) rice
1 packet of frozen peas
to garnish:
  strips of red pepper or chillies
  black or green olives, plain or
    stuffed

Joint the chicken into portions, skin and season well with salt and pepper; chop the onions finely; remove seeds from the pepper and cut into thin slices. Lift the trivet from the cooker, heat the butter, fry the joints all over until golden-brown and lift out. Gently fry the onion, garlic and pepper strips, add the hot stock (if cold allow the cooker to cool), the beer and seasonings, stir well, allow to boil, throw in the rice and peas. Bring to pressure in the usual way, cook for 5 minutes and allow the pressure to reduce at room temperature. Serve in a deep dish, lifting out the chicken, rice and vegetables; boil the sauce in the open pan until a thick consistency, tasting and correcting the seasoning. Garnish with the strips of pepper and olives dotted over the surface.

Sweden

Köttbullar
Pressure-cooking time: 10 minutes

1 tablespoon butter
1 small, finely chopped onion
325 g (¾ lb) finely minced steak
100 g (4 oz) minced veal
100 g (4 oz) minced pork or ham
3 tablespoons fine white
  breadcrumbs soaked in 1·5 dl
  (¼ pt) soured cream*

salt and pepper
1 egg
1·5 dl (¼ pt) water
1·5 dl (¼ pt) vinegar
1 teaspoon dry mustard
2 tablespoons brown sugar
pinch of ground cloves

Lift the trivet from the cooker, heat the butter and fry the onion until golden-brown. Lift out and mix with the meats, the breadcrumbs, seasoning and beaten egg to give a firm consistency that will form easily into meat balls. If the mixture is too dry, add a little milk as necessary. Form into 8 balls and stand on one side for at least an hour. Put the vinegar and water into the cooker, add the mustard, sugar and cloves and boil, stirring all the time, until the sugar is dissolved. Toss the meat balls in seasoned flour, put into the liquid, bring to pressure, cook 10 minutes and allow the pressure to reduce at room temperature. Lift the meat balls into a serving dish and keep hot. Boil the stock rapidly until thickening, taste and correct seasoning and pour into the dish.

9 Vegetarian and invalid dishes

A section such as this in a general cookery book cannot cover the particular requirements of these two groups entirely, but the following recipes give an idea of how useful your pressure cooker can be when special diets are a necessity or just a matter of choice.

For vegetarians, who have to ensure an adequate supply of protein in their diet, the quick, complete cooking of the pulse vegetables such as beans, split peas and lentils is a guarantee of the full retention of their flavours and the softness which makes for easy digestion. Again, the short cooking time for fresh vegetables leads to the higher retention of vitamins and other nutrients, and the concentrated cooking liquid need never be wasted. To make vegetarian dishes appetizing and to give variety they should be well seasoned and pepped up with herbs, spices, garlic, onions and so on, or with something tart such as fruit sauces or, if permissible, sour cream. As they also lack fats, these should be added in the form of a vegetable oil, either in preliminary frying of the ingredients or by addition before serving. To obtain a balanced diet, desserts to follow should be of fresh, tinned or stewed fruit rather than further cereals.

For invalids, the many advantages of having a pressure cooker must by now be obvious. All the delicate dishes, tender and well flavoured to encourage a flagging appetite, with all their goodness to help build up strength, can be done in a matter of minutes. Small quantities present no problem as, using cups, small boilable plastic bowls or deep saucers, individual portions of savoury and sweet dishes can be cooked together.

Many of the following recipes are interchangeable; many others suitable will be found in previous sections. For those who have been ill and are trying to get back to normal food, the suggestions for infant feeding might prove helpful.

Vegetarian dishes

Vegetarian stock
Pressure-cooking time: 30 minutes

225 g (8 oz) large haricot beans
outside stalks of 1 head of celery
1 large onion
1 large carrot
bouquet garni*
a few white peppercorns
salt
a strip of lemon peel
1·2 litres (2 pt) water

Presoak the beans as given in the instructions on p 64. Cut the vegetables up into rough 1-cm ($\frac{1}{2}$-in) dice. Lift the trivet from the cooker, put in the water in which the beans were soaked, made up to 1·2 litres (2 pt), the vegetables and seasonings and bring to the boil. Add the beans, stir, bring to pressure in the usual way, cook for 30 minutes and allow the pressure to reduce at room temperature. Strain the stock for use.

Corn chowder
Pressure-cooking time: 4 minutes

2 tablespoons vegetable oil
1 peeled, chopped onion
6 dl (1 pt) creamed sweet corn*
2 large potatoes cut in 5-mm
   (¼-in) dice
6 dl (1 pt) water

2–3 tablespoons blended flour for
   thickening
3 dl (½ pt) hot milk
a good knob of butter
to garnish:
   chopped watercress
croûtons* to hand separately

Lift the trivet from the cooker, heat the oil and allow the onion to cook until golden. Add the corn, potatoes and water, stir well, bring to pressure, cook for 4 minutes and reduce the pressure with cold water. Add the flour blended with the milk, stir until boiling; put the knob of butter on the top and seasoning to taste and allow to cook for a minute or two. Serve, sprinkled thickly with chopped watercress and hand the croûtons separately.

Vegetable chowder
Pressure-cooking time: 5 minutes

1 teaspoon granulated sugar
2 tablespoons vegetable oil
2 onions, diced
2 carrots, diced
½ white cabbage, shredded
4 sticks celery, diced
1 small turnip, diced

3 dl (½ pt) vegetable stock
3 dl (½ pt) tomato juice
extra stock if necessary
salt and pepper
1 sour green apple, peeled and
   grated

Lift the trivet from the cooker, put in the sugar and, over a low heat, allow it to turn dark brown but not to burn. Put in the oil and all the vegetables and cook, stirring gently, until all are lightly browned. Add the stock, tomato juice and seasoning, bring to pressure, cook for 5 minutes and reduce the pressure with cold water. Stir the soup, add a little more stock if necessary, taste and correct seasoning; stir in the grated apple, reheat and serve.

Variations
Rice is excellent with this chowder; 1 cupful can be added after the liquid, which should be increased by 3 dl (½ pt) and allowed to boil before the rice is thrown in.

Dumplings turn this soup almost into a meal on its own; make these in the usual way but add a little very finely diced onion and ¼ teaspoon thyme or marjoram to the mixture. After pressure has been reduced, bring the soup to the boil, drop in the dumplings and boil for 10 minutes with a plate on top to serve as a cover.

For a summer chowder, coarsely shredded French or runner beans, fresh peas and small, whole new potatoes can be added to the vegetables, but do not use leafy green vegetables as they would overcook.

Cauliflower amande
Pressure-cooking time: 4 minutes

1 large cauliflower	fried breadcrumbs
3 dl (½ pt) water for the cooker	chopped parsley
1 egg	1 tablespoon butter
3 dl (½ pt) white sauce*	50 g (2 oz) shredded almonds

Wash and trim the cauliflower, divide in half and cut away small triangles from the thick stems. Put the water and the trivet in the cooker, the halved cauliflower and the egg for hard-boiling. Bring to pressure, cook for 4 minutes and reduce the pressure with cold water. During this cooking, make the white sauce, fry the breadcrumbs and stir in the chopped parsley. Lift the halves of cauliflower on to the serving dish, fitting them together to look whole again, or serve portions on to individual dishes, and keep hot. Chop the egg, add to the sauce, reheat and check seasoning, pour over the cauliflower, sprinkle thickly with the breadcrumbs and keep hot again. Melt the butter in a small pan and while it is still foaming stir in the almonds, then quickly spread them over the cauliflower and serve at once. A salad of sliced tomatoes, sprinkled liberally with very finely chopped raw onions and sprinkled with chopped chives would go well with this dish and give an attractive colour.

Egg and mushroom pie
Pressure-cooking time: 5 minutes

3 dl (½ pt) water for the cooker	100 g (4 oz) button mushrooms
4 eggs	2 tablespoons butter
1 cup rice	6 dl (1 pt) rich cheese sauce*
2 cups water	a little grated cheese
salt	a few golden crumbs

Lift the trivet from the cooker, put in the water, the eggs and the rice and water in a covered bowl. Bring to pressure, cook for 5 minutes and allow the pressure to reduce at room temperature. During this cooking, slice the mushrooms very finely and cook gently in the butter but without browning. Lift out, but leave the butter in the pan. Have some boiling water ready; light the grill; make the sauce. Drop the eggs into cold water. Put the rice in a colander, pour the boiling water over, shake well, turn into the frying pan and stir, over a low heat, until well coated with the butter. Shell the eggs and slice them. Into a greased ovenproof dish put alternate layers of rice, mushrooms and egg, finishing with a layer of egg. Pour over the sauce, sprinkle with cheese and crumbs and leave under the grill until golden-brown. This dish is delicious served with a salad of hearts of lettuce and sprigs of watercress, with spoonfuls of redcurrant or cranberry jelly or mango chutney.

Lentil rollettes
Pressure-cooking time: 20 minutes

150 g (6 oz) lentils	golden crumbs
1 onion, sliced	fat for frying
salt and pepper	*to garnish:*
1 level tablespoon nut butter	fried parsley*
yolk of 1 large egg	quick piquant sauce* to hand
beaten egg or a little milk	separately

Prepare, presoak and cook the lentils as instructed on p 64, with the sliced onion. When the lentils are strained, put back into the cooker and toss over a low heat until quite dry. Sieve, mix with the seasoning, nut butter, egg and seasoning, and form into small rolls. Allow to cool. Pass twice through the egg and golden crumbs, fry in hot fat until golden-brown. Drain on kitchen paper, serve with the fried parsley and hand the sauce separately.

Vegetable galantine
Pressure-cooking time: 20 minutes and 20 minutes

225 g (8 oz) small haricot beans
1 egg for hard-boiling
2 diced onions
a little vegetable oil
1 large tin of tomatoes
100 g (4 oz) stale bread soaked
  in a little milk
salt and pepper

pinch of mixed herbs
1 egg, separated
4·5 dl (¾ pt) water with a little
  lemon juice or vinegar for the
  cooker
3 dl (½ pt) tomato sauce* with a
  little extra tomato purée
golden crumbs

Prepare and cook the beans as given on p 64. During this cooking, hard-boil the egg and fry the onions lightly in a little heated oil. Sieve the beans with the strained tomatoes (keeping the juice on one side) and beat well until really creamy. Squeeze the excess milk from the bread into the tomato juice; add the bread, onions, diced hard-boiled egg, seasoning and herbs to the bean and tomato purée and stir carefully with the yolk of egg. Beat the egg white until stiff and fold into the mixture. Grease a seamless loaf tin or mould, fill with the mixture and cover securely with a double sheet of greased greaseproof paper. When the water in the cooker is boiling, put in the trivet and the galantine, bring to pressure, cook for 20 minutes and allow the pressure to reduce at room temperature for 10 minutes. During this cooking, use the tomato juice to make a tomato sauce as on p 268, adding a little concentrated tomato purée to strengthen the flavour. Preheat the oven to Gas No 4, 190°C (375°F), and have ready the middle shelf. Carefully turn out the galantine on to the serving dish, coat with the golden crumbs and put into the oven while the accompanying green vegetables are pressure cooked. Pour the tomato sauce over the galantine or hand separately.

Invalid dishes

Barley broth
Pressure-cooking time: 35 minutes and 20 minutes

The stock for this broth should be cooked in the evening for use next day.

450 g (1 lb) neck of lamb
9 dl (1½ pt) water
2 tablespoons barley
1 onion
1 carrot

1 turnip
piece of celery
salt and pepper
to garnish:
    chopped parsley

Wipe the meat and cut into small joints. Lift the trivet from the cooker, put in the water and the joints, bring to pressure, cook for 35 minutes and allow the pressure to reduce at room temperature. Lift out the joints, cut off the meat and keep covered in a cool place until required. Put the stock into a bowl and leave overnight. Next day remove the fat, put 6 dl (1 pt) stock into the cooker and bring to the boil. Throw in the barley and the finely diced meat and vegetables, add seasonings, bring to pressure in the usual way. cook for 20 minutes and allow the pressure to reduce at room temperature. Serve sprinkled with chopped parsley. This will give two appetizing and nutritious helpings of broth which will be a meal in themselves.

Barley cream
As a variation with even greater food value, the rest of the stock can also be pressure cooked with barley and vegetables and, when pressure has been reduced and the seasoning corrected, a beaten egg can be added and the soup carefully reheated; do not allow to boil, or it will curdle.

Barley water
Pressure-cooking time: 45 minutes

12 dl (2 pt) water
75 g (3 oz) pearl barley
1 large lemon
sugar to taste

Lift the trivet from the cooker, put in the water, bring to the boil, throw in the barley, bring to pressure, cook for 45 minutes and allow the pressure to reduce at room temperature. Strain off the barley water, return to the cooker and boil rapidly for 5 minutes in the open pan. Add the strained lemon juice and sugar to taste. Allow to cool completely before drinking; keep in a covered container in a cool place.

Beef tea
Pressure-cooking time: 30 minutes

100 g (4 oz) very lean beef
pinch of salt
4·5 dl (¾ pt) water with a little lemon juice or vinegar for the cooker

Wipe the meat, shred or scrape as finely as possible and put with the salt into a Kilner jar, a heatproof basin or boilable plastic bowl. Cover with a saucer, bring to pressure, cook for 30 minutes and allow the pressure to reduce at room temperature. Lift out the container, press the meat against the sides with a wooden spoon as hard as possible to extract all the liquid. Put into a strainer and again press hard, but do not scrape the strainer as the beef tea should remain a clear liquid. Remove all traces of fat while hot with small pieces of jagged kitchen paper dragged across the top, or allow to cool and lift off. Taste and correct seasoning, and reheat before serving with small fingers of dry toast.

Scalloped chicken
Pressure-cooking time: 8 minutes

You are sure to have some left-overs from a boiled chicken and this is a delicious way to disguise it and to vary the diet.

1 tablespoon chopped celery
small slice soaked bread, well
    squeezed, or 1 tablespoon
    fresh breadcrumbs
1 tablespoon parsley
1 portion sliced cooked chicken
1 egg
1·5 dl (¼ pt) chicken stock*
salt and pepper
3 dl (½ pt) water with a little lemon
    juice or vinegar for the cooker
golden crumbs and dabs of butter
accompanying vegetables to
    choice

Mix together the celery, bread and parsley; grease an individual deep dish, small bowl or cup, put in the chicken and the celery mixture in layers. Beat the egg, add the hot chicken stock and seasoning and pour into the dish. Put the water and the trivet in the cooker, then the dish covered with greaseproof paper and the accompanying vegetables. (If you had a little steamed or rice pudding left over, this also could be reheated in a covered cup.) Bring to pressure, cook for 8 minutes and allow the pressure to reduce at room temperature. Lift out the dish of chicken, put the cover back on the cooker to keep the vegetables hot. If the chicken is not in an individual dish, turn it out; sprinkle with golden crumbs, dot with butter and brown quickly for no more than a moment under a hot grill. Serve with vegetables tossed in melted butter.

Sole véronique
Pressure-cooking time: 4 minutes

1 medium sole, filleted	3 dl ($\frac{1}{2}$ pt) water for the cooker
salt and pepper	*for thickening:*
a little lemon juice	1 small tablespoon butter
knobs of butter	1 level tablespoon flour
8 white grapes	1 tablespoon cream (optional)
50 g (2 oz) button mushrooms	*to garnish:*
1·5 dl ($\frac{1}{4}$ pt) milk	sprigs of parsley
	a little paprika

Skin the fillets, sprinkle with salt, pepper and lemon juice on the skinned side, put a little knob of butter on each and roll up. Put the fish with the skinned and pipped grapes and mushrooms into an ovenproof dish that will fit in the cooker and add the milk. Put the water and the trivet in the cooker, then the dish covered with a piece of greaseproof paper, bring to pressure, cook for 4 minutes and reduce the pressure with cold water. During this cooking, melt the butter in a small saucepan, add the flour and allow to cook for a minute or two without colouring. Lift out the dish, strain off the milk and add to the saucepan, stirring until the sauce thickens. Taste and correct seasoning and add cream. Reheat but do not allow to boil again.

Two fillets will probably be enough for one invalid meal, so lift these on to a small serving dish, garnish with the grapes and mushrooms and pour over a little of the sauce, garnishing with sprigs of parsley and a line of paprika.

For another meal, the other two fillets, when cold, can be flaked, stirred into the remainder of the sauce, piled into a scallop shell or individual heatproof dish, sprinkled with grated cheese and dabs of butter and then grilled until golden-brown. One or two slices of skinned tomatoes could garnish the top to add colour.

COMPLETE MEAL To cook **Sole Véronique** as part of a complete meal, put the dish directly into the water in the bottom of the cooker with the trivet on top; on this put potatoes, a perforated separator with some green vegetables, such as peas, beans, broccoli or asparagus, fresh or frozen, and then a cup of fruit and one or two cups of custard (for preparation, see **Infant Feeding**).

Cook extra potatoes to mash and pipe around the **Fish Scallop**, prepared as already described, for another meal.

Timbales of fish
Pressure-cooking time: 5 minutes

This is another way to serve the sole fillets from the preceding recipe; alternatively a little cooked plaice, turbot or halibut from a family meal could be used instead.

1 large egg	3 dl ($\frac{1}{2}$ pt) water with a little lemon
salt and pepper	juice or vinegar for the cooker
1·5 dl ($\frac{1}{4}$ pt) milk	accompanying vegetables to
a little anchovy essence (optional)	choice
a little cooked fish	1 tablespoon mayonnaise* or
	tartare sauce*

Grease two cups well with butter. Beat the egg with the seasoning, heat the milk, add the anchovy essence if used and pour over the beaten eggs. Flake the fish and divide into the cups; pour the custard over and stir gently. Put the water and trivet in the cooker, then the cups of fish covered with greaseproof paper, and the accompanying vegetables. Bring to pressure, cook for 5 minutes and reduce the pressure with cold water. Turn the timbale into the centre of an individual dish, surround with the vegetables; quickly heat the sauce without boiling, pour over the timbale and serve at once.

Lamb cutlet with tomato
Pressure-cooking time: 6 minutes

Season the cutlet well with salt and pepper, put in a deep saucer with a little butter and a slice of tomato on top. Cover with greaseproof paper and continue as for **Sole Véronique**, giving 6 minutes' pressure-cooking time. Take off the bone, mince the meat and tomato, moisten with a little of the stock and serve with accompanying vegetables, cooked at the same time, or piled on a buttered round of toast. A little meat extract may be added to the stock for extra flavour before mixing with the minced meat if it is to be served with vegetables, or may be spread lightly on the toast after buttering.

10 Infant and child feeding

Nowadays there are many ready-made baby foods in great variety, easily obtainable and with the assurance of adequate food value, but they do tend to be rather expensive, especially as quite a selection has to be bought to vary the diet. With your pressure cooker you can do all that is necessary with the minimum effort in work and time and with considerable economy.

Make the most of it from the very first day; you will find instructions to sterilize the baby's bottles, teats and feeds in the following section; when your baby needs his food sieved or puréed you can cook a selection of different vegetables each day with a little chicken, liver or fish, and prunes or other fruits so that he becomes accustomed to a wide range of flavours, making it easier to join in family meals later on. When this stage is reached the pressure-cooked food will be so tender and full of flavour that the child will easily become accustomed to it and you will know that it is full of nutrients.

Food for small children should be plain, with much less salt than for adults, and it is generally helpful for purées, pulps and dicing to cook the food just a minute or so longer than the times given in the

rest of the book. Because pressure cooking is so quick and therefore less harmful to the nutrients in the food, there is no reason
why suitable foods such as meat, fish, fruit and puddings set aside
from a previous meal should not be kept, well covered, at the
bottom of the refrigerator and be brought up to pressure only to
reheat them through for the baby's meal next day. This does not
apply to vegetables; these are such a necessary source of vitamins
and other food essentials in a baby's diet and should be cooked
fresh each time – only a matter of minutes in the pressure cooker.

The great standby for this sort of feeding is ordinary teacups or
individual boilable bowls. Several composite meals for Baby using
these are set out, but these are only a very few of the many choices
and combinations which you will soon discover for yourself.

Nowadays, most mothers do not find it necessary to sterilize
feeding bottles and baby foods, as there are so many suitable and
safe disinfectants available and recommended, but should this need
to be done the following instructions have been tested and approved
as giving complete safety. The feeding bottles and teats can be
sterilized on their own or already filled with the correct amount
for each feed. This can be made up from any type of milk or milk
powder which will be completely sterilized in a matter of minutes,
with no more loss of vitamins or nutritional content than the
longer process by ordinary heating. This sterilization must be done
in a cooker fitted with M pressure to give an internal temperature
of 115°C (240°F); all the feeds for 24 hours can be done at the one
time. Just follow this simple procedure:

Wash the bottles and teats thoroughly. If sterilizing the feeds as
well, make these up according to the instructions and fill into the
bottles. Put the teats into a cup or small bowl and cover lightly
with a double piece of greaseproof paper.

Have ready in the pressure cooker 3 dl ($\frac{1}{2}$ pt) water with a little
lemon juice or vinegar and the trivet. Put in the bottles and cover
across the top with a double thickness of greaseproof paper. Put
the covered cup or bowl in the centre.

Bring to M pressure, maintain this carefully for 5 minutes and
allow the pressure to reduce at room temperature, being very careful when moving the cooker from the heat not to knock or jog it in
any way.

Lift out the bottles, covering again quickly with the paper and a piece of muslin or a clean tea-towel to prevent any germs or dust from entering.

It is best to have a small round tray or dish on to which to lift out the bottles so that they can all be covered over at once and lifted into the refrigerator when cool or stood on one side in a cool place, without uncovering them.

Of course, if the bottles are provided with their own caps, these should be used and not be removed until required to be filled or to have the teat fitted. Leave the bowl of teats covered when lifted from the cooker.

It is not recommended to sterilize bottles containing feeds with the teats in position as if the liquid boils up this may block them.

When a feed is due take out one of the bottles and fit the teat, taking care to replace the coverings at once. Stand the bottle in a jug of hot water until the required temperature is reached and shake the bottle well before using.

Meat and vegetable broth
Pressure-cooking time: 10 minutes

6 dl (1 pt) water
100 g (4 oz) finely minced beef
a little salt

a selection of vegetables such as carrot, potato, turnip, peas, beans etc: 1 tablespoon of each, cut up finely

Lift the trivet from the cooker, put in the water, meat and salt, bring to pressure, cook for 7 minutes, reduce the pressure with cold water. Strain off the meat, put back the stock and vegetables, bring to pressure again and cook for the last 3 minutes. Pass the vegetables through a sieve, return to the stock, stir well and warm just before feeding.

The mince can be used for an older child, stirred into gravy and served with fresh-cooked vegetables; can be added to stuffing for a marrow or, with the addition of a little tomato sauce, would be an excellent supper dish for one, on toast or with fried croûtons.

Puréed vegetables
Pressure cook as above but with 1·5 dl (¼ pt) water or thin gravy, and use a little of the liquid to moisten the vegetables after they have been sieved.

Complete meal: 1

Fish with tomatoes and vegetables;
Stewed apple and egg custard
Pressure-cooking time: 3 minutes

a small fillet of sole or plaice
a slice of tomato
1 teaspoon milk
small knob of butter
salt
1 apple, peeled, cored and sliced
sugar

1 egg
¾ cup milk
1·5 dl (¼ pt) water for the cooker
thin slices of potato, carrot,
    cabbage, and beans or peas, as
    available

Butter a saucer, put in the folded fillet with the slice of tomato, milk, butter and a pinch of salt. In a cup put the apple, without water but with a little sugar; in another buttered cup, beat the egg with a little sugar and add the heated milk. Put into the cooker 1·5 dl (¼ pt) water and the trivet. On this put the saucer with the fish, the cups of apple and custard covered with a piece of grease-proof paper, and the vegetables with a pinch of salt. Bring to pressure, cook for 3 minutes and allow the pressure to reduce at room temperature. Lift out the fish and mash with a fork into the juice. Serve with the vegetables, mashed or put through a sieve. Serve half the custard and the apple, mashed or sieved, keeping the rest for the next day.

Complete meal: 2

Diced chicken with vegetables; rice custard
Pressure-cooking time: 4 minutes

Prepare this when you have a tablespoon of cooked rice left over from another dish.

a small piece of chicken breast
  brushed with butter
1 tablespoon milk, or white sauce*
  if available
selection of vegetables including
  pieces of potato or carrot
  and sprouts

¾ cup milk
1 egg and a little sugar
1 tablespoon cooked rice
1 dessertspoon seedless raisins
  (optional)
3 dl (½ pt) water for the cooker

Put the chicken brushed with butter on a saucer and add a spoon-ful of milk or white sauce if any is available. Prepare the vegetables. Heat the milk and pour slowly on to the beaten egg and sugar. Stir in the rice and if the child is old enough, a few seedless raisins can be added. Divide this into 2 buttered cups. Put the water and the trivet in the cooker, then the saucer of chicken, the vegetables and the 2 cups covered with a piece of greaseproof paper. Bring to pressure, cook for 4 minutes and allow the pressure to reduce at room temperature. Cut the chicken finely, mix with the mashed or sieved vegetables and moisten with the liquid from the saucer. Serve one cup of rice custard, saving the other for another day.

Complete meal: 3

Liver in gravy with vegetables; chocolate cream
Pressure-cooking time: 3 minutes

a small piece of calf's liver
a little gravy
2 slices tomato
a selection of vegetables including
  thin slices of potato and carrot,
  a floweret of cauliflower or
  green vegetable

4–6 squares plain or milk
  chocolate
¾ cup milk
1 egg
a little sugar
3 dl (½ pt) water for the cooker

Chop the liver finely and put in a cup with the gravy and tomatoes. Prepare the vegetables. Put the broken-up chocolate into a small saucepan, add a drop of milk, stir over a low heat until melted, add the rest of the milk and heat, pour over the beaten egg and sugar and put into 2 buttered cups. Put the water and the trivet in the cooker, then the cups of liver and chocolate cream covered with a piece of greaseproof paper, and the vegetables with a pinch of salt.

Bring to pressure, cook for 3 minutes and allow the pressure to reduce at room temperature. Mash the vegetables in with the liver. Use one of the custards and put the other away for another day.

Complete meal: 4

Egg and spinach with mashed potato; stewed apricots
Pressure-cooking time: 3 minutes

5–6 dried apricots with sugar for sweetening
1 tablespoon creamed spinach (or other puréed green vegetable)
1 egg
pinch of salt

a little cheese (optional)
2 small potatoes
knob of butter
1 tablespoon milk
3 dl ($\frac{1}{2}$ pt) water for the cooker

Soak the apricots in 1·5 dl ($\frac{1}{4}$ pt) boiling water for at least half an hour before required. Butter a cup, put in the spinach, break the egg on top, put in a pinch of salt and grated cheese, if liked. Cut the apricots up into very small pieces, put into 2 cups with sufficient of the soaking water to cover and add sugar to sweeten. Peel the potatoes, slice very finely and put on a saucer with a knob of butter and a spoonful of milk. Put the water and trivet in the cooker, then the cups and saucer covered with a piece of greaseproof paper. Bring to pressure, cook for 3 minutes and reduce the pressure with cold water. Mash the potatoes with the liquid. Turn out the egg and mash into the potatoes.

Feed the apricots as they are, mashed or puréed with a little top of the milk or thinned cream.

11 Preservation
of fruit and vegetables

This is a section that perhaps you will consider wasted on you, feeling that you would never have time to make your own marmalade, jam or chutney, or that living in a town it would not be economical to bottle fruit. But with pressure cooking you will find it is so easy and quick to make a batch of marmalade, to do a couple of bottles of strawberries or pears, that the small amount of trouble involved is well worth while. Even in these days of high-quality shop produce there is a certain glow of pride in home preserving.

With modern pressure cookers, it is not of course possible to make preserves or do bottling on the grand scale; if you live in a town a simple system is to start in the spring and obtain small quantities of fruit just when it is at its best and cheapest in the shops, when you are in the country or from friends with gardens. When you think of all the fruits which follow on one after the other, you will realize that even using just 900 g (2 lb) at a time with your pressure cooker, by the season's end you could have

Fruit	Season	Type of preserve
Seville or bitter oranges	January, February, March	Thick or jelly marmalade
Gooseberries	April–May	Jam, jelly, chutney, bottled, canned
Rhubarb	April–June	Bottled, canned
(forced garden)	May onwards	Jam, chutney, sauce, bottled, canned
Limes	May–June	Jelly marmalade
Apricots (imported)	May–July	Rather expensive but make excellent jam; bottled, canned
Apricots (dried)	All the year round	Jam
Cherries	June onwards	Most varieties not suitable for jam; some varieties good for bottling and canning but others tend to lose colour
Currants (black)	June and onwards	Jam, jelly, bottled, canned, syrup
Currants (red)	June and onwards	Jam, jelly, bottled, canned
Raspberries	June onwards	Jam, but not using a pressure cooker; bottled, canned
Strawberries	June onwards	Jam, but not using a pressure cooker; bottled, canned
Loganberries	June onwards	Jam, jelly, bottled, canned
Peaches (imported)	June onwards	Expensive and not too satisfactory for jam; bottled and canned if special varieties are used, others do not keep a good colour; chutney
Mulberries	July and August	Jam and jelly
Greengages	July–September	Not easily set for jam; tend to cloud when bottled or canned
Plums	August onwards	Jam, chutney, bottled and canned
Tomatoes (ripe)	August onwards	Jam, chutney, sauce, juice, bottled, canned
Tomatoes (green)	August onwards	Chutney
Pears (home-grown)	August onwards	Chutney, bottled, canned
Damsons	September and October	Jam, jelly, cheese, bottled, canned
Blackberries (cultivated)	August and September	Jam alone or with apple; jelly, bottled, canned
Blackberries (wild)	September and October	Jam with apple; jelly
Crab apples	September and October	Jelly
Whortle- and elderberries	September and October	Jam with apple or blackberries
Tangerines	November onwards	Jelly marmalade
Grapefruit	All the year round	Marmalade
Lemons	All the year round	Thick and jelly marmalade
Oranges (sweet)	All the year round	Marmalade with lemons and grapefruit

Fruit	Season	Type of preserve
Apples (cooking)	All the year round	Jam, jelly, cheese and butters, chutney; jelly for adding to other jams; bottled and canned as pulp, purée or in quarters

13·50 kg (30 lb) or so of marmalade and jam made and prepared, just while you are about the ordinary daily cooking and work.

Whether you have a small or a large garden, you are still sure to find your pressure cooker invaluable for preservation. Fruit and vegetables retain their colour, flavour and vitamin content at the highest level if they can be preserved as soon as possible after picking: it is therefore very convenient to have available a means of preserving small quantities just as they are ripe and ready, perhaps doing this daily in the season, rather than keeping them until you have enough for one big, all-out effort – by which time some may have passed their best.

No elaborate equipment or years of experience is necessary to be successful; just an understanding of the principles, careful following of the instructions – and a little bit of luck – and you will be surprised when you see and taste the results.

In the following sections this principle of through-the-year preserving has been followed.

Among the different methods of preserving fruit are the following:

Jams: With fresh or dried fruits.
Jellies: With fresh fruits cooked to a pulp and strained through a jelly bag, the juice being used alone or with thin shreds of peel in marmalades.
Cheeses and butters: With fresh, acid fruits, sieved to a pulp. As they require a large amount of fruit in proportion to the end product they are usually made only by those who have plenty of fruit available or when there is a glut. They are usually served as an accompaniment with meats.
Marmalades: Using citrus fruits, either thick or jelly types.
Pickles and chutneys: Using certain firm and sound fruits, but as these need not be necessarily of good quality it is a useful method for keeping rough or windfall fruit.

Sauces: Using ripe tomatoes with spices, etc.
Bottling: Almost every fruit can be satisfactorily preserved in this way.
Deep-freezing: This is dealt with in a separate section, p 253.

Jams, jellies and marmalades

The most important point to remember is that these preserves are meant to keep and, if they are to remain in good condition during storage, care must be taken in the choosing of the fruit and in making sure that the essential ingredients – sugar to preserve, acid to improve the colour and flavour and help prevent crystallization of the sugar, and pectin to obtain a set – are present in the correct proportions. A good recipe should have decided all this for you, but it is as well to know something about the principles involved so that every stage of the process is understood.

First, about the pressure cooker itself: made of aluminium, it is perfectly suitable for jam and marmalade making and indeed tests have shown that preserves cooked in this material, or in stainless steel, keep a higher proportion of their vitamin C content.

The pressure cooker's role is to soften the fruit in the required amount of water before the sugar is added. Once the sugar has been put in, the preserve has to be allowed to boil in an open pan – that is, in the pressure cooker without the cover – so that it can thicken and the setting point can be tested.

The recommended pressure for the precooking of fruit for jams and marmalades is M. While a fixed H pressure can be used for marmalades (as these contain a high proportion of acid and pectin and it is therefore easy to obtain a good set), it is rather too high a pressure and temperature for the softer fruits and its use may result in a lower yield and a slight loss in colour and flavour. If your model of pressure cooker has only a fixed weight you may find that on application to the manufacturer a variable set of weights can be supplied at a reasonable cost.

The pressure cooker should not be more than two-thirds full when the sugar has been added and is dissolved. At this point the preserve should be boiled as fast as possible and if enough room is not left in the pan to do this the jam will either boil over or will have to boil slowly, which will darken it in colour and probably spoil its flavour. For this reason, the recipes are for 900 g or 1·35 kg (2 or 3 lb) of fruit only at a time; if a large saucepan is available it is quite a good idea when making jam or marmalade to pressure cook several lots one after the other, adding each into the big pan and then adding all the sugar, as this will still save a considerable amount of time and fuel.

The fruit chosen should be of good quality, as fresh as possible, under- rather than over-ripe, and without any sort of blemish. All fruits except the very soft varieties should be cooked first to soften the skins and break down the cell walls to extract the pectin before the sugar is added. In the pressure cooker most fruits require no more than a few minutes to be reduced to a pulp and, because there is little loss by evaporation, only a minimum of water need be added. This keeps the fruit and juice concentrated so that a shorter boiling time is necessary after the addition of the sugar, leading to a jam with the best possible colour and flavour. Fruits which do not require presoftening such as strawberries and raspberries are therefore not included among these recipes. A certain amount of water must be added with the fruit and the quantity given in these recipes is correct for pressure cooking and is approximately one-third of the amount given for normal cooking.

The **acid** necessary is present in many of the fruits from which preserves are made, but if there is none or too little, then more must be added; the easiest to use and most readily available is lemon juice. While there can be no hard-and-fast rule about how much is needed, an average amount would be 1 tablespoon to each 900 g (2 lb) of fruit. Not only does the acid content vary according to the fruit itself, but it can also be affected by the ripeness of the fruit and how dry it is, so the condition of the fruit is very important. Fruits with little acid are late blackberries (which is why apples are usually added to this jam or jelly) and pears and cherries, from which a satisfactory jam cannot really be made, as the addition of lemon or apple juice overrides their own flavours. When additional acid is required in jam it is added for the softening process.

Pectin is a natural setting property found in the cell walls of fruits and released when fruit is cooked. Like acid, it is present in varying quantities and quality and, if a fruit is very deficient in it, there is no point in trying to make it into jam unless one is prepared to add a commercial pectin or it is possible to use the juice of apples, lemons or redcurrants without spoiling the original flavour. Fruits deficient in pectin are usually those also lacking acid, such as blackberries, cherries and pears; neither rhubarb, though acid, nor marrow will set without the addition of lemon juice, for example.

Sugar is added to preserves to ensure their keeping qualities. Preserving sugar is the most easily dissolved and so it is the easiest to use when available, but lump or granulated sugar will do equally well and will make no difference to the jam in storage. It is a help if the sugar is warmed first before being added to the jam as it will dissolve more quickly and cool the jam down less, so that boiling point is more quickly reached. The jam must be stirred over a low heat until the sugar is dissolved, then brought to the boil as quickly as possible and boiled rapidly until setting point is reached without further stirring. Again, there is no hard-and-fast rule about how much sugar should be added but an average is 450 g (1 lb) to each 450 g (1 lb) of fruit or fruit juice; however, if a fruit is known to be rich in pectin, for example blackcurrants, 550 g ($1\frac{1}{4}$ lb) can be added for each 450 g (1 lb) of fruit. There is no need to skim the jam during cooking; if necessary scum can be removed after setting point is reached.

Setting point, providing that the fruit has been well softened before the addition of the sugar, should be between 5 and 10 minutes but seldom longer than 20; prolonged boiling when the jam shows no sign of setting after this time will not necessarily produce a set. The easiest way to test for a set is to dip a wooden spoon in the jam, lift it out and twist it for a moment or two to allow the jam to cool. Hold the spoon edge down so that jam runs off; if it is ready, the last drop left on the spoon will stay as a blob of jelly hanging from the edge. Lift the pan from the heat immediately and skim if necessary, using a skimmer or perforated spoon dipped in hot water and wiped just before use.

Finishing the jam is also very important. It should be poured, or filled with a ladle, into clean, dry, warm jars; if it contains whole fruit, it must be left until a skin forms to show that the jelly is thickening slightly, otherwise the fruit will rise to the top of the jars, giving a very uneven jam. Because preserves shrink as they cool, each jar must be filled literally to overflowing; a waxed circle must be gently pressed on to cover the whole surface and the rim of the jar wiped with a clean cloth dipped each time in hot water. The final cellophane circle should be put on immediately each jar has been filled or else left off until the jam is quite cold, during which time the jars should be covered with a piece of greaseproof paper just laid over the tops. If preserves are covered when only warm, moulds may grow in the warm pocket of air between the waxed circle and the top cover.

A simple method of testing whether your jam making has been successful is to work out an easy sum based on the amount of sugar used and the amount of jam resulting. This can be done as soon as you know how much sugar you are going to use so that you have some idea of what quantity of jam you are aiming for; a little experience of using your cooker as a preserving pan will enable you to judge whether you have about the right amount. What you have to remember is that an average yield is $\frac{5}{3}$ of the amount of sugar: i.e. if you are adding 3 units of sugar, your sum will be $\frac{5}{3} \times 3 = 5$. If you have much more than this, then the jam will be too runny, and if much less, then the jam will probably be much too thick. It is not always worth while to try and correct either of these; you will know better next time.

Storage of the jam should be in a dry place to prevent moulds growing, in a cool place to prevent fermentation and shrinkage and in a dark place to preserve the colour. Label the jam with its contents and the date and be sure that you keep your preserves on the move, putting the latest made to the back and bringing the earliest forward so that they are used while still at their best.

TO SUMMARIZE THE PROCESS OF JAM MAKING The fruit chosen should be firm, sound, without blemish and as dry as possible.

Acid, pectin and sugar should be present in the correct proportions and this has been worked out as accurately as possible in the following recipes.

All fruit, except the very soft varieties such as strawberries and raspberries, should be precooked to soften the skins and break down the cell walls to release the pectin. This is the pressure cooker's job.

The sugar should be added, warm if possible, to the boiling fruit and stirred over a low heat until dissolved, when the jam must be allowed to boil as rapidly as possible until setting point is reached.

For this reason, the pressure cooker here is used as an open pan and must not be more than two-thirds full.

The jam should not be skimmed during boiling; do this, if necessary, just before potting the jam.

Setting point is when the last drop on a wooden spoon, held edgeways, does not drop off but stays as a blob of jelly.

The jam should be potted immediately into clean, dry, warm jars unless it contains whole fruit or peel, when it should be left until a thin skin forms.

Each jar should be filled to the very top and covered immediately with a waxed disc.

The final covering should be put on immediately or left until the jam is quite cold.

Jars should be stored in an airy, cool, dry and dark space.

FAULTS WHICH MAY OCCUR

Overboiling, which can cause a sticky jam, dark in colour and with a burnt flavour.

Underboiling, when the preserve will be runny even when cold.

Insufficient pectin or acid or too high a proportion of sugar to fruit, when the preserve does not set and there is no sign of a jell.

Fermentation giving a fizzy taste because too little sugar has been used.

Mould because the jar was not filled right to the top and has been stored in a warm damp place. This will not be harmful as long as every little bit is carefully lifted away before the jam is used.

Crystallization, due to insufficient acid (if the crystals are like rice grains) or too much acid (if it is a solid mass). To get rid of it, just take off the cover and stand the jar in a gently boiling saucepan of water, then allow the jam to set again and use at once.

Shrinkage caused by being kept in too warm a place or too long.

Cloudiness because the scum has been stirred in during the cooking or not removed entirely after cooking.

Fruit rising in the jars because the preserve has not been allowed to cool a little before potting or was put in when the jars were too hot.

M pressure is recommended for jams. The trivet is not used. The pressure is allowed to reduce at room temperature.

Gooseberry jam
Pressure-cooking time: 3 minutes

900 g (2 lb) gooseberries, still green
3 dl (½ pt) water
1·1 kg (2½ lb) sugar

Top, tail and wash gooseberries. Put the water and fruit in the cooker and continue as given in the instructions. The colour of the finished jam will depend on the type and ripeness of the fruit; the longer the boiling, the pinker the jam will be.

Yield: approx. 2 kg (4½ lb).

Rhubarb jam with ginger
Pressure-cooking time: to pressure only

1·1 kg (2½ lb) rhubarb
50 g (2 oz) root ginger or 100 g (4 oz) preserved ginger
juice and rind of 2 lemons
900 g (2 lb) sugar

Wash the rhubarb, cut into 5-cm (2-in) lengths, run cold water over and put into cooker without allowing to drain; add the finely chopped peel and juice of the lemons. Bring to the boil, press down well with a potato masher. Bring to pressure only, add the bruised root ginger loosely tied in a piece of muslin, or the preserved ginger cut into dice, and the sugar. Before potting, lift out the muslin bag.

Yield: approx. 1·5 kg (3½ lb).

Fresh apricot jam
Pressure-cooking time: 4 minutes

900 g (2 lb) apricots, weighed when stoned
3 dl (½ pt) water
900 g (2 lb) sugar

Wash the fruit, halve, and remove the stones. If liked, some of these can be cracked, the kernels blanched by dipping in boiling water and then halved. Put the water, fruit and kernels in the cooker and continue as given in the instructions.

Yield: approx. 1·5 kg (3½ lb).

Fresh peach jam
Pressure-cooking time: 4 minutes

1·35 kg (3 lb) peaches, weighed when stoned
3 dl (½ pt) water
strained juice of 2 lemons
1·35 kg (3 lb) sugar

Prepare and cook as for **Fresh Apricot Jam**, adding the lemon juice to the cooker with the water and fruit.

Yield: approx. 2·25 kg (5 lb).

Dried apricot jam at H pressure
Pressure-cooking time: 10 minutes

450 g (1 lb) dried apricots
1·2 litres (2 pt) boiling water
juice of 1 large lemon

1·35 kg (3 lb) sugar
50–75 g (2–3 oz) blanched, shredded almonds (optional)

Cut the apricots into small pieces and put in the cooker, pour over the boiling water and leave, covered, for about 1 hour. Bring to pressure, cook for 10 minutes and allow the pressure to reduce at room temperature. Add the lemon juice, almonds if used and the warmed sugar and continue as given in the instructions. This will be a thick jam, more of a purée than a jelly and is excellent for cooking with steamed puddings, serving with rice puddings, as a filling for tartlets and flans or as a sauce over ice-cream.

Yield: approx. 2·25 kg (5 lb).

Blackcurrant jam
Pressure-cooking time: 3–4 minutes

900 g (2 lb) blackcurrants
6 dl (1 pt) water
1·35 kg (3 lb) sugar

String the fruit and wash well. Put the water and fruit in the cooker and continue as given in the instructions.

Yield: approx. 2·25 kg (5 lb).

Loganberry jam

Pressure-cooking time: to pressure only

1·35 kg (3 lb) loganberries
1·35 kg (3 lb) sugar

Pick over the fruit, put in a colander and run cold water over. Put straight into the cooker without allowing to drain. Bring to the boil and press down well with a potato masher. Bring to pressure only and continue as given in the instructions.

Yield: approx. 2·25 kg (5 lb).

Plum jam

Pressure-cooking time: 5 minutes

900 g (2 lb) plums, weighed when stoned
1·5 dl ($\frac{1}{4}$ pt) water
900 g (2 lb) sugar

Wash and stone the fruit, holding the fruit over the cooker so that no juice is lost. (If a lot of the fruit is left on the stones, tie these loosely in a piece of muslin and cook them with the fruit but add a little more water as some will be taken up by the cloth. Squeeze the bag well by pressing it against the side of the cooker before lifting it out.) Continue as given in the instructions. If the plums are of a sweet variety, 1 tablespoon lemon juice should be added before the cooking to help to obtain a good set.

Yield: approx. 1·5 kg ($3\frac{1}{2}$ lb).

Damson jam

Pressure-cooking time: 5 minutes

1 kg ($2\frac{1}{4}$ lb) damsons
1·5 dl ($\frac{1}{4}$ pt) water
1·35 kg (3 lb) sugar

Wash the fruit. Put the water and the fruit in the cooker and continue as given in the instructions. Remove as many of the stones as possible during the cooking, straining back any jam that may be taken out as well; a small piece of butter put on the surface after setting point has been reached and before potting will help to bring the last ones to the top.

Yield: approx. 2·25 kg (5 lb).

Blackberry and apple
Pressure-cooking time: 7 minutes

900 g (2 lb) blackberries
325 g (12 oz) green cooking apples, weighed when peeled and cored
1·5 dl (¼ pt) water
1·35 kg (3 lb) sugar

Pick over blackberries, wash and drain. Remove peel and cores of apples and put these in a muslin bag. Put the blackberries, cut-up apples and water in the cooker and continue as given in the instructions. Lift out the muslin bag and squeeze well before adding sugar.

Yield: approx. 2·25 kg (5 lb).

If **Blackberry Jam** is preferred on its own, then use 900 g (2 lb) fruit, 900 g (2 lb) sugar, 1·5 dl (¼ pt) of water and 2 tablespoons lemon juice (adding this for the pressure cooking). Continue as given in the instructions.

If the **Blackberry Jam** is preferred seedless, then sufficient blackberries must be pressure cooked to give at least 900 g (2 lb) pulp when sieved. Using the strained juice, pressure cook the apples as for **Blackberry and Apple**, on their own. Weigh the combined pulps and use an equal weight of sugar. Continue as given in the instructions.

Apple ginger
Pressure-cooking time: 5 minutes

1·35 kg (3 lb) apples   ground ginger
4·5 dl (¾ pt) water   sugar
rind and juice of 1 large lemon

Wash the apples, cut in quarters, put into cooker with the water and the rind and juice of lemon, bring to pressure in the usual way, cook for 5 minutes and allow the pressure to reduce at room temperature. Sieve the pulp, measure, add 1 level teaspoon ground

ginger and 450 g (1 lb) sugar to each 6 dl (1 pt) sieved apple, bring
to the boil and continue as given in the instructions.
Yield: approx. 1·8 kg (4 lb).

Marrow and ginger jam
Pressure-cooking time: 2 minutes

900 g (2 lb) marrow, weighed after preparation	25 g (1 oz) root ginger
	900 g (2 lb) sugar
rind and juice of 2 lemons	

Peel the marrow, remove seeds and cut the pulp into 2-cm (1-in)
squares. Tie the brushed ginger and lemon rinds loosely in a piece
of muslin. Put the lemon juice and marrow into the cooker, heat
gently until enough liquid is extracted from the marrow to just
cover the bottom of the cooker, put in the muslin bag and pressure
cook for 2 minutes. Allow the pressure to reduce at room temperature, add the sugar, stir and leave in a covered bowl for 24 hours.
Lift out the bag and squeeze well; continue as given in the instructions. This jam may require up to 30 minutes' boiling, when the
marrow should be transparent and the syrup have thickened. It
will not set as most jams do.
Yield: approx. 1·35 kg (3 lb).

Jellies

The principles and instructions given for jams apply equally to
jelly making, but the fruit chosen must be plentiful, as only the
juice is used; it must be rich in pectin and acid or else must be
combined with another which has these properties, and should
have a distinctive flavour. Such fruits as cherries, pears, strawberries would not therefore be suitable as so much pectin and acid
would have to be added that they would lose their own flavour.
  Fruit for jelly making should be washed and carefully looked
over but does not require peeling, stalking and so on, as the juice
will be strained. This makes it a quick and easy process, particularly with gooseberries and currants, and is excellent for windfall
fruits, though apples usually need another fruit with them as they
tend to be insipid; this, however, makes them a good source of

acid and pectin for setting other fruits which may be slightly deficient by themselves.

When making jelly it is essential that the fruit be completely broken down to release the acid and pectin into the water and your pressure cooker is just the thing for this. After pressure has been reduced, mash the fruit up well until it is a complete pulp before putting it into a jelly bag.

This is an essential piece of equipment for jelly making; you may be able to buy one made of felt or flannel; if not you could make one yourself, using a smooth but thick tea-towel and sewing tapes at each corner. An upturned chair or stool with the tapes tied to the legs and a large bowl into which the juice can drain will then be quite satisfactory. The jelly bag must have a kettle of boiling water poured through it just before the pulp is put in.

It is not possible to give the exact proportions of fruit, water or sugar for jelly making; with a pressure cooker the fruit should not more than half fill the base, the water should be 3–6 dl ($\frac{1}{2}$–1 pt), depending on the type of fruit, and the sugar measured according to the amount of strained juice obtained.

With fruits very rich in pectin, such as blackcurrants and apples, a second extract of juice may be made by returning the fruit to the cooker after the first straining, adding half the amount of water originally used, giving the same pressure cooking time, and adding the second extract to the first.

The pulp should be allowed to drain for about 1 hour, and the bag must never be squeezed, otherwise the jelly will be cloudy.

The warmed sugar is added and dissolved, as for jam, and then the jelly must boil rapidly until setting point is reached. At this moment (which may be as little as 1 minute for redcurrant jelly and certainly no more than 10 minutes after a jelly first begins to boil), quick action is necessary, otherwise the jelly will start to set in the pan and its appearance in the jars will be spoiled. All scum should be quickly removed, with a spoon dipped in boiling water if there is a lot, or with pieces of kitchen paper torn with ragged edges and drawn along the surface if there is only a little.

The jelly should then be poured into the warmed jars at once and quickly covered with a wax disc. Small containers are the best as jelly is better eaten as soon as possible after it is opened.

TO SUMMARIZE THE PROCESS OF JELLY MAKING

The fruit should be ripe, well picked over and washed, but does not need any other preparation.

It should be thoroughly cooked and well broken down before being strained.

The pulp should be allowed to drain for about an hour, the jelly bag should not be squeezed and the jelly should be finished off the same day.

A second extract may be made from those fruits known to be rich in pectin and acid.

The warmed sugar should be added to the strained juice when it is at boiling point, except for pale extracts such as apple and gooseberry when the longer cooking while the sugar dissolves tends to give a deeper colour.

After setting point has been reached, the scum should be quickly removed and the jelly poured into small containers as quickly as possible.

The jars should not be moved until the jelly has set.

FAULTS WHICH MAY OCCUR

Air bubbles in the jar because the jelly has been stirred during boiling or not poured into the jars quickly enough.

Cloudy jelly because the texture of the jelly bag was not fine enough or the bag was squeezed.

Weepy jelly because there was too much acid in the fruit.

Only a few samples of jellies are given here because there are so many that can be made from fruits on their own or combined with others that it is rather fun to try out your own 'mixtures', depending on the fruit available; in fact, as long as a good jelling-juice is obtained there is no limit to the varieties that can be made. No yield is given as this will depend on the amount of juice obtained, but it should still be $\frac{5}{3}$, approximately, of the amount of sugar added.

Blackcurrant jelly
Pressure-cooking time: 5 minutes

about 1·35 kg (3 lb) blackcurrants
1·2 litres (2 pt) water
sugar in the proportion of 450 g (1 lb) to each 6 dl (1 pt) strained juice

Be sure to mash the fruit well before straining.

Crab apple jelly
Pressure-cooking time: 8 minutes

about 1·35 kg (3 lb) crab apples
water
sugar in the proportion of 450 g (1 lb) to each 6 dl (1 pt) strained juice

Cut the apples across; when they are in the cooker add sufficient water just to show through the top layer.

Gooseberry jelly
Pressure-cooking time: 5 minutes

1·35 kg (3 lb) gooseberries
6 dl (1 pt) water
sugar in the proportion of 450 g (1 lb) to each 6 dl (1 pt) strained juice

A delicious combination is **Gooseberry and Strawberry,** replacing 450 g (1 lb) gooseberries with 450 g (1 lb) strawberries.

Gooseberry mint jelly
Pressure-cooking time: 5 minutes

As gooseberries are in season when mint is at its youngest and best, you may find you prefer this jelly to the more usual one made with apples, available when the mint is getting towards the end of its season's growth.

900 g (2 lb) gooseberries
1·5 dl (¼ pt) water
sugar in the proportion of 450 g (1 lb) to each 6 dl (1 pt) strained juice

bunch of fresh mint
chopped mint
a little green colouring

Make the strained gooseberry juice following the instructions (p 230), return to the cooker, add sugar and when dissolved and the jelly is boiling again put in a good bunch of bruised mint tied loosely together with string. After 5 minutes or so, or when the jelly looks nearly ready to set, lift out the mint and continue boiling until setting point is reached. Allow to stand until a thin skin forms, then gently stir in the finely chopped mint and the colouring. Pour into small containers and cover as usual.

Redcurrant jelly

Pressure-cooking time: 1 minute

about 1·35 kg (3 lb) redcurrants
water just to show through the top layer
sugar in the proportion of 550 g (1¼ lb) to each 6 dl (1 pt) of strained
  juice

Be sure to mash the fruit well before straining. After adding the sugar, no more than 1 to 2 minutes' quick boiling, stirring all the time, will be necessary to reach setting point and then it must be potted immediately. A second extract can certainly be made from the same fruit.

A proportion of raspberries will make a delicious **Raspberry and Redcurrant Jelly.**

Apple jelly

Pressure-cooking time: 5 minutes

about 1·35 kg (3 lb) apples of a good flavour
6 dl (1 pt) water
sugar in the proportion of 450 g (1 lb) to each 6 dl (1 pt) of strained
  juice

If to be on its own, flavourings such as lemon peel, ginger or cloves may be added for the pressure cooking.

Variations of **Apple Jelly** can be made with equal quantities of **Mulberries, Elderberries, Whortleberries, Cranberries** and so on.

If a fruit juice (apple, gooseberry or redcurrant) is required for adding to jams with a poor set, pressure cook the fruit as for making jelly and use the strained juice in the proportion of 2 tablespoons to 900 g (2 lb) fruit.

Marmalades

Here again, the principles and general instructions are the same as for jams and jellies. The thick peel needs thorough cooking, a job the pressure cooker will do in a fraction of the normal time necessary. With citrus fruits the pectin required to obtain a set is mostly contained in the white pith and the pips and it is for this reason that the best oranges for marmalade making are Sevilles. If the pith is not wanted in the finished product it can be cut off the peel, but must be tied loosely with the pips in a muslin bag and added during the cooking, being lifted out and well squeezed before the sugar is added.

It really is not necessary to remove the pulp when you have a pressure cooker as it is so thoroughly cooked that it is never unpleasant in the finished product. If you prefer a marmalade with less fruit, then one of the jelly types could be chosen.

So many citrus fruits such as lemons, grapefruit and sweet oranges now reach us seedless and with thin skins that it is not easy to obtain a marmalade with plenty of jelly round the fruit; it is quite a good idea therefore when you have in mind to make one of these marmalades to start saving the pips a while in advance – from oranges squeezed for juice, from lemons used in cooking and from grapefruit prepared for breakfast. Put them as you get them into a small cup or egg-cup and just cover them with water, adding them and the extract in a muslin bag to the fruit just before pressure cooking.

Using a pressure cooker, there is no need whatever to soak the fruit overnight; this will have no effect in the way of better flavour or setting as is often thought.

Even though one may think of citrus fruits as being very acid, a little lemon juice is usually added as marmalade fruits are bulky, rich in pectin and can take twice as much sugar as other fruits so that the proportion of acid is considerably less than in jams.

TO SUMMARIZE THE PROCESS OF MARMALADE MAKING

Either **M** or **H** pressure can be used.

The fruit should be fresh and must be well washed.

All pith must be included with the pips in the cooking.

Only half the amount of water should be used for the cooking, the rest added with the sugar. This will prevent the fruit and juice boiling out during the cooking.

The fruit must be soft before the sugar is added.

The lemon juice can be added either for the cooking or with the sugar.

The scum should be removed after setting point has been reached.

The marmalade should be allowed to stand a little before potting, otherwise the fruit will rise in the jars.

The waxed circle should be put on as each jar is filled, the final covering when the marmalade is really cold.

Thick marmalades

Seville orange marmalade
Pressure-cooking time: 10 minutes

900 g (2 lb) Seville oranges
juice of 2 lemons
1·2 litres (2 pt) water
1·75 kg (4 lb) sugar

Wash the fruit. Depending on the type of marmalade wanted the fruit can be:

1 Cut in quarters, the pips removed and tied loosely in a muslin bag, the fruit cut, chopped or minced after the cooking and the bag squeezed and lifted out before the sugar is added.

2 Peeled, the pith cut off with a knife, roughly chopped up and added with the pips in a muslin bag as above. The fruit should be roughly chopped up too and the peel cut up, chopped or minced after cooking.

3 Skinned, the pith removed and the peel cut as required before cooking. The peel, cut-up fruit and the chopped pith and pips, in a muslin bag as above, are then all cooked together.

Put the fruit, peel and muslin bag with *half* the water into the cooker, bring to pressure in the usual way, cook for 10 minutes and allow the pressure to reduce at room temperature. Lift out the muslin bag and squeeze well; strain the fruit, putting the juice back into the cooker, and cut up the peel. Add this to the cooker with the other *half* of the water and the lemon juice, bring to the boil on a high heat, add the sugar and stir until dissolved over a low heat. Bring to the boil quickly again and boil rapidly until setting point is reached. Skim if necessary, allow to stand until a skin has formed, pot, cover at once with a waxed disc. Allow to get cold, cover and tie down, label and store.

Yield: approx. 2·5–3 kg (6½–7 lb).

Lemon marmalade
Pressure-cooking time: 7 minutes

900 g (2 lb) lemons
6 dl (1 pt) water
1·75 kg (4 lb) sugar

As for **Seville Orange Marmalade**.
Yield: approx. 2·5–3 kg (6½–7 lb).

Grapefruit marmalade
Pressure-cooking time: 10 minutes

675 g (1½ lb) grapefruit
225 g (½ lb) lemons
6 dl (1 pt) water
1·75 kg (4 lb) sugar

As for **Seville Orange Marmalade**, but use all of the lemon and not just the juice.
Yield: approx. 2·5– 3 kg (6½–7 lb).

Sweet orange marmalade
Pressure-cooking time: 8 minutes

675 g (1½ lb) sweet oranges
325 g (¾ lb) lemons
6 dl (1 pt) water
1·75 kg (4 lb) sugar

As for **Seville Orange Marmalade**, but use all the lemons, not just the juice. This marmalade may have a cloudy appearance when potted, depending on the kind of oranges used.
Yield: approx. 2·5 kg (6½ lb).

Three fruit marmalade
Pressure-cooking time: 10 minutes

2 oranges, 1 grapefruit and 2 lemons to weigh 900 g (2 lb)
9 dl (1½ pt) water
1·75 kg (4 lb) sugar

As for **Seville Orange Marmalade**.
 Yield: approx. 2·5–3 kg (6½–7 lb).

Jelly marmalades

Orange shred
Pressure-cooking time: 8 minutes

900 g (2 lb) Seville oranges
juice of 2 small lemons
7·5 dl (1¼ pt) water
1·35 kg (3 lb) sugar

Peel four of the oranges finely, remove the pith very carefully, shred the peel finely and tie loosely in a muslin bag. Chop the rest of the fruit and all the pith roughly, put into the cooker with the water, the lemon juice and the muslin bag, bring to pressure in the usual way, cook for 8 minutes and allow the pressure to reduce at room temperature. Lift out the muslin bag, put the shreds into a strainer and pour a kettle of boiling water over them. Strain the rest through a jelly bag and continue as for jelly making (p 230) until just before setting point, then skim the marmalade, add the shredded peel and continue boiling until setting point is reached. Continue as given for thick marmalades.
 Yield: approx. 2·25 kg (5 lb).

Lemon shred
Pressure-cooking time: 8 minutes

900 g (2 lb) lemons
7·5 dl (1¼ pt) water
1·35 kg (3 lb) sugar

As for **Orange Shred**.

Lime jelly marmalade

Pressure-cooking time: 10 minutes

450 g (1 lb) limes (about 8)
juice of 1 lemon
9 dl (1½ pt) water
675 g (1½ lb) sugar

Although the colour of the marmalade will not be good, it will be less bitter and with a better set if the limes are used when they are beginning to turn yellow.

Wash the limes, peel off the rind with a potato peeler and shred it finely. Take off as much pith as possible from the fruit, cut the fruit in half, take away the pips which should not be cooked, squeeze out the juice and add it to the peel with the strained lemon juice and leave overnight. Cut up the pulp, tie in a muslin bag, put in the cooker with the peel, juice and water, bring to pressure, cook for 8 minutes and allow the pressure to reduce at room temperature. Lift out the muslin bag, squeeze very gently, add the sugar and continue as given for thick marmalade.

Yield: approx. 1 kg (2¼ lb).

Tangerine jelly

675 g (1½ lb) tangerines
½ grapefruit and 1–2 lemons to weigh 225 g (½ lb)
9 dl (1½ pt) water
1 kg (2¼ lb) sugar

As for **Orange Shred.**

Fruit cheeses and butters

Cranberry cheese

Pressure-cooking time: 3 minutes

900 g (2 lb) cranberries
3 dl (½ pt) water
sugar in the proportion of 325 g (12 oz) for each 450 g (1 lb) pulp

Wash the cranberries, put into the cooker with the water, bring to pressure, cook for 3 minutes and allow the pressure to reduce at room temperature. Sieve the fruit, weigh the pulp and juice, return to the pan and boil until it is really thick. Add sugar and continue cooking, stirring all the time until the fruit holds on the spoon without dropping off. Pot and cover at once.

This is an excellent preserve to serve with Roast Turkey, Turkey Pilaff and Curried Turkey.

Damson cheese
Pressure-cooking time: 8 minutes

900 g (2 lb) damsons
1·5 dl (¼ pt) water
sugar

Make as for **Cranberry Cheese.**

Lemon curd or cheese
Pressure-cooking time: 10 minutes

2 large or 3 standard eggs
225 g (8 oz) caster sugar
finely grated rind of 2 lemons
strained juice of 1 lemon

50–75 g (2–3 oz) unsalted butter
3 dl (½ pt) water and ½ squeezed lemon for the cooker

Beat the eggs lightly and strain into a china, earthenware or oven-proof bowl that will fit into the cooker. Add the sugar and stir until well mixed. Put in the lemon rind and juice and lastly the butter in small knobs, and stir well again. Put the water and trivet in the cooker, stand the bowl in it and cover with a double thickness of greaseproof paper. Bring to **H** pressure, cook for 10 minutes and allow the pressure to reduce for 10 minutes. Lift out the bowl, stir the curd well, pour into a warm jar and cover with a waxed disc. Seal when cold. Lemon curd should have the consistency of thick cream and coat the back of the spoon with a thin film when it is cooked. It will thicken as it cools. This quantity will make a 450-g (1-lb) jar; no more should be made at one time as Lemon Curd does not keep for more than 5 to 6 weeks, as it has no preservative added to it.

Orange curd
Use the same method as for **Lemon Curd** but with the grated rind of 2 oranges and 2 tablespoons of mixed orange and lemon juice.

As orange peel does not grate as finely as lemon, the curd when cooked should be put through a sieve if a smoother consistency is preferred.

Pickles and chutneys

These are very simple to make and again almost any combination of available fruits or vegetables is suitable. Your pressure cooker will once more be invaluable for the rapid and complete softening of the ingredients, though the thickening to reduce the contents to the correct consistency must always be done in the open pan, stirring all the time. These preserves require H pressure.

For storage, care must be taken that the jars are well sealed or else the vinegar will evaporate, but it must not be allowed to come into direct contact with metal, otherwise it will lead to rusting. A cover of greaseproof paper will not be sufficient. If jars with metal screw or push-on tops are chosen, a waxed disc should go on first, then a circle of cardboard and, if possible, the inside of the metal tops should be given a coating of clear lacquer a few days previously. It is possible to buy plastic push-on covers now to fit 450-g (1-lb) or 900-g (2-lb) jars, and these are both suitable and practical as they can be used over and over again. A form of synthetic skin which can be purchased is excellent too as a cover over a waxed disc.

Mustard pickle
Pressure-cooking time: 1 minute

1·35 kg (3 lb) vegetables made up of cucumber, marrow, french or runner beans, small onions or shallots, cauliflower, unripe green tomatoes
225 g (8 oz) kitchen salt
2·4 litres (4 pt) water

6 dl (1 pt) white vinegar
100 g (4 oz) brown sugar
1½ level tablespoons dry mustard
2 level tablespoons ground ginger
2 tablespoons flour
2 tablespoons turmeric

Prepare the vegetables by dicing, leave the cauliflower in flowerets and cut the tomatoes into eight. Dissolve the salt in the water and put this brine and the vegetables into a large bowl and leave overnight. A weighted plate should be put into the bowl to make sure all the vegetables remain covered. The next day, rinse the vegetables well.

Put the strained vegetables into the cooker with 4·5 dl ($\frac{3}{4}$ pt) of the vinegar, the sugar, mustard and ginger, bring to pressure in the usual way, cook for 1 minute and reduce the pressure with cold water. During the cooking blend the flour and turmeric with the rest of the vinegar. Carefully lift a selection of each vegetable into the jars with a straining spoon, add the thickening to the liquid in the cooker, bring to the boil, cook for 2 minutes until really thick, then pour into the jars, using a round-bladed knife to make sure the sauce gets round, down and through the vegetables. Cover immediately.

Yield: approx. 4 × 450-g (1-lb) jars.

If liked the vinegar can be boiled separately for about 5 minutes with 1 tablespoon pickling spice and then strained before being put in the cooker.

Green tomato chutney
Pressure-cooking time: 10 minutes

900 g (2 lb) green tomatoes	1 tablespoon salt
2 apples	6 dl (1 pt) vinegar
2 onions	225 g (8 oz) brown sugar
100 g (4 oz) sultanas or seedless raisins	1 teaspoon cayenne pepper
	1 tablespoon ground ginger
3 heaped teaspoons pickling spice tied in muslin	

Cut up the tomatoes, the peeled and cored apples and the onions and chop the raisins. Put these with the pickling spice, the salt, and 3 dl ($\frac{1}{2}$ pt) of the vinegar in the cooker, bring to pressure, cook for 10 minutes and reduce the pressure with cold water. Put in the rest of the vinegar, lift out the bag of spices, add the sugar, the pepper and the ginger and stir until boiling, cooking until the chutney thickens. Pour into the jars and cover immediately.

Marrow chutney
Pressure-cooking time: 8 minutes

1·35 kg (3 lb) marrow
2 tablespoons salt
450 g (1 lb) green apples
225 g (8 oz) onions or shallots

1 heaped tablespoon pickling spice
6 dl (1 pt) malt vinegar
325 g (12 oz) brown sugar
1 teaspoon turmeric

Peel the marrow, remove the pips and cut into small pieces. Leave to soak overnight in layers sprinkled with 1 tablespoon salt. Next day, drain well, then put into the cooker with the peeled and chopped apples and onions, the spices tied loosely in muslin, the remaining salt and half the vinegar. Bring to pressure, cook for 8 minutes, reduce the pressure with cold water and lift out the muslin bag. Add the sugar, turmeric and the rest of the vinegar and cook, stirring frequently, until the consistency of thick jam. Pot and seal immediately.

Beetroot relish
Pressure-cooking time: 15–20 minutes and 5 minutes

450 g (1 lb) beetroot
450 g (1 lb) chopped cabbage
1 heaped tablespoon horseradish sauce or freshly grated horseradish

1 tablespoon dry mustard
1 teaspoon salt
pinch of cayenne pepper
3 dl ($\frac{1}{2}$ pt) vinegar
225 g (8 oz) white sugar

Pressure cook the beetroots whole, according to their size, for 15–20 minutes. Peel and chop into fine dice; throw away the water. Return to the cooker with all the other ingredients except the sugar, bring to pressure again, cook for 5 minutes and reduce the pressure with cold water. Add the sugar and cook, stirring frequently, until the relish thickens. Pot and seal immediately.

Sweet apple chutney
Pressure-cooking time: 10 minutes

1·35 kg (3 lb) sour apples
2 cloves garlic, crushed
6 dl (1 pt) malt vinegar
100 g (4 oz) crystallized ginger
1 level teaspoon cayenne pepper

1 level teaspoon salt
2 level teaspoons mixed spice
325 g (12 oz) brown sugar
225 g (8 oz) sultanas

Peel, core and cut up the apples and put into the cooker with the garlic and half the vinegar. Bring to pressure in the usual way, cook for 10 minutes and allow the pressure to reduce at room temperature. Add the chopped ginger, the pepper, salt, spice, sugar and sultanas and cook, stirring frequently, until the consistency of thick jam. Pot and seal immediately.

Sauces and ketchups

If these are to be kept for any length of time they should be poured, while still boiling, into heated 450-g (1-lb) Kilner jars which can be sealed, leaving 5 cm (2 in) headspace. The instructions for sealing fruit purées, p 252, should then be followed. If for immediate use, well washed and dried sauce bottles can be used. Pour the sauce while still boiling into the hot jars, each one being capped immediately with the original cap, scrupulously clean and dry and tied down with a double thickness of greaseproof paper.

Tomato sauce
Pressure-cooking time: 3 minutes

1·75 kg (4 lb) ripe red tomatoes   pinch of cayenne pepper
1·5 dl (¼ pt) white vinegar   salt
½ teaspoon each ground ginger,   225 g (8 oz) white sugar
    ground cloves, ground mace

Slice the tomatoes, put into the cooker with the vinegar, bring to pressure, cook for 3 minutes and allow the pressure to reduce at room temperature. Rub the tomatoes through a fine sieve, return to the cooker, add all the other ingredients and cook, stirring frequently, until the desired consistency. Bottle as given in instructions on pp 248–9.

Yield: approx. 1 litre (2 pt).

Tomato ketchup
Pressure-cooking time: 10 minutes

900 g (2 lb) ripe tomatoes
1 large cooking apple
1 medium onion
1·5 dl ($\frac{1}{4}$ pt) white wine vinegar

1 dessertspoon pickling spice,
  tied in muslin
good pinch of cayenne pepper
salt
100 g (4 oz) white sugar

Put the quartered tomatoes, cored and quartered apple and chopped onion into the cooker with the vinegar and spice, bring to pressure, cook for 10 minutes and reduce the pressure with cold water. Put through a sieve, return to the cooker and boil, stirring all the time, until thick. Add the seasonings and sugar and cook a further 10 minutes. Taste and correct seasoning and bottle at once according to the instructions given on pp 248–9.

Rose hip syrup
Pressure-cooking time: 2 minutes

900 g (2 lb) rose hips
1·2 litres (2 pt) water
225 g (8 oz) sugar

Put the rose hips through a coarse mincer and then directly into 6 dl (1 pt) fast boiling water in the cooker. Bring to pressure in the usual way, cook for 2 minutes and allow the pressure to reduce at room temperature. Strain through a jelly bag. Rinse out the cooker, put back the syrup, add 6 dl (1 pt) boiling water, then the sugar, and allow to boil for 5 minutes. This syrup must now be treated like bottled fruit if it is to keep, so pour immediately into clean, hot, 450-g (1-lb) Kilner jars leaving at least 5 cm (2 in) headspace and continuing as given in the instructions on p 248, bringing to pressure only and allowing the pressure to reduce at room temperature before tightening the jars.

    This syrup will not keep for more than a week or so once it is opened.

Fruit sterilization

The bottling of fruit, contrary to what many cooks may think, is a very simple process; now that you have a pressure cooker you can be sure it will also be quick and completely safe. Its purpose is to allow you, when fruit is at its best or cheapest, to preserve it for the times when fresh fruit is scarce and expensive. It requires very little equipment, so little time that a couple of jars can be processed in a matter of minutes and the satisfaction of having a lovely shelf of home bottled fruit is out of all proportion to the time and effort involved. Even though a wide choice of frozen and tinned fruit is now readily available and the town dweller would not find it economical to go out and buy large quantities of fruit for bottling, there will always come a day in the season when you may see lovely peaches, apricots, even pineapple, at just the right price and asking to be 'put away' for that special recipe. For the country cook it will be a comfort to know that the pressure cooker is just waiting to deal with a surplus of fruit when no one can eat another gooseberry or strawberry and if just sufficient is picked daily, at its best, for one lot of bottling at a time, it need never become a chore.

The theory behind fruit bottling is simply that fruit must be brought to a certain temperature high enough to kill the moulds and yeasts on it and to arrest the agents in it which normally would cause it to become overripe and then to rot. This particular temperature can be reached in a pressure cooker in a matter of minutes so that the fruit is sterilized in only a fraction of the time which used to be necessary; quick, simple, effective.

THE PRESSURE COOKER As most fruits are soft it is important that they should not be overcooked in the processing, so the recommended pressure for fruit bottling therefore is L; if H pressure is used the same bottling times must be kept to, so as to ensure complete sterilization, even though this may mean that not quite such a good result is obtained.

As it is important that your pressure cooker should be working completely efficiently for this purpose, now might be a good time to check that neither the gasket nor the safety plug is showing any signs of leakage.

THE BOTTLING JARS The most usual types of vacuum jars sold in this country are:

1 Screw-top jars, such as the Kilner with a specially surfaced metal cover fitted with a plastic ring and a screw-band. After the cover has been put on the screw-band is tightened down and then turned back a mere quarter turn to allow for any expansion of the jar during heating. After processing, the band is screwed down again as tightly as possible until the jar is ready to have the seal tested.

2 Clip-top jars have similar metal or glass covers with a separate rubber ring placed on the neck of the jar before the cover is positioned. The clip-top secures the cover, allowing it to lift slightly during the processing and then holding it firmly while cooling to form the vacuum.

Clip-tops are also available for use on 450-g (1-lb) and 900-g (2-lb) jam jars and are entirely satisfactory, though it must be remembered that jam jars are not designed for this purpose and may crack because of the higher temperature required for bottling.

All equipment must be carefully looked at each year before being used again: check that the jars have no cracks or chips round the neck that could prevent a seal forming and see that the covers are in good condition and the rings have not stretched or perished. It is essential that the clips should still have plenty of spring in them; if they appear to be loose, a good tip is to put a coin on the cover before putting on the clip, though this should be only a temporary remedy until new ones can be bought. Screw-bands should also be a good fit and to prevent them rusting, after the seal has been tested they should be washed, dried, wiped over with a little oil and put back loosely on the jars for storage.

THE FRUIT Choose fresh, firm but ripe fruits (with the exception of gooseberries which must be green and hard, otherwise they will overcook). Do not be tempted to bottle damaged or overripe fruit just to save it.

The fruit in each jar should be as uniform in size and ripeness as possible to ensure even cooking. Be sure to prepare enough to fill the number of jars you have decided to do, as there is always a certain amount of wastage from peeling, stoning and stringing.

Those fruits such as apples and pears which discolour when peeled should be dropped into a solution of 1 teaspoon salt to 6 dl (1 pt) water and just before packing thoroughly rinsed in cold water.

As the bottling time is so short, hard fruits such as cooking pears may not be softened enough during the processing so they should be brought up to pressure in the cooker before being packed into the jars.

Fruits that need skinning, such as tomatoes and peaches, should be left in boiling water for about half a minute so that they can be easily peeled.

Soft fruits, such as strawberries, which shrink a lot when heated are best preserved according to the special instructions given as this ensures a good colour and a properly filled jar.

Bulky fruits or those which are over-plentiful such as apples, tomatoes, may be economically packed, following the instructions given, as purées or pulps.

THE SYRUP Bottling fruit in water does not give such a good flavour or colour to fruit which is to be stored for any length of time, and as fruit is acid, it is more economical in the end to use a syrup as the fruit then takes up the sweetening in the jars and requires less sugar to be added before serving. If a very heavy syrup is used this may cause the fruit to rise in the jars, but this is only a matter of looks and can often be avoided by careful packing of the jars. Syrups may be average or thick; a good suggestion is to decide when bottling what the fruit is likely to be used for and let this decide the strength of the syrup. For instance: pie fruit, using an average syrup of 150–225 g (6–8 oz) per 6 dl (1 pt) water would be fruit that is to be cooked again, in pies, tarts, suet puddings, so that it can be further sweetened if necessary; dessert fruit, using a heavy syrup of 250–325 g (10–12 oz) per 6 dl (1 pt) of water would be fruit that could be turned straight out of the jars for serving.

Granulated or loaf sugar can be used and should be dissolved in the water in a small saucepan with a lip to make it easy to pour out, and be allowed to boil for at least 1 minute just before use. Do not leave it boiling away madly for any length of time or it will evaporate.

If strawberries have been presoaked or pears precooked, the syrup should be strained and reboiled before filling into the jars.

ADJUSTMENTS FOR ALTITUDE If fruit bottling or canning at an altitude of more than 1,000 m (3,000 ft) above sea-level use M pressure instead of L, or increase the timings by 4 minutes if using H pressure.

Instructions

Check that the jars are clean, heat by pouring in a little warm water and stand them, ready for packing, in a large bowl half filled with boiling water.

Have ready in the cooker, the trivet, 9 dl ($1\frac{1}{2}$ pt) water to which has been added a spoonful of vinegar, and put to boil.

Make the syrup and put to boil.

Put the covers and rubber rings into a small bowl and cover with boiling water.

Pack the jars firmly with the prepared fruit, layer upon layer, working around the edges but always remembering to keep the centre filled in and just a little higher than the outsides. Except for very small or soft fruits such as currants and raspberries, each piece should be put in separately; always manage to get just one more in than you thought you possibly could. Only a tight pack with firm fruits such as cherries, halved apricots and peaches, pears, gooseberries, rhubarb in lengths, will ensure a full, good-looking result which is the kind that will give the most satisfaction.

Soft fruits such as berries and apples cannot be tightly packed and will therefore always tend to float in syrup.

Tomatoes in brine may squash a little during the processing so the jar may show some space at the top.

When the jars are packed to the very top, fill with the boiling syrup, leaving at least 5 mm ($\frac{1}{4}$ in) headspace. To remove the air bubbles which may get caught among the fruit, only pour a little in at a time and twist the jar sharply from side to side before adding any more. Space must be left above the syrup as the fruit will make some juice of its own and if the jar is completely filled, the syrup may boil out and be wasted.

Wipe the rim of the jar before putting on the cover and adjust the screw-band or clip. After screwing the band down tightly, unscrew a mere quarter turn.

Lift the packed jars, filled with the boiling syrup, from the boiling water in the bowl into the boiling water in the cooker. This pre-heating of the jars will prevent them from cracking when being heated quickly as the cooker is brought to pressure. The jars should not be allowed to touch each other or the sides of the cooker.

Bring to pressure on a medium heat, cook for the time given and leave the pressure to reduce at room temperature for at least 5 minutes.

Lift the jars out and if screw-bands have been used, screw them down as tightly as possible, doing this again at least once more before leaving the jars on one side to cool.

The next day, test the jars to make sure the seals have taken. Un-screw the bands or remove the clips and see if the covers can be lifted. If they are firm, the jars are ready for storage. If a vacuum has not been formed and the cover can be taken off, use the fruit at once and check the jar, cover and screw-band or clip before using again.

For storage, wipe the jar and cover, wash the screw-band and clip, dry, then smear them and the cover with a little oil to prevent rus-ting. The clips should be put away; the screw bands can be put back just resting on the jars but should not be screwed down in case any deterioration of the fruit should take place, when this will allow the covers to lift instead of the jars bursting. Label the jars with the date of bottling so that they are used in the right order and keep in a cool place, and preferably in the dark, to conserve the colour of the fruit.

When canning, use the same method for preparation of the fruit and syrup and the same pressure-cooking time as for bottling, but follow the canning machine manufacturer's instructions for clos-ing the cans. These may be laid on their sides when packing into the cooker if this allows more to be processed at one time.

SOLID PACK FOR BERRIES Prepare the fruit and lay in a single layer in a large bowl.

Fruit	Preparation	Minutes at L pressure[1]
Apples	Peel, core, cut in quarters or slices. Put in brine solution, until packed, then rinse well with cold water	1 minute
Apricots	Rinse fruit in cold water. If left whole, prick with fork once or twice; if halved, remove stones	1 minute
Blackberries	Wash if necessary. May be packed with sliced apples ready for pies or tarts	1 minute
Blackcurrants	String, rinse in cold water, drain	1 minute
Cherries	Wash and stalk; whole; if stoned add juice from fruit to syrup and reboil	1 minute
Damsons	Rinse in cold water; leave whole, prick once or twice with a fork	1 minute
Gooseberries	Rinse in cold water. Must be hard and green or will burst in the cooking	1 minute
Greengages	Rinse in cold water; leave whole, prick once or twice with a fork	1 minute
Loganberries	Pick over very carefully, rinse and drain. Follow instructions for soft fruit pack	3 minutes
Mulberries	As above	3 minutes
Peaches	Peel by leaving in boiling water ½–1 minute. Halve and stone. If large, cut in quarters or slices	3 minutes (halved) 1 minute (sliced)
Pears	Peel and core and put in brine solution until ready for packing, rinse with cold water If hard-cooking variety, pressure cook in syrup at H for 1–3 minutes, reboil the syrup before pouring over the fruit in the jars	3 minutes 3 minutes
Pineapple	Cut in 1-cm (½-in) slices, cut away skin, remove eyes, leave in slices or cut in cubes	3 minutes
Plums	Remove stalks, wash in cold water. If left whole, prick once or twice with fork. If halved, remove stones	1 minute
Raspberries	Follow instructions for soft fruit pack, unless bottling with redcurrants, when use equal quantity of the fruits and pack loosely	3 minutes 1 minute

Fruit	Preparation	Minutes at **L** pressure[1]
Redcurrants	Stalk, rinse with cold water and drain	1 minute
Rhubarb	Cut off leaves and base of stem. Wipe and cut into even lengths just to reach the shoulders of the jar for the outside pieces and the top of the jar for the centre pieces. Squeeze in as many lengths as you can as rhubarb shrinks a great deal when cooked	1 minute (forced) 2 minutes (garden)
Strawberries	Follow instructions for soft fruit	3 minutes
Tomatoes	Small, whole, unpeeled. Add boiling brine, 1 level teaspoon salt, pinch of sugar per 6 dl (1 pt) water instead of syrup Peeled by leaving in boiling water for $\frac{1}{2}$–1 minute; pack small ones whole, large may be halved or quartered. Do not add liquid; sprinkle each layer with a little salt and a pinch of sugar	3 minutes
Fruit Salad	If several different fruits have been bottled and there are enough pieces left over to make up one or two jars, these can be processed as fresh fruit salad, giving the time for the fruit which requires the longest cooking	

[1] The times given are for 450- and 900-g (1- and 2-lb) jars and for 900-g (1-lb) cans.

Boil a heavy syrup, pour over the fruit, cover and leave overnight. Next day, lift the fruit carefully into the jars, packing them as given in the general instructions (p 248) and leaving as much syrup behind as possible.

Reboil the syrup, fill the jars slowly, twisting them to get rid of any air bubbles.

Continue as given in the general instructions, processing for 3 minutes.

These fruits will keep a good colour for 3 to 4 months if each jar is stored individually in a brown paper bag to be sure that the light is kept out. For longer storage, add a little artificial colouring to the syrup before boiling.

FRUIT PULP Prepare the fruit as for stewing, put into the cooker with 3 dl ($\frac{1}{2}$ pt) water but no sugar, bring to pressure in the usual way, cook for the required time (see table, p 250) and allow the pressure to reduce at room temperature. During the cooking, have the jars etc ready as given in the general instructions. Mash the fruit to a pulp and pour the pulp immediately, while still boiling hot, into the jars. Be sure that each rim is wiped before putting on the cover, then continue as given in the general instructions (p 249), processing for 1 minute.

FRUIT PURÉE Follow instructions for pulp but when the pressure is reduced, sieve the fruit; then reboil the purée and pour at once into the jars, leaving at least 1 cm ($\frac{1}{2}$ in) headspace. Be sure that the rim of the jar is wiped clean before putting on the cover. Continue as given in the general instructions, processing for 3 minutes for fruit, 5 minutes for tomato purée.

Citrus fruits such as Seville oranges, grapefruit, lemons, for marmalade making may be in season or at their cheapest when you still have sufficient marmalade from previous years or are too busy to spare the time to make more. To preserve these fruits for later use weigh, prepare and cut them up in the usual way and pack loosely into the jars, leaving 1 cm (1 in) headspace and do not add any liquid. Process for 15 minutes according to the instructions. Label each jar with its actual weight of fruit and when making into marmalade add sufficient water to bring the juice up to the required quantity and add the correct proportion of sugar, as given on pp 235–8. The pulp will not require further softening.

FAULTS WHICH MAY OCCUR If a jar has not sealed: the jar, cover and band or clip should be checked; care should be taken to tighten the screw-band immediately after processing.

Poor colour of fruit: it may have been under- or over-ripe, have been processed too long or the jars may not have been stored in the cool and the dark.

Discolouration of fruit at the top of the jar: while the jar may have sealed all the air has not been expelled – just what would happen if the fruit was left peeled or cut and uncovered in the kitchen. Care must be taken to get rid of the air bubbles when filling with syrup, the screw-bands must be loosened slightly for processing and the correct cooking time must be given. Check, too, that the inside of the cover, against the fruit, is not rusted or corroded.

Fruit rising in the jar: the fruit was over-ripe and has over-cooked; the jar was not packed tightly enough or, if a very heavy syrup has been used, the fruit itself is lighter and just simply floats.

Air bubbles in tight packs such as strawberries: this can be avoided by adding the syrup as the jar is packed, covering each layer in turn.

Cloudy fluid in the jars: the fruit was dirty or over-ripe.

Sediment in the jars: probably the water used for the syrup was very hard. This will not be harmful.

Mould on fruit or fermentation: jars not processed for long enough or at the full, correct pressure; a slight leak round the jar which will eventually loosen the cover. Open the jar at once, being careful when doing this if it has fermented because it will open like a bottle of pop, and discard the contents.

Blanching vegetables ready for deep freezing

When deep freezing vegetables, the first process must be blanching or scalding, otherwise the vegetables may develop unpleasant flavours from the action of the enzymes which they contain and they may not retain a good colour in storage. After the young, tender vegetables have been cleaned and picked over, they are blanched in the normal way in a large quantity of boiling water for a given time, then are plunged into cold water to prevent over-cooking and to cool them as quickly as possible so that they can be handled and the process continued.

For full instructions, follow those given by the manufacturers of your deep freezer; for certain of the larger, longer-cooking vegetables, blanching can be done quickly and satisfactorily with your pressure cooker saving time and fuel.

Only vegetables which are suited to blanching with the pressure cooker are included in the following table: have 3 dl ($\frac{1}{2}$ pt) hot water in the cooker before putting in the vegetables, and use the trivet.

	Pressure	Blanching time
Asparagus (thick stems)	L	1 minute
Beans		
(broad)	L	To pressure only
(french or runner)	L	To pressure only
Beetroot (unskinned)	H	5–15 minutes, according to size
Broccoli	L	To pressure only
Brussels sprouts	L	1 minute
Carrots (unpeeled)	H	2 minutes
Corn-on-the-cob	H	2 minutes
Peas	L	To pressure only

Reduce pressure immediately, with cold water, as soon as the blanching time is up.

12 Your pressure cooker out and about

When you reach this chapter, I am sure you will not need to be convinced that for an outdoor holiday – camping, caravanning, boating – a pressure cooker is a must. Just think of all the advantages its use will bring: complete meals in one pan, so handy when a small stove or one burner is all that you have; so sparing of fuel when this has to be carried; so economical on food bills, important if you are holidaying on a budget; so safe on small stoves or on tossing boats as everything is sealed in the pan and even if the cooker is toppled over it will not spill; so light on water supplies which may be restricted – indeed, in these and many other ways the pressure cooker has proved itself and found its way to many strange places such as the Himalayas with the Everest expedition, a lone Atlantic crossing in a rowing boat and overland to the Far East and Australia.

The recipes given here are mostly composite ones, to serve a substantial dish out of the one pan for four, and could most suitably be followed by fresh fruit, bought pastries etc, or by a pudding, pressure cooked first and kept hot in a bowl of boiling water or to be served cold.

Where tinned foods are to be served, meat and pasta are best turned into a solid container for reheating putting at least 3 dl ($\frac{1}{2}$ pt) water in the cooker itself, bringing to pressure and cooking for 1–3 minutes according to the type of food and the time recommended. Vegetables should be opened, strained and heated through, in a perforated container for the larger ones such as potatoes, carrots etc, or in a solid container for peas, beans etc, when they will be less likely to become overcooked if being done with other foods. It is not essential to turn out of the tins, which can be successfully reheated unopened, allowing about one-third of the time given on the tin, but this way they take up quite a lot of room and probably not enough can be reheated at once to satisfy the family. If using two containers, put a solid one first in the water in the bottom of the cooker, using the trivet as a platform on which to stand the second container. The top one, if solid, should then be covered with a piece of greaseproof paper (from round the butter or margarine would be fine) to prevent the steam from falling back into the container as liquid when pressure is reduced.

Nowadays there are so many easily carried and packed cooking aids to save extra work and saucepans that it is a good idea to take a selection of them with you. Among these would be packets of bouquet garni, white and various sauces, gravy powder, grated cheese, suet crust mixes, dehydrated vegetables and a selection of packet soups which, by their various flavours, can make a basic stew or dish seem different every day.

These could be added or substituted for ingredients given in the following recipes.

As a final bonus for those cooking out and about – when the cooker is stood in a bowl of water to reduce the pressure it will heat the water, which will then be most useful for the washing up.

Baked beans with pork or ham
Pressure-cooking time: 20 minutes

225 g (8 oz) haricot beans	1 teaspoon dry mustard
6 dl (1 pt) water	3 tablespoons brown sugar
4 thick slices fat bacon or salt pork cut into 2-cm (1-in) pieces	2 tablespoons diced green pepper if available
1 large onion, peeled and sliced	salt and pepper

The previous night, or in the morning after breakfast, boil the water, pour over the beans, cover and leave to soak. Lift the trivet from the cooker and fry the meat until golden-brown. Add the onion and mustard and leave for a minute or two, then put in the beans with the soaking water, the sugar, green pepper and the seasoning. Bring to pressure, cook for 20 minutes and leave the pressure to reduce of its own accord.

Chicken with dumplings
Pressure-cooking time: 5 minutes; ordinary cooking time: 10 minutes

1 boiling chicken
6 dl (1 pt) water with chicken
  stock cube
salt and pepper

for the dumplings:
  8 tablespoons flour
  4 tablespoons shredded suet
  salt
  cold water to mix
2 tablespoons flour blended with
  a little stock for thickening

Joint the chicken; lift out the trivet, put in the liquid, the chicken pieces and the seasoning, bring to pressure, cook for 5 minutes and reduce the pressure with cold water. During this cooking, prepare the dumplings (a packet of suet pudding mixture may be used here) and shape into eight balls. Put in the peas, return the pan to the heat and allow the liquid to boil, add the dumplings and boil for for 10 minutes, during which time the cooker should be just covered with a plate. Lift out the dumplings and the chicken pieces, add the thickening, reboil, taste and correct seasoning and cook for a minute or two. Serve with some of the sauce poured over the chicken, the rest kept hot in the cooker until required.

Gipsy stew
Pressure-cooking time: 10 minutes or 10 minutes per 450 g (1 lb)

675 g (1½ lb) veal pieces, or a piece
  of veal on the bone weighing
  1–1·35 kg (2½–3 lb)
salt and pepper
1 onion
2 slices streaky bacon
a little butter

6 dl (1 pt) water
1 tin (or packet of frozen) peas
sufficient potatoes, cut to cook
  in 4 minutes
1 small tin of tomatoes or tomato
  purée or paste
flour for thickening if necessary

Toss the veal pieces in seasoning or sprinkle seasoning over the joint. Dice the onion and bacon. Lift the trivet from the cooker. Melt the butter, lightly fry the bacon and onion, put in the veal and the water, bring to pressure and cook for all but 4 minutes of the cooking time. If the meat is on the bone, lift out, take off the meat and cut into large dice. Put back into the cooker with the peas and potatoes, bring to pressure again, cook for the remaining 4 minutes and reduce the pressure with cold water. Lift out the meat and potatoes, add the tomatoes or purée to taste, correct the seasoning, add the thickening if necessary, reboil and cook for a minute or two and pour over the meat and vegetables.

The veal bone can be cooked again with 6 dl (1 pt) water, some vegetables and seasoning to make some good stock for another soup or meat dish.

Macaroni picnic
Pressure-cooking time: 6 minutes

6 dl (1 pt) water	1 small tin of tomato soup
½ teaspoon salt	pepper
225 g (8 oz) macaroni	1 teaspoon sugar
1 tablespoon butter or margarine	grated cheese
1 level tablespoon flour	

Lift the trivet from the cooker, put in the salted water, allow to boil, throw in the macaroni, bring to pressure, cook for 6 minutes and reduce the pressure with cold water. Strain the macaroni, saving the water, and keep hot by covering with the cooker lid. Melt the fat in the pan, add the flour and cook without colouring; add the tomato soup and the sugar, reboil and cook until it thickens, if necessary adding a little of the macaroni water to obtain the correct consistency of a pouring sauce. Taste and correct seasoning, stir in the macaroni, reheat and serve sprinkled thickly with cheese.

Meat or cooked sausages left over from another meal or a small tin of corned beef can be chopped and added with the macaroni when reheating.

Meat loaf dinner
Pressure-cooking time: 15 minutes

This loaf is best made early in the day so that it has time to become firm before cooking.

2 slices of dry bread soaked in hot water
2 onions
450g (1 lb) minced beef
salt and pepper
pinch of mixed herbs
1 egg

2 tablespoons fat
3 dl (½ pt) water
sufficient potatoes, carrots or other vegetables, cut to cook in 5 minutes
thickening and colouring as required for gravy

Press the excess water from the bread; dice the onions finely and combine thoroughly with the meat, seasonings, herbs and bread. Bind firmly but not too moistly with egg, roll tightly in a piece of greaseproof paper and allow to stand. Lift the trivet from the cooker, heat the fat and fry the meat roll all over until really brown. Lift out and roll again loosely in the paper. Put the water and trivet in the cooker, then the roll, bring to pressure, cook for 10 minutes and reduce the pressure with cold water. Lift out the roll, pile in the potatoes, carrots etc and season well. Put back the roll, bring to pressure again, cook for 5 minutes and reduce the pressure with cold water. Lift out the roll, serve the vegetables, take out the trivet, thicken and colour the gravy as required, reboil, taste and correct seasoning and cook for 2–3 minutes. Unwrap the roll and serve with some of the gravy poured over or cut into slices, put a portion on each plate with a little gravy and keep the rest hot, until required, in the cooker.

Pork chops – American style
Pressure-cooking time: 7–8 minutes

4 pork chops about 2 cm (1 in) thick
salt and pepper
2 onions
4 hard eating apples
2 tablespoons ready-made stuffing
4 cloves

sufficient medium potatoes for 4
2 tablespoons dripping or fat
3 dl (½ pt) stock or water
packet of frozen peas (thawed out)
flour for thickening
gravy colouring if necessary

Wipe, trim the chops and season well. Peel and slice the onions. Wash, peel and core the apples; fill the centres two-thirds full with stuffing and stick each with a clove. Prepare the potatoes. Lift the trivet from the cooker, heat the fat, brown the chops well on both sides and lift out. Brown the onions, add the hot liquid (if cold, allow the cooker to cool), the trivet, then the chops and on top the potatoes in a perforated container. Bring to pressure, cook for 7–8 minutes; reduce the pressure with cold water. Put in the thawed-out peas in a perforated container, cover with a piece of foil or greaseproof paper, put in the apples, bring to pressure again, remove immediately and allow the pressure to reduce of its own accord. Lift out the apples and peas; serve a portion of potatoes and a chop with an apple on top surrounded with peas on each plate. Lift out the trivet, add the blended flour and colouring if necessary, reboil the gravy, taste to correct seasoning and cook a few moments. Pour a little carefully round the chops and leave the rest in the cooker to keep hot until required.

Short-cut risotto
Pressure-cooking time: 10 minutes

2 tablespoons margarine or oil	225 g (8 oz) tomatoes, skinned and quartered
2 or 3 bacon rinds or slices of streaky bacon	2 tablespoons sultanas
1 medium onion, sliced	2 tablespoons tomato (or other) sauce
1 small tin mushrooms	
1 large cup rice	bay leaf (optional)
6 dl (1 pt) water (liquid from tinned mushrooms can be included)	salt and pepper
	1 small tin of spam or luncheon meat
1 small apple, sliced	2 tablespoons grated cheese

Lift the trivet from the cooker, heat the fat and fry the bacon rinds or chopped bacon until golden. Add the onion, mushrooms and rice and allow to cook a moment or two in the fat. Add the liquid, apple, tomatoes, sultanas, sauce, seasonings and the meat cut into 1-cm ($\frac{1}{2}$-in) dice. Stir well, bring to pressure in the usual way, cook for 10 minutes and reduce the pressure with cold water. Lift out the bacon rinds and bay leaf, taste and correct seasoning and serve, handing the grated cheese separately or sprinkling it over the top.

Coffee dessert

Even on an outdoor holiday, one may still want a special meal. This recipe will make a really extravagant dessert and can be served even round the camp fire. The basis of caramelized milk must be prepared overnight.

Pressure-cooking time: 1¼ hours

1 tin sweetened condensed milk
9 dl (1½ pt) water with a little
  lemon juice or vinegar for the
  cooker
for the crumb pastry shell:
  20 rich tea biscuits
  3 tablespoons melted butter
  2 tablespoons sugar

1·5 dl (¼ pt) hot, very strong coffee
2 tablespoons chopped nuts
  (optional)
for decoration:
  sweetened whipped cream
  pieces of glacé cherry

Put the water, trivet and the unopened tin of condensed milk into the cooker. Bring to pressure in the usual way, cook for 1¼ hours, allow the pressure to reduce at room temperature, lift out the tin and leave overnight. Next morning, make the pastry shell, mixing the finely crushed biscuits and sugar in a basin with the melted butter. Press this mixture evenly on to a deep plate or pie dish and leave to set while making the filling. Turn the caramelized milk out of the tin into a large bowl, slowly stir in the hot coffee, add the chopped nuts and beat until quite smooth. Pile on the pastry shell, allow to cool and just before serving decorate with the whipped cream, cherries etc.

Concentrated fruit juice can be used instead of coffee flavour, or sliced bananas can be stirred in after the mixture has been beaten, a few being reserved for decoration.

If you have no glacé cherries, take three or four children's fruit jellies, halve them and set them in the cream, cut side up, to give colour.

Madeleines

Pressure-cooking time: 5 minutes' steaming; 10 minutes at H

Here is a quick way of having your own home-made cakes for tea.

3 eggs and their weight in butter, sugar and flour

a little vanilla essence

4·5 dl (¾ pt) water with a little lemon juice or vinegar for the cooker

some red jam diluted with a very little water

desiccated coconut

glacé cherries and angelica

Use small greased teacups and fill each only half full. This quantity should make eight to ten madeleines and they can be cooked with four standing in the water in the cooker covered with a double thickness of greased greaseproof paper, then the trivet, then four more cups, covered as before. Make the madeleines as given for **Canary Pudding**, and cook as given in the instructions on p 152. When the cakes are cold, trim them so that they stand level and are of even height (any cake trimmings could be used for the **Golden Crumble** recipe). Warm the jam with the water in a small saucepan, put each cake in turn on a skewer and dip into the jam, turning round to coat all over evenly, then roll in the coconut. Dip halved cherries and little angelica leaves in the jam and decorate the top of each madeleine.

13 Miscellaneous

Sauces

However much care and attention has gone into the preparation of a dish, it can always be improved in flavour and food value by a well-made sauce. Very often it is indeed 'the sauce that makes the dish'. Nowadays, there is a large selection of ready-made sauces which are invaluable if time is short, but the concentrated stocks and juices from pressure cooking form an ideal base and should never be wasted.

Even the plainest food can be made more appetizing by the clever choice of a sauce; other sauces, which may be traditional, are served as an aid to digestion, to bring out a particular flavour or to improve the appearance of the main dish.

Accompanying sauces are prepared separately in an ordinary saucepan as they require stirring during the cooking. When made, they may be kept hot by standing them in a larger saucepan or dish one-third filled with hot water, over a low heat, so that they will not overcook or burn. To prevent a skin from forming, lay a circle of dampened greaseproof paper over the top until required for serving.

Sauces may be divided for easy reference into groups: white, brown, mayonnaise, sweet and miscellaneous; examples of these, following a basic foundation sauce for each type, are given here.

As a general rule, sauces are made in two consistencies, either a coating sauce requiring 1 heaped tablespoon flour to 3 dl ($\frac{1}{2}$ pt) liquid or a pouring sauce requiring 1 level tablespoon flour to 3 dl ($\frac{1}{2}$ pt) liquid. Thickened gravies to accompany pot roasts, stuffed joints, hot meat rolls and so on require 1 dessertspoon flour to 3 dl ($\frac{1}{2}$ pt) liquid. Other thickening agents, for special sauces, are cream and yolks of egg.

For all sauces accompanying savoury dishes, the liquid used should include some of the stock or liquid from the food cooked, so as to make sure that none of the goodness is wasted.

Foundation white sauce

1 tablespoon butter or margarine
1 tablespoon flour
3 dl ($\frac{1}{2}$ pt) liquid (milk and liquid from the cooking)
salt and pepper

In a small saucepan, allow the fat to melt without colouring. Add the flour and cook gently, stirring over a low heat for a minute or two, again without allowing to colour. Remove from the heat, add the liquid gradually, stirring all the time; return to the heat, bring to the boil and cook for 2–3 minutes, still stirring. Add the seasoning, taste to check flavour and keep hot until ready to serve.

In many of the preceding recipes the sauce is begun during the pressure cooking, using milk or stock as half the liquid and adding the cooking liquid, after pressure has been reduced, to give the required consistency.

Variations
ANCHOVY: With fish stock and anchovy essence added to taste.
CAPER: With fish stock and 1 tablespoon chopped capers.
EGG: With 1 finely chopped hard-boiled egg.

MUSTARD: With 1 teaspoon dry mustard added with the flour. A little vinegar may also be added for sharpness.

PARSLEY: With 1–2 dessertspoons finely chopped fresh parsley.

Béchamel

A slightly richer white sauce requiring that, before addition to the white roux, the milk is boiled with an onion stuck with 2 cloves and a piece of carrot for 20 minutes or so, in a covered saucepan. The rest of the liquid may be fish, meat, poultry or game stock or from the cooked dish; add 1 tablespoon cream just before serving.

Variations

CELERY: With 225 g (8 oz) celery purée and 1·5 dl ($\frac{1}{4}$ pt) celery stock.

MORNAY OR CHEESE: With the addition of 2–3 tablespoons grated or Parmesan cheese. A little dry, white wine may also be added.

SOUBISE OR ONION: With 2 large sliced or puréed boiled onions, a little nutmeg and cream.

SUPRÊME OR MUSHROOM: With sliced fresh, cooked mushrooms and their liquor or sliced tinned mushrooms and the juice of $\frac{1}{4}$ lemon.

Quick tomato cream sauce

3 dl ($\frac{1}{2}$ pt) white sauce
1 small tin of tomatoes or tomato juice
a little cream

Make the white sauce and keep hot. If using tinned tomatoes, drain and sieve to give a thick purée. Heat this but do not boil, then stir in one or two spoonfuls of cream. Add this to the white sauce, whisk well together, reheat, but do not allow to boil.

This sauce is excellent with fish for an invalid or infant dish, with savoury meat rolls and balls and for cereal and pasta dishes.

Foundation brown sauce

1 tablespoon dripping
1 small onion, chopped
1–2 tablespoons flour

3 dl ($\frac{1}{2}$ pt) stock or cooking liquid
salt and pepper

In a small saucepan, melt the dripping and fry the onion until golden. Add the flour and cook over a low heat, stirring all the time, until dark brown but not burnt. Remove from the heat, gradually add the liquid, stirring all the time, return to the heat and cook for 2–3 minutes until thick, still stirring. Add the seasoning, taste to check and keep hot until required.

For use with fish, add 1 teaspoon vinegar.

Variations

ESPAGNOLE: A piece of streaky bacon, a tomato and a pinch of herbs should be allowed to cook gently with the onion for 5 minutes or so. Sieve the sauce before serving, add 1 or 2 tablespoons sherry, reheat, but do not allow to boil.

MADEIRA: With 2 tablespoons tomato purée, reheat and add 2 tablespoons madeira but do not allow to boil.

REFORME: With 1 tablespoon sherry, 1 dessertspoon redcurrant jelly, 1 tablespoon port wine and a pinch of cayenne added while the sauce is simmered for 10 minutes or so before serving.

Egg sauces

The basis of these sauces is yolk of egg and butter whisked together, the volume increasing as more butter is added. Great care must be taken as they can easily curdle and patience is needed to achieve the correct result, which is well worth while. At least half an hour must be allowed for making a sauce of this kind and all one's attention must be given to it. A small milk saucepan, a small heatproof basin or one of the boilable plastic bowls and a small wire whisk are the equipment required. It is best to make only small quantities as these sauces are very rich and difficult to reheat to serve a second time.

Hollandaise

Have ready a small saucepan about half full of hot, not boiling, water and over a very low heat. Throughout the cooking the water must not boil (this may be found easier if an asbestos mat is used). Put into the bowl 1 dessertspoon strained lemon juice, 1 teaspoon cold water and 1 tablespoon butter. When this is melted, whisk in the beaten yolk of a large egg and continue whisking until the sauce begins to thicken slightly. Then add another 2 tablespoons butter, piece by piece, whisking continuously in between each addition until the sauce thickens, leaves a trail and is shiny like mayonnaise. Remove the basin from the heat and continue stirring while adding salt, pepper and more strained lemon juice to taste until the bowl is just warm. Cover, stand on one side until required, then give a final stir.

Variation

MOUSSELINE For savoury dishes: add 1 tablespoon thick whipped cream and beat in, just before serving.

For sweet dishes: use 1 dessertspoon maraschino instead of the lemon juice, 1 dessertspoon sugar instead of seasoning; a whipped white of egg can be beaten in with the cream just before serving.

If any hollandaise or savoury mousseline sauce is left over, stir in some chopped chives, parsley, gherkins as available, and allow to get cold. If put into a screw-top jar and kept in the refrigerator it will make a delicious substitute for mayonnaise with meat, fish or vegetable salads.

Mayonnaise

Most of us take fright at the thought of making our own mayonnaise as we have heard of the difficulty and hard work involved but it is not really as bad as all that – a good recipe and a little care and one's trouble is well rewarded. If you have a refrigerator, decide to do double or triple quantity while you are at it and store it in an airtight container on the bottom shelf. If you have an electric mixer, then follow the manufacturer's instructions. Remember that fresh, good-quality oil is essential for a perfect tasting result.

1 egg yolk	$\frac{1}{4}$ teaspoon caster sugar
$\frac{1}{2}$ teaspoon dry mustard	2–3 teaspoons vinegar or lemon juice
a little salt and pepper	1·5 dl ($\frac{1}{4}$ pt) salad or olive oil

Put the yolk of egg in a small bowl, add the dry ingredients and mix together well with a wooden spoon. Add a bare half teaspoon of vinegar to moisten and then the oil, literally drop by drop, stirring steadily all the time so that the mayonnaise turns and thickens. As this keeps both hands busy and one cannot hold the bowl, stand it on a cloth to prevent it from turning. Should the mayonnaise show signs of curdling because the oil has been added too fast, quickly stir in a drop or two of cold water or, if very bad, beat another yolk of egg in another bowl and stir the mayonnaise into it. Once the mayonnaise has thickened, the rest of the oil can be added in a thin stream with a little vinegar added from time to time to keep the correct consistency. A tablespoon of cream may be added at the last, for extra richness.

Variations

TARTARE: Stir in 1 dessertspoon each of capers, parsley, chives and red pepper if available and 1 teaspoon each of finely chopped gherkins and shallots.

CHAUDFROID: This should be mayonnaise of a flowing consistency and to make it set when cold a 6-g ($\frac{1}{4}$-oz) packet of gelatine must be dissolved in 1·5 dl ($\frac{1}{4}$ pt) slightly warm aspic jelly (this can be bought), and be added to 6 dl (1 pt) mayonnaise which also must be slightly warm. The sauce should then be put through a sieve and 1 tablespoon of cream added. To prevent the sauce setting if not used at once it should be stood in a bowl of hot water.

Tomato sauce
Pressure-cooking time: 5 minutes

12 g ($\frac{1}{2}$ oz) butter	bay leaf
1 small rasher streaky bacon	salt and pepper
1 onion, sliced	pinch of sugar (optional)
1 carrot, sliced	3 dl ($\frac{1}{2}$ pt) white stock*
225 g (8 oz) fresh or 3 dl ($\frac{1}{2}$ pt) tinned tomatoes	2 teaspoons cornflour blended with a little extra stock
1 teaspoon tomato purée	

If the pressure cooker is not in use, the sauce can be made in it as follows: lift out the trivet, melt the butter and gently fry the chopped bacon. Put in the onion and carrot and cook without allowing to colour. Add the tomatoes, stirring well to mash them if they are fresh ones. Put in the tomato purée, the seasonings and sugar and lastly the stock. Bring to pressure in the usual way, cook for 5 minutes and reduce the pressure immediately. If the sauce is to be made while other foods are being pressure cooked, prepare in the same way but leave to simmer in a covered saucepan for 30 minutes. Sieve the sauce, return to the pan, add the blended cornflour and stir until boiling. Taste and correct seasoning. If the sauce is to be served with fish, leave out the bacon and use fish stock.

Apple sauce

This can be made loose in the pressure cooker by cooking the apples with 1·5 dl ($\frac{1}{4}$ pt) water for 2–3 minutes without the trivet, or can be done in a solid container without any added water and at the same time as the accompanying vegetables to be served with the meat. 2 cloves to 4 apples can be added for the cooking if liked. When pressure has been reduced the apples should be beaten until smooth with 1 tablespoon butter and a little sugar to taste.

Bread sauce

Simmer an onion stuck with 2 cloves, with a blade of mace in 3 dl ($\frac{1}{2}$ pt) milk for half an hour. Pour the flavoured milk over 4 table-spoons fresh white breadcrumbs; add 1 tablespoon of butter, salt and pepper and leave to stand for at least half an hour. A little more milk may be added if too thick. Taste and correct seasoning and reheat just before serving.

Mint sauce

Chop 1 small handful washed and dried fresh mint leaves with 1 heaped teaspoon sugar. Put in a small jug or dish, pour over 1 dessertspoon boiling water and add 1·5 dl ($\frac{1}{4}$ pt) vinegar. Mint sauce should stand on one side for at least an hour and be well stirred before serving.

Vinaigrette dresssing

Mix $\frac{1}{4}$ teaspoon each of salt, pepper and mustard in a small basin with 3 tablespoons olive oil, then whisk in 1 tablespoon vinegar. This dressing should be kept in a stoppered or screw-top bottle so that it can be well shaken each time before use. A squeeze of lemon juice may be added to taste.

Quick piquant sauce

1 tablespoon butter	$\frac{1}{2}$ green pepper, diced
1 onion, diced	small bay leaf
1 clove garlic, crushed	1 tin tomatoes or tomato purée

Heat the butter in a frying pan, cook the onion for a few minutes until transparent, add the garlic, pepper and bay leaf and allow to cook gently. If using the tin of tomatoes, strain and sieve to give a purée; add this to the rest of the ingredients, allow to boil. Add

water or stock to give the correct consistency, a little meat or vegetable extract if liked for extra flavouring; taste and correct seasoning, lift out bay leaf and serve.

This sauce would be just right to serve with stuffed vegetable
dishes such as marrow, onions or tomatoes, to accompany rice and
pasta dishes and so on.

Sweet white sauce

Use the foundation white sauce with 2 teaspoons sugar instead of
seasoning and a little vanilla or other flavouring to taste.

Chocolate sauce

50 g (2 oz) plain chocolate or 1
  level tablespoon cocoa
1 tablespoon caster sugar
3 dl ($\frac{1}{2}$ pt) water

2 teaspoons cornflour blended
  with a little water
1 tablespoon sherry if liked

Melt the chocolate and sugar in the water and boil for a moment
or two stirring until smooth. Add the blended cornflour, stir until
boiling; cook for 2–3 minutes and add sherry before serving.

Custard sauce

1 teaspoon cornflour
3 dl ($\frac{1}{2}$ pt) milk with a strip of lemon peel
1 teaspoon sugar
1 egg

Blend the cornflour with a little of the milk, boil the rest and pour
over the blended flour. Return to the pan, add the sugar and bring
to the boil, stirring all the time. Take from the heat, add the beaten
egg, then stir over a low heat until the custard thickens, but do not
allow to boil.

To make this custard into a mousse-like sauce, a stiffly beaten
white of egg may be folded in when the custard has cooled a little.

Jam sauce

1·5 dl ($\frac{1}{4}$ pt) water
2 tablespoons jam or marmalade
1 teaspoon cornflour blended with a little water
a few drops of lemon juice

Boil the water with the jam gently for a few minutes, add the blended cornflour, stir until boiling, and while cooking for 2–3 minutes add lemon juice, and colouring if necessary.

Marmalade sauce
See recipe under Orange Castles, p 154.

Orange or lemon sauce

thin shreds of orange (or lemon) rind
1·5 dl (¼ pt) water
1 teaspoon cornflour blended with a little water

1 tablespoon sugar
juice of ½ orange (or lemon)

Boil the shreds of fruit in the water until tender. Add the blended cornflour, stir until thickened, add the sugar and strained juice and serve.

Garnishes and accompaniments

Bacon rolls
Use thin slices of streaky bacon. Stretch each slice by running the back of a kitchen knife along it, cut into three or four pieces, roll and put on skewers. Can be grilled, turning once; fried in fat in the cooker, before putting in other ingredients; or cooked in a roasting tin in the oven, as when browning a chicken after pressure cooking.

Bouquet garni
This is a mixture of dried herbs which can now be bought in muslin bags or sachets from most grocers. If you wish to make your own so that the selection can be varied or fresh herbs can be used, a basic selection would be: 1 bay leaf, 1 blade of mace, 1 pinch of mixed herbs, a few black or white peppercorns, a sprig of parsley. Tie into a small square of butter muslin, put in for the cooking and lift out before serving.

Brandy butter
For serving with Christmas Pudding: cream 100 g (4 oz) unsalted butter until white, beat in 150 g (6 oz) finely sieved icing sugar, then brandy (4 to 8 dessertspoons, to taste). Put in a refrigerator or cool place to harden.

Browned crumbs

For garnishing cauliflower and the tops of savoury dishes: melt about 25 g (1 oz) butter or oil in a frying pan, add 3 tablespoons fresh white breadcrumbs and stir with a metal spoon until golden-brown. Only a medium heat should be used and care must be taken that they do not get dark or burnt. Season with salt and pepper before using.

French bread

As an accompaniment to any savoury dish: cut 15-cm (6-in) pieces diagonally from a long French loaf and slit diagonally at 2·5-cm (1-in) intervals almost through to the bottom crust. Spread these cuts with butter, place the bread on a baking tray and leave in a slow oven, Gas No 2, 150°C (300°F), for about 5 minutes until warmed through.

Fried croûtons

Use white bread, slice thinly and cut off the crusts. Dice into small squares by cutting 6-mm ($\frac{1}{4}$-in) strips in one direction and then across, or into triangles by cutting diagonally from corner to corner. Have hot fat ready in the frying pan, throw in the croûtons and keep turning them so that they brown evenly on all sides. They should be a gingery brown and crisp but not brittle. Lift on to kitchen paper to drain. Diced croûtons may be served plain on a savoury doily and handed separately; triangles may be half dipped in chopped parsley and used to garnish the dish.

Fried onion rings

To garnish fish and other savoury and made-up dishes: use large onions, peel, cut into thinnish slices and separate each into rings. Toss in seasoned flour and fry in hot fat until golden-brown. Drain on kitchen paper.

Fried parsley

For garnishing fish, grilled and made-up dishes: pick over fresh, bushy parsley sprigs, pinching off the stems; wash and toss in a tea-towel to dry. Fry in hot fat before it reaches hazing point, until the spluttering ceases. Fried parsley should be crisp but still bright green.

Gherkin fans
To garnish fish, boiled rice: make parallel cuts down almost the full length of each gherkin, then spread out like a fan.

Lemon baskets
As a garnish for fish, joints or pasta dishes, very effective for special occasions: place the lemon sideways to you, cut a slit about 3 mm ($\frac{1}{8}$ in) off centre to half-way down, then cut across from the end to meet this, thus taking away a quarter wedge of the lemon. Repeat on the other side; the 6 mm ($\frac{1}{4}$ in) left in the centre will now be the handle of the basket. Clean this and the basket itself of the lemon pulp and fill with cooked peas to garnish fish, mint jelly for lamb or cranberry jelly for turkey and poultry dishes.

Lemon butterflies
To garnish fish and cheese dishes: cut thin slices of lemon in half, remove any pips, make a cut almost to the centre and spread to form a butterfly. When on the dish lay flat, or twist and put a small sprig of parsley in the centre.

Lemon shells
Cut thin slices of lemon, remove any pips, make a slit to the centre, take hold of each edge and move them in opposite directions so that they overlap to form a cone. When on the dish, put a small sprig of parsley in each.

Various stuffings

When stuffing pressure-cooked foods, keep the texture dry because excess moisture will not be driven off as in the oven. This should apply particularly when packet stuffing is being used: add less than the recommended quantity of liquid.

When using stuffing, pack loosely as it will swell during the cooking.

Plain stuffing for meats and fish
4 tablespoons fresh breadcrumbs or 2 slices bread, crusts cut off, soaked in hot water and then pressed in a strainer to take away all excess liquid; 1 tablespoon chopped suet, 1 tablespoon finely chop-

ped parsley, a pinch of mixed herbs, a little grated lemon rind mixed well together with sufficient milk or beaten egg to bind but with a dry (not moist) consistency.

Cheese or meat stuffing

For vegetables such as onions and tomatoes: 50 g (2 oz) grated cheese or minced, cooked meat, 2 tablespoons fresh breadcrumbs or soaked bread, 2 tablespoons crisp, chopped fried bacon, plenty of seasoning and a little egg to moisten. To this should be added the chopped centres of the vegetables themselves.

Rice stuffing

For red or green peppers, marrows, cucumbers: fry 1 small diced onion in a little butter, add 2 peeled, chopped tomatoes, cook for a minute or two, add 50 g (2 oz) cooked diced meat or ham and 1 large tablespoon rice with plenty of salt and pepper. Pack loosely to allow for the expansion of the rice.

Unclassified recipes

Marinade

Used for meats and pieces of poultry and game to enrich the flavour before cooking. Mix together in a deep bowl 1·5 dl ($\frac{1}{4}$ pt) red wine, 2 tablespoons vinegar, 1 tablespoon olive oil, 1 clove garlic, crushed, 1 medium onion, sliced, a few peppercorns, a bay leaf, a pinch of thyme or mixed herbs and seasoning. Put in the meat, cover the bowl and turn the meat at least once (and preferably more often), while leaving it to soak for 12–24 hours. Before cooking, the meat should be dried with kitchen paper.

Mirepoix

A bed of vegetables on which food to be braised is placed. Melt 1 tablespoon butter and fry 1 slice chopped bacon until the fat runs out. Add 2 to 3 large carrots and turnips, 2 large onions, 2 to 3 sticks of celery cut into large pieces; fry until brown. Pour off the fat, add sufficient stock to come halfway up vegetables (but not less than 3 dl [$\frac{1}{2}$ pt]), a bouquet garni and plenty of seasoning. Place meat or food to be braised on top.

Soured cream

For special dishes such as **Beef Strogonoff*** or **Pork Fillets*** or as a sauce coating for carrots, parsnips, beetroot etc: to 1·5 dl (¼ pt) double cream add 2 teaspoons strained lemon juice, stir well and allow to stand for at least 3–4 hours in a warm place. Soured cream with chopped chives or capers is excellent as a coating for green beans, cucumbers and tomatoes.

To hard-boil eggs

Pressure-cooking time: 3–5 minutes

If a number are required for salad, for scotch eggs or just for a picnic, put 3 dl (½ pt) water in the cooker without the trivet, put in the eggs (which should not just have been lifted from the refrigerator, or they may crack), bring to pressure in the usual way, cook for 5 minutes, reduce the pressure with cold water, take out the eggs and drop into cold water until cool.

If one or two are required for an accompanying sauce or as garnish, they may be wrapped in greaseproof paper or aluminium foil and cooked in with the dish, then be dropped, unwrapped, into cold water until cool. For curries where they are to be served in a sauce, allow cold water to run over the wrapping, then unwrap, shell and put straight back into the sauce.

Food for pets

Although there are now so many prepared and canned foods for dogs and cats, many people still like their pets to have fresh foods as part of their diet; but the cheap cuts of meat, horseflesh and coarse fish require a lot of cooking and often make for unpleasant, pervasive odours in the house. Be sure to use your pressure cooker for this purpose, increasing cooking times as experience will soon show you is necessary, saving fuel and cooking smells and still being quite certain that, with the high temperatures reached, your pressure cooker will be safe and sterile for the family meals as well.

Conversion tables

International conversion tables

The weights and measures used throughout this book are based on British Imperial standards and the nearest workable metric units.

International Measures

Measure	UK	Australia	New Zealand	Canada
1 pint	20 fl oz	20 fl oz	20 fl oz	20 fl oz
1 cup	10 fl oz	8 fl oz	8 fl oz	8 fl oz
1 tablespoon	$\frac{5}{8}$ fl oz	$\frac{1}{2}$ fl oz	$\frac{1}{2}$ fl oz	$\frac{1}{2}$ fl oz
1 dessertspoon	$\frac{2}{5}$ fl oz	no official measure	—	—
1 teaspoon	$\frac{1}{5}$ fl oz	$\frac{1}{8}$ fl oz	$\frac{1}{6}$ fl oz	$\frac{1}{6}$ fl oz

Conversion of fluid ounces to metric

1 fl oz	= 28·4 millilitres
35 fl oz (approx 1$\frac{3}{4}$ Imperial pints)	= 1 litre (1000 ml or 10 decilitres)
1 Imperial pint (20 fl oz)	= approx 600 ml (6 dl)
$\frac{1}{2}$ Imperial pint (10 fl oz)	= 300 ml (3 dl)
$\frac{1}{4}$ Imperial pint (5 fl oz)	= 150 ml (1·5 dl)
4 tablespoons (2$\frac{1}{2}$ fl oz)	= 70 ml (7 centilitres)
2 tablespoons (1$\frac{1}{4}$ fl oz)	= 35 ml (3·5 cl)
1 tablespoon ($\frac{5}{8}$ fl oz)	= 18 ml (2 cl)
1 dessertspoon ($\frac{2}{3}$ fl oz)	= 12 ml
1 teaspoon ($\frac{1}{5}$ fl oz)	= 6 ml

(All the above metric equivalents are approximate)

Equivalents
1 UK (old BSI standard) cup equals 1$\frac{1}{4}$ cups in Commonwealth countries

4 UK tablespoons equal 5 Commonwealth tablespoons
5 UK teaspoons equal 6 New Zealand or 6 Canada or 8 Australia
1 UK dessertspoon equals $\frac{2}{3}$ UK tablespoon or 2 UK teaspoons
In British cookery books, a gill is usually 5 fl oz ($\frac{1}{4}$ pint), but in a few localities in the UK it can mean 10 fl oz ($\frac{1}{2}$ pint)
Other non-standardized measures include:
Breakfast cup = approx 10 fl oz (3 dl)
Tea cup   = 5 fl oz (1·5 dl)
Coffee cup   = 3 fl oz (0·9 dl)

Liquids

Minimum for pressure cooking	English $\frac{1}{2}$ pint	American $\frac{1}{2}$ pint	Nearest metric equivalent 3 dl

Pressures

(1 metric bar=1 kg per sq cm at sea level)

	lb per sq in	kg per sq cm
L	5	0·35
M	10	0·70
H	15	1
	8	0·56 (most low-pressure cookers)

Oven temperatures	Gas regulo	Fahrenheit	Centigrade
Cool	$\frac{1}{2}$	250°	121°
Slow	2	300°	150°
Moderate	4	375°	190°
Hot	6–7	450°	233°

Quick check timetable for meats

Joints suitable (1·35 kg or 3 lb) or under	Preparation
Pot-roasting (with trivet)	
Beef: topside, brisket, rolled rib	Trim, remove fat, tie securely. Weigh. Brown lightly in hot fat, in open pan,
Veal: stuffed shoulder, loin	over medium heat. Lift out, season with salt and pepper. Drain off fat.
Mutton or Lamb: stuffed, rolled breast	Add required amount of hot liquid
Boiling (without trivet)	
Beef: brisket, silverside	Sufficient water to half fill cooker
Veal: knuckle	Sufficient water to half fill cooker
Mutton: leg	Sufficient water to half fill cooker
Pork: pickled leg, hand, belly	Sufficient water to half fill cooker
Ham: gammon, hock, collar, flank	Sufficient water to half fill cooker. On trivet, water according to cooking time
Pig's trotters	Use 1·5 dl ($\frac{1}{4}$ pt) vinegar, 1·5 dl ($\frac{1}{4}$ pt) water
Braising (without trivet)	
Beef: chuck, rump	Brown in hot fat, over medium heat in open pan. Prepare mirepoix*. Drain off fat. Add liquid to just show through vegetables
Oxtail	Fry onions, then joints in hot fat: 7·5 dl (1$\frac{1}{4}$ pt) boiling liquid
Veal: rolled, stuffed breast	Stuff, roll tightly, tie or skewer, weigh; continue as for beef stew
Mutton or Lamb: chops and cutlets	As for beef stew
Hearts	Clean out, three-quarter fill with stuffing, secure loosely, continue as for beef stew

Pressure-cooking time	Accompaniments
12–15 minutes per 450 g (lb)	Thin gravy, horseradish sauce
12–14 minutes per 450 g (lb)	Thickened gravy, bacon rolls, lemon
10–12 minutes per 450 g (lb)	Thickened gravy, mint or onion sauce
15 minutes per 450 g (lb)	Mustard sauce, garnish of vegetables
10 minutes per 450 g (lb)	Boiled rice, bacon rolls, lemon
15 minutes per 450 g (lb)	Caper sauce
18 minutes per 450 g (lb)	Thickened gravy, haricot beans
12 minutes per 450 g (lb)	Cooking liquor or parsley sauce, hot
12 minutes per 450 g (lb)	Coated with golden crumbs, salad, cold
30 minutes	Garnish of vegetables, brown gravy
10 minutes	Mashed vegetables from mirepoix, thickened gravy
40 minutes	Redcurrant jelly, thickened gravy
12 minutes per 450 g (lb)	Brown quickly under hot grill, thickened gravy, bacon rolls, lemon
10 minutes	As for beef stew
30 minutes	As for beef stew

Joints suitable (1·35 kg or 3 lb) or under	Preparation
Liver	As for beef stew
Kidneys	Brown in bacon fat, add 3 dl ($\frac{1}{2}$ pt) hot liquid
Pork: chops, plain	As for beef stew
Stuffed	As for beef stew; brown small, whole onions, after lifting out chops
Ham: gammon slices 2 cm (1 in) thick	Brown in hot fat, top with pineapple rings, use juice as liquid
Stewing (without trivet)	
Beef: stewing steak cut into 2-cm (1-in) cubes	Toss lightly in seasoned flour; fry gently in hot fat, over medium heat, in open pan. Add vegetables and required amount of liquid
Mince	Fry gently as above
Tripe	Add onions; sufficient water to cover
Veal pieces	Seal in a little hot butter but without browning; add vegetables and 3 dl ($\frac{1}{2}$ pt) hot liquid
Sweetbreads	See recipe, p 103
Mutton or Lamb: best end of neck	Cut into chops or pieces
Meat and pastry dishes	
Steak and Kidney Pudding	See recipe, p 117
Suet Roll	See recipe, p 118
For Steak and Kidney Pie	Add 4·5 dl ($\frac{3}{4}$ pt) liquid
Cold meats	
Brawn: pig's head	See recipe, p 133
Galantine of Beef	See recipe, p 134
Pressed Tongue	Tie in muslin; sufficient water to half fill cooker

Pressure-cooking time	Accompaniments
5 minutes	As for beef stew
7 minutes	Brown sauce, with red wine added
10–12 minutes	As for beef stew, apple sauce or rings
12–15 minutes	Browned whole onions, thickened gravy
10 minutes	Parsley sauce, peas
15–20 minutes	Thickened gravy
7 minutes	Triangles of toast, chopped parsley
15 minutes	White sauce, fried croûtons
12 minutes	White sauce, bacon rolls, lemon, slices of hard-boiled egg, chopped parsley
6–8 minutes	Triangles of fried bread, lemon, parsley
10–12 minutes	Thickened sauce, chopped parsley
Steam 15 minutes Pressure cook 55 minutes	Mixed vegetables, extra gravy
Steam 10 minutes Pressure cook 35 minutes	Mixed vegetables, extra gravy
Pressure cook 10 minutes Oven bake 30 minutes	Mixed vegetables, extra gravy
35 minutes	Green salad, hard-boiled egg, gherkin
35 minutes	Press, coat with golden crumbs; salad
15 minutes per 450 g (lb)	Press; new potatoes, salad

Index